How to Make a FORTUNE on the Information Superhighway

How to Make a FORTUNE on the Information Superhighway

EVERYONE'S GUERRILLA GUIDE TO MARKETING

ON THE INTERNET AND OTHER ON-LINE SERVICES

Laurence A. Canter and Martha S. Siegel

HarperCollins*Publishers*

HarperCollins books may be purchased for educational, business, or sales promotional use. For information, please write: Special Markets Department, Harper-Collins Publishers, Inc., 10 East 53rd Street, New York, NY 10022.

FIRST EDITION

Designed by Nancy Singer

ISBN 0-06-270131-2
94 95 96 97 98 PS/RRD 10 9 8 7 6 5 4 3 2 1

CONTENTS

1

GETTING YOUR BEARINGS ON THE INFORMATION SUPERHIGHWAY

If you haven't heard the term "Information Superhighway," you can probably look up right now and see bats hanging upside-down from the ceiling of the cave in which you live. Never in recent memory has the media taken a pop phrase, blown it up so big, draped it with so much fancy rhetoric and played it back to the public with such repetitiveness. The interesting part of all the hype is that although almost everyone has heard the term "Information Superhighway" no one seems really to know what that is. Where is this so-called "highway?" Where does it lead? How do you get on it? What will you find as you travel along the Information Superhighway? If you have no answers to these questions, you are not alone by any means.

Maybe you are not wondering at all "What is the Information Superhighway?" Instead, perhaps the question that first comes to mind is "Who cares?" Of course, you probably wouldn't be reading this if you didn't care, and you should, for lots of reasons. The Information Superhighway is going to affect your life, whether you want it to or not. In the very near future you will talk to your friends and family, send letters, go shopping, get news, find answers to your questions, draw pictures, solve problems, even gamble, and more, all on the Information Superhighway. Not least, you can make a lot of money.

"But," you say, "I can do the things you've mentioned perfectly well already. Why should I bother learning a new way when things are working fine just as they are?" The answer to this very good question is, again, simple. The Information Superhighway is now, and for the foreseeable future, where the action is. If you join in the fun and excitement, not to mention the profit potential, of this great new resource, you'll benefit in more ways than you can imagine. We'll show you that taking advantage of all the Information Superhighway has to offer is easy. On the other hand, if you choose not to embrace this undeniable wave of the future, while nearly everyone else is busily climbing on the computer bandwagon, you will surely be left behind. There you will be, huddled in your cave, alone with your new best friends, the bats. Well, maybe that's an overstatement. Then again, maybe not.

There are endless numbers of missions you can accomplish while traveling the Information Superhighway, and we want you to know about all of them. But the one we want to tell you about most will help you to achieve a goal close to all our hearts—making money! Money. Is there ever enough of it? You know the answer. If you're anything like us, you've been looking for a good way to increase your money-making ability for a long time. We tried it, as many do, by going to college and learning a profession. Everyone thinks all lawyers are rich. If only it were true. Rich lawyers are rich. The rest struggle just like anyone else. And so we struggled. We wrote a book on immigration law (our specialty) and sold it for extra income. The book was a critical success and became very popular throughout the world, but it was expensive to promote and had a limited market. Contrary to what you read in the newspapers, not every living soul in the world wants to move to the United States. For that matter, not everyone who wants to move to the United States is willing or even able to read a book about it, especially one written in English. And so we went right on struggling. In the course of a lifetime, we came across lots of ideas on how to get rich. None of them, on close inspection, really made much sense. We wanted a change but couldn't figure out what change to make. We were doing all right by most people's standards, but we weren't where we wanted to be by a long shot. We were sure we could do better.

Then we took a good, hard look at our computer and an answer finally came. Would a spare $50,000 come in handy? How about an extra $100,000? That's what we made as a result of one night's work using our knowledge of the Information Superhighway. We're going to turn that knowledge over to you, so you can do the same thing we did. It's both easy and fascinating. You don't need to make a big investment. You don't need to be a brilliant "computer nerd," complete with glassy-eyed stare and pocket protector (although you might at some time want to hire just such a person to work for you). What you do need is some basic computer equipment and a working knowledge of the Information Superhighway. Let's put the equipment part aside for now. Instead, let's concentrate on your first orientation trip down the highway and into Cyberspace.

Learning the Jargon

Cyberspace? Another term of computer jargon that it's hard to avoid. Once again, you've probably heard it what seems like a million times, but you still don't know exactly what it means. We'll give you a definition a little later. First, however, it will be helpful to you as you go on your journey if you grasp the fact that jargon is important to computer people. They have worked hard to develop their own special lexicon. They delight in the debate and deliberation that precedes the birth of every new term, and they fancy themselves terribly clever. So besotted are they with using computer terms of art, even the simplest act is verbally glorified. You don't turn a computer on, you "boot it up." If, after you've booted, you want to connect to a computer network through your phone line, you don't call up, you "go on-line" and "log in." You never gather information from your computer, you "download" it. Conversely, when you are ready to send information out, that's right, you "upload." You will refrain from typing instructions into your computer. Instead, you will "execute commands." Maybe you'll even salute at the same time.

Over and above the fact that a developing technology probably does need some new vocabulary to work with, one of the main purposes of the jargon is to make the people who created it feel as if they are part of the computer world "in crowd." The existence of an "in" crowd would also suggest the existence of an "out" crowd. That, of course, would be you. They even have a name for people like you—"newbies." It doesn't take a genius to figure out what this means. It's not exactly the same as calling you a worthless idiot, but it's close enough. What's more, newbies are usually prime targets for flames. Flames are insults sent over the computer. Statements that someone with any sense or manners would never make to your face are sent over the Information Superhighway with great glee. This sort of silliness may be amusing to some for a while, but you're not here to goof around. You're here to make money. Therefore, our best advice is to ignore these clowns. (By clown, we mean the glassy-eyed nerd over there with the pocket protector.) The Information Superhighway is for everyone, even lawyers, even you. Plant your feet firmly on the road, hold your head up, and keep moving.

All right, you've still got to learn a few words of the language spoken here so you can converse with the natives. Soon these people will contribute their purchasing power to making you a financial success, so they are well worth talking to. First of all, you should probably realize the term "Information Superhighway," also known to the cognoscenti as the

Infobahn or I-way, is looked down upon by some of its more experienced travelers. That is because, along with the coining of the phrase, came a huge flood of the dreaded newbies. Where the term Information Superhighway actually first came from was a speech given by Vice President Albert Gore on December 21, 1993, when he addressed the National Press Club in Washington, D.C. That speech, and that phrase in particular, was the siren's song to the mass media. They took the idea and the terminology to heart and gave out the news that the Vice President had given birth to the watchword for the future of communications. Suddenly, because of one speech, nearly all those who walked the earth became aware of something that had in fact quietly existed for a long time. That "something" was the Internet.

The Internet can best be described as the main and most important branch of the I-way. In fact, to many people the Internet *is* the I-way. Very simply, the Internet is about thirty million computers all connected together and communicating with each other. Thirty million is a rough calculation. No one actually knows for sure. There are nearly three million computers officially registered on the Internet, but most of those have dozens or even hundreds of individual users accessing them. A typical Internet access provider, for example, a company whose job it is to connect people to the Internet, counts as only one computer, even though the provider may really account for 500 separate users. Reports on estimated numbers of Internet participants have shown ranges careening from as low as several million to as high as fifty million or more. Those claiming the lower number probably do not understand the meaning of a registered computer. Thirty million is the figure used most often and all indications are that this is a conservative estimate. So popular is the Internet now that the user group grows by thousands *every day*. The way all these connected computers communicate is over standard phone lines. That is why it is so easy and practical for you, sitting in your home or office, to link up. The Internet is what we used to make our fortune on the Information Superhighway, and it is the Internet that we will mainly be talking about in this book.

When we say the Internet is made up of thirty million computers, we mean all kinds of computers, both big and small. Most of the thirty million are plain old PCs consisting of a screen, a keyboard, and a monitor, just like the one probably sitting in your home or office right now. Some of the largest and most elaborate computers tied into the Internet are located at government offices and universities around the world. These larger machines act as central exchanges, allowing all the other, smaller ones to be in contact with each other. Still more computers linked to the Internet are storehouses of information. What sorts of information are we talking about? You name it. Everything from newspaper stories to medical information to sports to sex—well, as we said, you just name it and it's available out there on the Internet. These electronic information repositories in the computer are called *databases*. It's an extra added bonus that, because all this was started by the U.S. Government, almost anything and everything you get from Internet databases is free.

Another interesting concept that you should understand about the Internet is that there is no central authority running it. The Internet was deliberately arranged that way for a practical purpose. The Defense Department, which created it, anticipated that the Internet might be used as a critical communication tool in time of war. They wanted to be sure that there was no central operating mechanism that could disable it with one, well-placed bomb. Today, the practical need for decentralization has evolved into a philosophy that advocates governance from the bottom up, rather than the top down. Certain universities and private organizations voluntarily assume the administrative and technical tasks of keeping the Internet operational. As for the content of what goes on the Internet, there is nobody who exercises control. Human nature being what it is, philosophy or no philosophy, there are many who, as you will see, can't resist the urge to try directing operations. So far, however, no attempts at formal regulation have taken hold and, in theory at least, no one runs the Internet.

The Internet, usually referred to by those who know and love it simply as "the Net," is the big show on the I-way. It is not, however, the only one. The Gore concept was really meant to cover all the recently developed electronic resources that have increased to a blinding speed the exchange of information between people. This would included the commercial computer networks such as CompuServe, America Online, Delphi, Genie, and Prodigy. Each of these is a circle of computers unto itself and each one supplies its own unique assortment of databases. Unlike the Internet, using the commercial services is not free. Some commercial networks also include in their service packages a gateway to the Net. Although the Internet is our main concern in this book, there are money-making opportunities on the commercial networks, and we'll be telling you about some of them as well.

Finally, for the sake of thoroughness, the I-way concept also covers other, non-computer developments in telecommunications, such as the video telephone and interactive television. Breakthroughs like these are exciting to think and know about, but they are not in wide use yet, as is the I-way, and so they are of no real value to our purpose here.

Now that you understand what is really meant by the Information Superhighway, you are ready to tackle the all-time favorite computer pop phrase—Cyperspace. The term Cyberspace was first coined by William Gibson in his popular computer-based science fiction book *Neuromancer*. You will remember that we mentioned Cyberspace earlier as a world you were about to enter. Dyed-in-the-wool Internet devotees love to think of it that way, as an actual place to which you can go. The idea that you can be connected to so many people and so much information so easily creates in their minds a sense of wonder and mysticism which transcends planet earth. They picture themselves as Captain Kirk (or Captain Picard, if they are a little younger) daring to go where no man has ever gone before. They imagine they are brave explorers, riding their computer keyboards through electronic lollipop land. Go ahead and share the fantasy if you are of a mind to do so, but when you get ready to leave your little pink cloud and jump back down to the real world, realize that Cyberspace is just a convenient way of describing the huge number of electronic information paths and messages darting back and forth between people and computers on the Internet and other networks that make up the I-way.

When you become more familiar with the territory, you will begin to notice that drawing analogies between real-life activities and electronic I-way functions has developed into almost a popular art form. As you go on your journey down the I-way to wealth, take advantage of these conventions and enjoy them, but never lose sight, as many before you have, of where reality ends and figments of the imagination begin. Those who buy into the myth that Cyberspace is a real place also believe that this illusory locale houses a community, with a set of laws, rules, and ethics all its own. Unfortunately, the perceived behavior codes of Cyberspace are often in conflict with the laws of more substantive lands like, for instance, the United States of America. Later we'll show you how to separate fact from fiction and follow the laws that really count in your quest for fortune on the I-way. The Internet has for some time been in the hands of dreamers. It is time for you, the realist, to take hold.

Equipment: What Do You Need?

First of all, computer equipment isn't known as equipment. Call it hardware. There is such a vast array of computer hardware on the market today that some enterprising souls will charge you $100 an hour or more simply to tell you which computer to buy. Calling this an unnecessary expense would be an understatement. We'll tell you the details of what you need to know later on. Here, now, are the basics which will enable you to engage in all the money-making activities described in this book.

You'll need only four tools. First, you will require a PC of any flavor. Yes, even Uncle Bob's old, classic, original IBM PC will work, although it won't give you the power, speed and flexibility of the newer models. When we say a PC, we mean an entire system, including a viewing monitor, a keyboard, and the box with the brain, the central processing unit, that actually manipulates the data. These items can be sold either separately or as a unit. You can spend as much as you want on this, and there are certain benefits to having a high-powered system, but if you don't already own a PC and want to get started without squandering your child's college-tuition fund, used ones can be found through classifieds, sometimes for as little as $200.

The next items on the list of requirements are a modem and telephone line. The two are related. A modem is a device that enables your computer to communicate with other computers over standard phone lines. Most PCs being sold today have modems built into them, but if you need to buy one, they can be purchased at any electronic discount store for as little as $30. As for the telephone line, any garden-variety phone line will do. If you are a real pioneer, you can even access the Internet on your camping trip via a cellular phone connection, although this requires purchasing a special cellular modem.

Finally, you need a communications program that lets your computer talk to the modem. A program is a set of electronic instructions that tells your computer what to do. The computer itself is nothing but a pile of metal and plastic. Every time you want your computer to perform a particular task, you must see that you have a program for that task. When your computer can act as a telephone, a typewriter, a research tool, and a record keeper all in one day, it is through the use of a variety of programs. Remember hardware? Programs are called software. Modems are almost always sold with free communications software, as are the majority of computers. If you don't like the software you have, however, don't worry. Fabulous communications software programs are available, for *free*, on the Internet. In fact, you will find that the Internet is loaded with free programs of all kinds that you may actually find useful. This, in I-way parlance, is called freeware or shareware.

There is one other item you might want to consider seriously, although it is not an absolute marketing necessity. It is a printer. A printer will allow you to create hard copies of any data that comes into your computer. With the use of a word processing program, you can employ the computer as a high-tech typewriter. No business should be without one and, in fact, it is becoming harder and harder to find any that are.

Getting on the Net

To get on the Internet, you must have some sort of Internet link. You acquire this connection by opening an account with any one of the many institutions or companies that fall into the category of Internet access providers. The Internet is a global link of millions of computers. Your access provider has a computer that is tied directly to the Net. You hook up by going through the access provider's computer. When you get really ambitious, and have made your first fortune, you may want to consider being your own access provider. For now, you should choose an easier and cheaper route. For example, your employer may already offer Internet access to staff members who want it. Check it out, because it will probably be free. Likewise, if you are a student, your school may offer free access. Be careful, though, to ask if there are any restrictions on usage. Many companies and most academic institutions provide Internet access for research purposes only. Using it to make money might be frowned upon.

The other, more flexible option is to find a commercial access provider. In this case you simply pay someone to get you on the Net. There are many well-known commercial on-line providers, such as CompuServe, Prodigy, and America Online. Historically, these have been self-contained networks with direct access only to other people who have subscribed to that particular network. All are now in the process of providing some degree of Internet access. It is a commercial provider specializing in Internet access only, however, that will offer you the most Internet capabilities, and probably the lowest price. There are hundreds of such companies located the world over. Access providers charge fees, but to begin making money on the Information Superhighway, you should be able to get the Internet connection you need for about $20 per month, with unlimited usage. We'll give you full information on choosing an access provider later on in this book.

What to Do with the Net

Fine. We have discovered great networks of computers out there all tied together and ready to communicate with each other. Your computer equipment and Internet access are, likewise, set to go. Now we have to figure out what to do with this thing. Our main goal here is to make a fortune. In order to do this we must leave behind all the romance, all the wonderment, and move on to the practical uses of the Net.

There are actually four primary functions that can be accomplished on the Internet. You are probably familiar with the first. It is called e-mail. Ideas don't get much simpler than e-mail. You and everyone else who ties into the Internet gets a mailbox code. Then, by typing in your code on his or her keyboard, anyone connected to the Internet can send private messages to your computer and yours alone. You can send private messages back in the same way. These messages come over the phone lines and into the computer, where they wait until the owner of the computer turns it on and reads the messages on the computer screen. E-mail is a vital component of making money on the Internet. It is the primary way potential buyers of your product will contact you.

The second practical use of the Internet is as a source of information. We've already mentioned that there are endless numbers of databases out there covering almost any subject imaginable. If you like knowing things, and we all do, you may at first suffer from information overload, a grownup version of the kid-in-the-candy-store syndrome. There are literally thousands of databases that can be accessed by anyone on the Internet, usually for free. Existing databases include such diverse categories as this morning's newspaper, all the laws of a particular state or country, the card catalog of your favorite library, research reports, and every telephone directory known to mankind. There are even databases that do nothing more than list other available databases. All you need to access a particular database is its Internet electronic address, which is similar to a mailbox for the database. This creates a wondrous opportunity for the academician trying to understand the mating habits of killer bees, or for the sports enthusiast who wants statistics on his favorite team, from the present back to the stone age. More important, it creates an opportunity for you to make a fortune. How? You create your own database. Your database may be as simple as a list of your products or services, or it may include an entire catalog, complete with multi-media video and sound. We'll tell you exactly how to go about it.

The third practical function of the Net is to act as a public forum of ideas. This is done by a vehicle called the Usenet. To those hooked on it, the Usenet is the only part of the Internet that really matters. The Usenet is a collection of about 10,000 discussion groups, each devoted to a different topic. As with the other features of the Net, the range of subjects covered is enormous. Starting with computer and technical subjects, moving on to celebrity fan groups, to sex, to family problem-solving, to the just plain silly (two recent favorites on the Usenet are called *tonyaharding.whack.whack.whack* and *nancykerrigan.ouch.ouch.ouch*), the Usenet provides an opportunity to air your views in public on nearly anything.

The Usenet groups, called "Newsgroups," are actually run less like discussions and more like electronic bulletin boards. Someone will post a message to the group. Then, anyone who tunes in to read what is posted can see the other postings and respond. The Usenet offers one of the best ways we know for making money on the Net. Once again, we'll save the details for later. Meanwhile, try to think of what it would be like if suddenly millions of people could know you had a wonderful product to sell or an excellent service to offer, and how they could purchase it from you. Temporarily, we'll leave the outcome to your imagination.

The fourth and final practical use of the Internet is for talk or chat. This Internet function works much like a CB radio or perhaps a big conference call on the telephone. There are certain talk channels you can access with your computer. You are then able to "talk" with anyone else who happens to be on the channel at the same time, by typing your words into the computer. The typed messages appear immediately on the monitor of all those who are tuned in, and they can answer back in the same way. Often, the size of a group accessing a chat channel simultaneously is in the hundreds. You may even engage in private conversations, or go into private rooms for limited group discussions. Add a voice synthesizer to your computer and who needs Ma Bell? Think of the long-distance phone charges you can save. And making money through talk or chat? Well, what if you joined the conversation and told everyone about the wonderful product or service you have to sell? Do you think someone might be interested?

Communicate Your Way to Wealth through Cyberselling

By now, you've probably guessed that the secret to making a fortune on the I-way lies in the amazing communication ability you can use for presenting your goods and services to huge numbers of people at a very low cost. We're going to help you think of a product or service and then we'll explain how to use the various functions available on the Internet and other parts of the I-way to sell it. We'll also tell you how to select an access provider and choose a PC according to the type of marketing you want to do. You'll see that the methods we describe can be used not only to present products initially, but also to offer follow-up service and create long-lasting customer relations. We call all of this "cyberselling." When Ronald Reagan was President of the United States, people called him "The Great Communicator." His way of reaching out to embrace people drew them to his humanity, blinded them to his faults, and made him one of the most popular presidents in history. Even if he did nothing else well, he was startling effective at one thing—selling Ronald Reagan. As good a communicator as Reagan was, in our opinion, the greatest communicator of them all is not the former President but the computer. This machine that transmits so much information in so many different forms to someone sitting in the privacy and comfort of his or her own home has the ability to create an intimate and trusting relationship with the user that is ideal for selling. What's more, that person sitting at the computer is not simply a passive recipient of information. He or she can talk back. This presents the opportunity for your customer to ask questions and make comments about your product or service. Most important, that customer can place an order.

You can't effectively use the selling abilities of your computer unless you have something to sell. That is why we've included in our explanation of cyberselling the methods you'll need for finding a product or service that is tailor-made for marketing on the I-way. Put your great new product or service together with the high-powered, low-cost promotion capabilities of the computer and you have a new and easy way of cyberselling yourself into a happy and wealthy financial future.

A New Road to Wealth

It isn't often that you have an opportunity to take part in the development of a great new industry, but it's about to happen to you right now. By the time you finish this book, you'll be able to cybersell with the best of them. Huge, mega-corporations are just beginning to take advantage of the incredible marketing power cyberselling has to offer, so you are in on the ground floor. What is more, you can reach so many people so effectively and inexpensively using cyberselling techniques, that you can play in the same league with the big boys and come out a winner. Once you've learned the simple basics of cyberselling we're going to show you in the rest of this book, you'll be limited only by your own imagination and creativity.

It is our goal here to have you understand how to utilize the I-way for commercial purposes. It doesn't require a finely honed scientific mind. In fact, what you are about to read is written making the assumption that you know absolutely nothing about computers whatsoever. In explaining how to market on the I-way, we can't avoid touching on a certain amount that is technical, but we've kept it at entry-level information and avoided it wherever possible. We have not included here directions on how to operate your computer. If you need to learn that, read a manual or take a class at your local community college. Likewise, if you want to examine the workings of the Internet in depth from a technical standpoint, there are many excellent books on the topic already in existence. You can even choose to omit the process altogether by hiring a computer "geek" to carry out the technical end for you. What you should examine closely for yourself, however, are the ways you can use the I-way to gain wealth. That's what you're going to find out right now. If you employ the computer for this purpose, you will have the advantage of being among the first.

There is one last notion you must understand before you begin your trip down the I-way to financial success. We've talked about it earlier in a joking way, but now we want to be completely serious and very clear. Whatever you hear, whatever you read, whatever others may tell you, the computer is just a machine. It's not human. It's not a miracle. It's a machine. It can transfer huge amounts of information back and forth with lightning speed, but that's all it can do. Because this transfer of information tends to intensify the effects of communication, the result often is that a feeling of closeness develops between the people who give and receive it. As uplifting as this feeling may be, it's important to keep things in perspective. Popular nicknames like Cyberspace and Information Superhighway serve the purpose of making it easy for the average person to grasp and discuss complex electronic functions carried out by computers and computer networks, but don't get so carried away that you start believing the I-way is a real six-lane blacktop. As we mentioned earlier, some starry-eyed individuals who access the Net think of Cyberspace as a community, with rules, regulations and codes of behavior. Don't you believe it! There is no community. Perhaps there was some truth to that concept in the past, when the Internet was used exclusively by a small, homogeneous group of academics and corporate technical researchers. Today, with Internet access available to everyone, I-way travelers reflect every heterogeneous nuance of the world population. Along your journey, someone may try to tell you that in order to be a good Net "citizen," you must follow the rules of the Cyberspace community. Don't listen. The only laws and rules with which you should concern yourself are those passed by the country, state, and city in which you truly live. The only ethics you should adopt as you pursue wealth on the I-way are those dictated by the religious faith you have chosen to follow and your own good conscience.

Millions of people have gone out and bought computers. Buying a computer is no different than buying a television or a CD player. It's not a passport to another world. It's just a machine. You should not fear this machine. Although it might have taken a brilliant scientist to invent it, any normal mortal with average intelligence and a little effort can learn to use it. You have only to look at the reception desk of nearly every business in the modern world to know that this is true. You should use your computer to communicate, to make your life easier and better. Once you learn cyberselling, you can and should use your computer to make money. You should use it. That's what it was made for. Let's get started.

2

A BUSY NIGHT IN CYBERSPACE: THE GREEN CARD INCIDENT

Starting Out

It wasn't long ago that the following marital exchange took place late one evening in our bedroom.

Larry: (*walking in after saying a reluctant good night to his computer at about 12:30 A.M.*) "I think we've just hit the mother lode."

Martha: (*half asleep*) "Stop bothering me. Go to bed. It's late."

The next morning, however, we both got up and started out on what would turn into an incredible adventure that would change our lives. As CompuServe subscribers almost since it began, we had been on-line computer enthusiasts for more than ten years, but knew little about the Internet. We had been hearing about it on CompuServe as well as in the news, but we couldn't even find the Internet, let alone figure out how to use it. We thought it was a private network for universities to communicate with one another. Then, we read somewhere that the U.S. Supreme Court was making all of its decisions available on the Internet. Other federal and state agencies were offering access to their databases and publications, usually for free. Could we get the government information on immigration free via computer? Could we get rid of our outrageously expensive law library, and prevent the future destruction of hundreds of trees needed to generate all that paper? That's what made us start out on our first journey through Cyberspace and down the Information Superhighway. We hadn't yet recognized the riches that lay ahead.

We searched for everything available about the Internet. The biggest question seemed to be, "How do we access it?" Then, one day, like black magic, the name Computer Witchcraft mysteriously popped up on our CompuServe screen. We found out this was the name of some free software that would get us on the Internet. It was also the name of a company engaged in the business of providing Internet access. For the software to do you any good, you had to sign up with the company. We proceeded to download this software to our computer. Suddenly, our modem was dialing a number and we were connected. You could almost see some mystical, Disneyesque character in a huge turban shouting "Open Sesame" in a big, booming voice. We were asked to give a title we wished to use as our computer identity and without much thought chose cslaw. Our e-mail address would be cslaw@lcanter.win.net. Also, we were asked to provide a credit card which would be charged a minimum of $10 each month against per minute charges of about fifteen cents. We were on the I-way and hadn't even left the comfort of our home.

We had what was known as a UUCP account (Unix to Unix Copy). We'll be discussing this and other types of Internet accounts in Chapter 13. We soon learned that a UUCP account does not really connect directly to the Internet. Instead, with this type of system we got the ability to use a certain number of Internet features by employing Witchcraft as a middleman. A hookup such as this is inexpensive and easy to work with, provided you don't use your account very much.

The first thing we did with our new Internet account was check out something called the Usenet. Here was a collection of about ten thousand public discussion groups, called Newsgroups, on a huge number of topics. The way these "discussions" were carried on was that one person would decide to post a message from his or her computer for everyone else who tuned into the group to read. Then, others would respond by posting reply messages, which would, in turn, elicit more responses and so on. These back and forth exchanges were, we learned, called "threads." There could be many threads going on in one group.

Not surprisingly, the first Newsgroup to catch our attention was called *alt.visa.us.* What we found there was a list of several hundred questions that people around the world had posted concerning U.S. immigration. We knew the answers to all of them, and without much thought, posted a few replies. Then it happened. Within a day or so our electronic mailbox overflowed with individual immigration inquiries. People we had never met wanted to hire us as lawyers. We knew from our years of experience that, in the end, very few would actually part with their money for traditional legal services. Still, it made us wonder about the possibilities here.

Just how many people knew about this one little Newsgroup? Were there more places on the I-way where the particular service we offered might be of interest? Hopefully, we began to explore. Then came another major discovery: a collection of Newsgroups devoted to the cultures of different countries. There was *alt.culture.japan, alt.culture.hungary, alt.culture.france;* nearly one hundred in all. For practitioners of immigration law there could have been no more desirable a market.

Still, we were reluctant to try selling traditional legal services. Good legal work requires painstaking hours of labor, and that translates into high prices few can afford. Besides, we had learned that, at least as far as immigration work is concerned, few people really understood the value of the service offer. They believed, incorrectly, that getting a visa or green card was simply a matter of filling out a few forms. Even when their own efforts failed and they came to us for help, they still had difficulty grasping why a couple of minutes of advice would not tell them all they needed to know. We had spent fifteen years working against this misconception. We noticed that most messages posted to Usenet Newsgroups were fairly short. We realized that we were not, in a few brief paragraphs, going to overcome sales objections that we had been unable to deal with for the duration of our careers. We concluded that traditional immigration legal services were not the most promising product to sell in this medium.

They say it's all in the timing. It was for us. Just as we discovered an unbelievable place to market our immigration know-how, we were also beginning our annual undertaking of the Green Card Lottery. This is a program sponsored by the U.S. government, where applications are filled out in a particular technical manner specified by the Department of State. Completed applications are then fed into a computer and "winners" are selected randomly. Those who are lucky enough to have their names drawn receive Green Cards. Every year the government does its best to make the Green Card Lottery as confusing as possible. Still, compared to the standard types of immigration applications we normally file, the lottery was simple stuff. Where we might charge several thousand dollars for an average immigration case, we could complete a lottery application for about $100 and still see a profit if our promotion costs were not too high. Moreover, we had learned over the years that immigration clients just loved the Green Card Lottery. Even though it was a long shot, there was excitement to the gambling feature. Besides, where other, more traditional efforts to get Green Cards took time, money, and perseverance, the lottery was, if successful, a quick fix.

In the Green Card Lottery, we believed we had the perfect item to sell to our new-found computer market. We sat down and wrote a short (about

171 words) statement announcing the Green Card Lottery and posted it to all the *alt.culture* groups. We invited those who wanted more information to send their request to our e-mail account. Later we learned a way to post to numerous groups automatically, but we were still beginners at the time, and so this posting was done the long way. Each of the approximately 100 postings took about two minutes apiece.

The next morning we got up to see what had become of our little postings. It had been a busy night in Cyberspace. Hundreds of requests for additional information poured in. As more people woke up, turned on their computers and saw our messages, the flow increased to an avalanche. It kept up at this rate for days, before slackening off a bit. Still, a steady stream of inquiries kept coming even weeks later.

We also received our first "flames." Flames are computerese for insulting messages. A few individuals did not like the fact that we had posted our notices to a number of Newsgroups. We were informed that when you post to Newsgroups, you must post only on the topic of the group. "What," someone wanted to know, "does the Green Card Lottery have to do with *alt.culture.japan*?" Others advised us to look into "Netiquette," the informal code of behavior certain people believe must be observed when you operate in Cyberspace. Still others were not so polite. They called us "idiots" and "clueless," words we thought inaccurate descriptions of two experienced professionals who had several advanced degrees and had written two books. An official from Witchcraft called to tell us there had been some complaints. We advised him that these complaints had been duly noted, but represented only about five per cent of the responses we received. The messenger from Witchcraft said his company really didn't care what we did as long as it had no effect on their business, and in fact, they wished they had the nerve to do what we were doing.

For our part, we didn't see that much in the way of nerve was required. We knew we had broken no law. We were receiving a fantastic response to our posting. If someone out there didn't see why information on the Green Card Lottery was relevant to the readers of the Newsgroup on Japan, almost everyone else who read the group clearly understood very well. What we did find difficult to grasp was why these people were wasting everybody's time trying to inject themselves into matters that didn't concern them. We wondered who'd raised them to use language like that with strangers. We had little time, however, to ponder these questions. We were too busy sending Green Card Lottery information to those who'd requested it. By now they numbered in excess of one thousand.

Now the limitations of a Witchcraft type UUCP account became readily apparent. For what we were trying to accomplish, clearly we needed a more direct, and therefore more flexible and rapid connection to the Internet. Back we went to CompuServe, and learned about another company, which offered direct connections to the I-way with its own easy to use software. Again getting the software free through CompuServe, we were quickly connected to what was called "The Pipeline." We were asked online for our preferred e-mail account name, and again chose cslaw, now to be known as cslaw@pipeline.com. We got a message saying that people from Pipeline would call us within a few days to issue a password and finalize setting up the account.

The call came and we had our second Internet connection. A number of strange-sounding services were immediately made available: things called Gopher, Veronica, FTP, and Telnet, in addition to e-mail and Usenet. We found that Pipeline had access to many more Newsgroups than Witchcraft. We discovered an entire world of Newsgroups located outside the U.S. This seemed like a possible gold mine for immigration services. By now, we had already made enough money to buy two new computers. Then we got to thinking. Advertising to these groups was practically free. Since cost was not a factor, why not advertise to all the groups. We began posting, one at a time, to each group available through Pipeline. We were not disappointed. Mail began pouring in, including requests for information, sales orders, and many more flames. It all happened too fast. Pipeline had its own limitations. Pipeline was a new company. We found that our connection was slow, the software had bugs and that it could not handle the kind of volume we were generating. Our mail became choked in a traffic jam on Pipeline's very narrow lanes. Also, Pipeline was located in New York and it took a long distance telephone call to hook up with them. Staying on line for hours a day was getting very expensive. Besides, they were upset about the flames. They still had not developed a policy toward advertising and they were clearly reluctant to do so. They themselves, after all, were making money from the Internet. It would be hypocritical to criticize others for doing the same thing. On the other hand, some of their customers were offended. They wanted us to ease up. We had to find better access.

Doing some research in various books about the Internet, we learned of a California company called Netcom that provided Internet access, with local dial up numbers in many different cities, including our own, Phoenix. We quickly signed up, with an account name of cslaw, e-mail address cslaw@netcom.com. We soon learned that Netcom had access to about 8,000 Newsgroups, many more than the other companies we had tried. We were beginning to feel a bit overwhelmed, however. Netcom, unlike Pipeline and Witchcraft, did not have its own simple graphical software to use. Instead, we were faced with a blank computer screen and told to execute commands from a Unix shell, whatever that was. Not having the vaguest idea of how to proceed, we began looking for someone who did, a consultant who would get everything running smoothly, and teach us what to do. All we needed was to find the right person, and, after several failed efforts, find him we did. He had long, light brown hair. He wore an old T-shirt with a picture by Escher, the "impossible triangle" artist worshipped by the Tech crowd. He was skinny. He was spacey. He had a girlfriend and an attitude. He was twenty years old and he had exactly the information we required.

We went through Netcom's Newsgroup list and picked out about 1000 groups with the help of our newly hired computer geek. We stayed up all night one Friday feverishly posting to each of them. The next morning, our phone started ringing. Irate people, claiming to be systems administrators and owners of other networks, complained that we were overloading their systems. Junk e-mail started to fill our mailbox. But requests for information also poured in. Hundreds of them came within a matter of hours. Then, it stopped. We were locked out of the account by Netcom. They sent a message to us to call them on Monday. We did and they read us the riot act on how what we had done was irresponsible and rude. We didn't see it that way. In any event, they agreed to turn our account back on, but only if we promised never to use their system for advertising on the Net again. Reluctantly, we agreed.

The Lunch Meat Hits the Fan

Mail from the Netcom posting continued to pour in. People began hiring us as well. This was looking very promising, but it was only March and the lottery wouldn't even take place until June. We had to do more advertising. We knew that the final government rules for the program would be released in a few weeks and that this would be the perfect time for one more posting. We also knew that so far we weren't having much luck finding a cooperative access provider. We did more research and discovered hundreds of Internet access providers all over the country, including several with local telephone numbers in Phoenix. A telephone call to one of them, Internet Direct, opened an account instantaneously. We were asked for our preferred e-mail address (what else—cslaw, now cslaw@in-direct.com). We were given a password, and told how to dial-up on the phone. We gave a credit card number to charge our $20 per month fee. There were no additional charges. We could stay on-line for 24 hours a day if we wished.

There was one last matter to take care of. We wanted no more roadblocks from access providers. Therefore, we set up a meeting with officials at Internet Direct. We told them exactly what we wanted to do. We warned them that there would be loud cries of protest to say nothing of an outpouring of e-mail attacks. We told them we did not want to proceed without assurance that we could have their cooperation in this matter. Internet Direct told us they could handle all our traffic. Their link to the I-way, unlike Pipeline's was a full-fledged, multi-lane freeway. They laughed when we told them that some of our previous providers had difficulties handling the mail traffic we received. They could do it, no problem.

With respect to policy, Bill Fisher, an Internet Direct official, gave us a memo outlining what the company would or would not do. In summary, the memo said that while "Internet Direct cannot take a pro-active stance" on the issues we raised, they would "continue to treat [us] with the respect [we] deserve as an Internet Direct customer." The memo let us know that Internet Direct did not "pre-censor information" and, more importantly (to us at least) assured us that "[Internet Direct] will not stop you from doing anything unless we believe it to be illegal." The memo went on to say that if the company received reports that our actions were having "deleterious effects" upon its system and the other users of Internet Direct, we would then be asked to "cease performing [those] actions" **and if we didn't stop,** "further action to halt problems" would be taken.

We made up our minds to go ahead.

Now we were faced with a technical problem. It had taken some doing in terms of time spent to sit down at the computer and send postings to each of about 1000 Newsgroups, as we had before with our Netcom account. We wanted it done automatically but we didn't know how to accomplish this. We were not professional programmers or technicians. We were certainly not "hackers," self-trained computer buffs, mainly in their teens and early twenties, who spent every waking hour trying to either build their own systems or destroy those of others. Although we didn't know how to solve our own problem, we knew enough about how computers worked to figure that it could indeed be solved. Computers were, after all, made to do simple, repetitious tasks like the one we had in mind. We called on our friend the geek. He wrote a program to do what we wanted in one night and then, mercifully, he disappeared.

Now we were ready. We went through the complete list of available Newsgroups. We sifted out the obvious no-winners such as the joke and flame groups. (Yes, there are even some Newsgroups where the participants dedicate themselves solely to the activity of insulting each other and anyone else who comes within their sites.) When we were finished, we had a list of about 6000 groups. It was by far the biggest mass posting of any kind done on the Usenet. We sat down at our computer about 12:30 a.m. We chose that hour because computer traffic was low at that time of night and we were less likely to meet with an electronic jam up from the huge dissemination of information we were about to attempt.

Then we pushed a single key. The program started operation. We watched, almost hypnotized by the steady rhythmic flashing and movement on the screen that signaled the launching of each message around the globe. We watched as the lights continued to blink like small, green stars in the middle of the night. At first, we were tense, concerned that the program would somehow break down before the job was done. Our fears were proven unfounded. The program moved through the list smoothly, flawlessly. Then the work was done. In ninety minutes we had sent our message to millions of people in every corner of the world. We went to bed and waited for whatever reaction was to come.

We got up early that next morning and went to work. The phones were already ringing off the hook. We had asked those who were interested to respond to us by e-mail, but we'd also put our office phone number on the message just in case someone wanted to speak to us directly. They wanted to speak to us all right. Call after call came complaining about what we had done. "What the hell do you think you're doing. You've put your message on every god damn Newsgroup on the face of the planet, you idiots," they screeched into the receiver. Nearly all the callers sounded young. Nearly all were male. We had never heard so many emotionally disturbed voices. Even the tone of those who tried to register their dissatisfaction politely were tinged with something approximating hysteria.

We turned on the computer. The messages were rolling into our e-mail box at a dizzying pace. In fact, they were coming in by the thousands. Here, too, there were shrill messages of protest. The use of four-letter words was more than liberal. The amount of mail was particularly staggering because a number of protesters decided to do more than just apply bad language to the situation. Instead, they sent mailbombs, huge electronic files of junk designed to clog up our computer by their sheer size. We were absolutely amazed that there were people who could become so distraught over the appearance of a simple, commercial message on their computer screens.

But that wasn't all. Among the wails of protest, the waves of profanity, the threats, and assorted electronic garbage were huge numbers of requests for further information on the Green Card Lottery. On our screen we read over and over, "Please send me your information on the Green Card Lottery as soon as possible. Thank you." Many of these requests also contained details of the writer's personal immigration situation and asked specific questions about what to do. On the telephone, as well, calls came from everywhere, asking questions and requesting more information. We began attempting to deal with the staggering amount of data before us. As quickly as we could, we sorted through the messages, deleting the complaints and putting the legitimate inquiries in a separate file for future response.

Then something we had not expected happened. Our link to the Internet shut off. Internet Direct, the company that had promised not to stop us unless we did something illegal, the company that had assured us they could handle the expected heavy load of messages, ignored our agreed upon procedure and cut our connection.

Looking back on it, we shouldn't have been surprised. Even when we reached an agreement with these people we were skeptical. We had chosen them in large part because they were local. Remember that all computer communications presently go over phone lines. It is important to have a local dial-up number. Otherwise, you have to pay long-distance charges every time you are on-line. There are some companies that have dial-up numbers in many places, irrespective of the company's home base location. Netcom was one such company. But access providers with that kind of broad service were few and far between. This is a brand new industry. Most access providers have been in existence only a year or two. The local Phoenix outfit we were now using had been in business even less time than that. Actually, we had once set up an account with them early on but gave up on it quickly. We found that we were never sure when we might be able to use their services and when we might not. Their system was crashing on us on a regular basis. We found that their phone lines were eternally tied up and that they were perpetually repairing something already installed or configuring something new. Our early experiences with them made us question the wisdom of dealing with them at all.

Still, economy dictated that we stick with a local dial-up number. Besides, given the somewhat controversial nature of what we wanted to do, we thought it best to deal with someone who was close by. That way, if there were problems, we could work them out on a face-to-face basis. Unfortunately, the face presented to us belonged to Bill Fisher, a twenty-something, khaki-swathed smart aleck. He was the one with whom we had met when we had tried to avoid the very result we were now experiencing. At that meeting, we had watched as Fisher slouched down in his chair, listing to one side in what appeared to be a poor William F. Buckley imitation. He had then proceeded to give behaving like a grown-up his best shot. His first move was to look at his watch and announce he could grant us only twenty minutes of his time. Ignoring the incredible rudeness of this remark as well as the transparently affected body language, we explained in detail what we wanted to do and what some of the backlash might be. Fisher said he would take it up with his associates. Later, we learned his associates were made up of owner Mike March, another individual in his twenties who was reputed to have gotten the start-up funds for Internet Direct from his parents, and technician Jeffrey Wheelhouse, a frighteningly precise clone of the twenty-year-old earth-bound space cadet who had written our mass posting program. Our close encounter with Internet Direct added to what we had already heard about the reliability of their service did little to inspire confidence. Nonetheless, a week later we had received our memo from Bill Fisher saying they would not stop us.

Now that the hour of reckoning had come, in spite of what had been said either in person or in memos, the empty screen where large numbers of messages had appeared moments before was now blank. We immediately called Fisher. By this time, his carefully crafted, cool persona was in shambles. He was shrieking uncontrollably. His system was overloaded. His phone was ringing off the hook. His company was being blamed by the angry hoards for our actions. Internet Direct's system was crashing under the weight of the huge number of messages being received. Wheelhouse was beside himself trying to handle the problem. No, they would not turn our connection back on, memo or no memo.

We, too, were upset. After all the effort we'd spent trying to create a smooth operation, and preparing for what was coming, a small access company was going to cost us thousands of dollars in lost business. We began to receive phone calls from potential clients who were unable to get through because Internet Direct had closed off our account. They wanted an explanation of why we had not answered their e-mail requests for more information on the Green Card Lottery. We responded as best we could, promising to send the information by regular mail, dubbed snail mail by those who reside in computerland. Meanwhile, we dispatched our lawyers to try and reason with Internet Direct. Eventually, after several days of wrangling, they were persuaded to forward our incoming mail to Netcom, where we still had an account in place.

As the day following our posting dawned, the phone was still ringing incessantly, with both protesters and potential immigration clients. By this time, we had also begun to receive death threats and certain enterprising individuals had started sending us hundreds of junk faxes. We turned on our computer and utilized the Netcom account to read the messages posted on some of the Newsgroups. Nearly all of them were about us. From that day forward, the Internet never stopped discussing us. Everything we did was tracked. Every action we took was dissected and examined. Our motives and thought processes were analyzed. A long discussion ensued on the need for a name to be given to the practice of mass-posting messages on the Net. After lengthy deliberation, it was decided to call the practice "spamming" in honor of a well-known skit by Monty Python's Flying Circus, the famous British comedy group. We were unfamiliar with the skit, but apparently it involved throwing lunch meat at a wall. The skit seemed to be a favorite among the university denizens and tech people who were our main detractors.

The hysteria continued. Soon it was impossible to keep track of everything that was being said about us, let alone answer back. Finally, we stopped trying. The volume of discussion about us became so great that to some we began to seem like celebrities. Someone posted a message saying that having our e-mail address was like having the private phone number of Mel Gibson or the playmate of the month. We looked in the mirror and failed to see either a Hollywood hunk or Miss January looking back. Oh, well. It was a nice thought.

Tales of the Fourth Estate

Then things took an even more bizarre turn. The phone rang again, but this time it was neither an immigrant seeking a Green Card nor a shrill protester. Instead, it was Peter Lewis, the technical writer for *The New York Times*. We were flabbergasted. We could not believe that what we had done would be of interest to the country's leading newspaper. We talked to Lewis on the phone at length. He seemed like a nice guy. Our amazement continued as Lewis dispatched a photographer so that his story could be accompanied by a picture, giving everyone the opportunity to see what the most notorious couple in Cyberspace looked like. Two days later, we saw ourselves staring back from the front page of *The New York Times* business section under the headline "An Ad (Gasp!) in Cyberspace." True to our impressions of him on the phone, the story he wrote was fair and balanced. The wryly humorous tone of the headline reflected our own take on the matter. It was still hard to understand why something as innocuous as a small commercial posting on a public electronic bulletin board seemed to be driving substantial numbers of people into a rage so profound they would actually consider doing physical harm to another person in retribution.

Like the endless discussions of our behavior on the Net itself, from that day on the newspaper stories never let up. Following immediately on the heels of Peter Lewis was *Washington Post* reporter John Burgess. In the weeks and months that followed we spoke to every major publication in the country repeatedly. At first, we did each interview as a team. Then the novelty began to wear off. Being interviewed became a full-time job. In an effort to accomplish something other than honing our skills at fashioning sound bites, we began to divvy up the interviewee duties. The press got one or the other of us, but not both at the same time.

Often, we would read a story from a particular reporter that claimed to quote us. What we were supposed to have said sometimes looked strangely unfamiliar. We also noticed that inaccuracies in reporting of the facts were a common occurrence. It was written that we had been kicked off the Net, when we weren't. Several reporters made it sound as if every response we received was a criticism, ignoring the by now awesome number of requests for immigration information that kept pouring in. We began to see why so many people in the public eye hated the press. We began to understand why Cher had sued the *National Inquirer*.

In this particular case, though, the press took heat as well, from none other than our highly energetic and ever-vigilant opponents on the Net. As each story came out, it was broadcast on the Net itself by individuals who took it upon themselves to spread the word and alert their comrades-in-arms to the latest diabolical statements Canter and Siegel were making. It was not without effect. A fairly new breed of journalists had been dispatched to cover this story. They were young technical reporters, hatched directly from the same spawning grounds whence came our most vocal Net critics. These reporters knew they were supposed to follow the universally recognized press ethic of impartiality. Still, it was tough with their constituents on the Net screaming for blood.

In short order, we observed that unbiased reporting was being abandoned for slanted attacks. We soon learned that when a reporter wants to skewer someone while still being able to claim objectivity, there are standard tricks to be used. Since editorial comments can't come from the reporter himself, he will instead get others to state his opinions for him and then print them as quotes. Statements matching the reporter's view will then be featured at the beginning of the story. Any opposing views are placed at the end, in hopes that the reader will look only at the first few paragraphs and miss the rest. Finally, the validity of the favored quotes are never questioned. They are treated as fact. The opposing statements, however, are always called "claims." We noticed that anything the computer crowd had to say, no matter how outlandish, was reported as gospel, while our comments never rose above the level of claims. One young reporter who wrote a computer column for the Phoenix afternoon paper felt the need one day to put an anti–Canter and Siegel item in his column and, absent any discernible news peg, managed to do so by quoting an unknown college student who, since the "Green Card Incident" had forsaken his real name and taken to calling himself Spam.

The rage of some appeared especially to bother Peter Lewis. In what was now about his fourth interview with us, he noted that his own e-mail box was overflowing with flames. Impartiality would not do for the Netters. Lewis had failed to characterized us as sufficiently heinous and he was being pressed hard to see the error of his ways. Apparently, the plan worked. Where Lewis's previous stories about us had been straightforward reporting, the next one described us as "sneering pariahs." He characterized us as hard-bitten publicity mongers who were lapping up media attention, forgetting that he was the one who had first called us. He went on to say that we were impervious to the death threats and continuous personal attacks that came over the computer on a regular basis, even though we had certainly never exhibited such behavior or expressed such sentiments to Lewis or anyone else. Nonetheless, Lewis appeared to want to blast us, and he did so. For the first time since all of this had started, we answered back. We wrote a letter to Tim Race, Lewis's boss and detailed the numerous inaccuracies and overstatements contained in Lewis's article. We never heard back from either Lewis or Race until the next time Lewis called to interview us in the ongoing saga. The subsequent story he wrote was again the model of objectivity. Probably the biggest irony of this tale is that after Lewis's pariah story was released, he again was criticized by die-hards on the Internet. To them, it still wasn't critical enough.

Another press victim of the Netters' penchant for dirty fighting was Jared Sandberg of *The Wall Street Journal*. Actually, Sandberg had contacted us the day before Peter Lewis, but we had not been in when his call came. We had intended to call him back, but before we got the chance, someone identifying himself as an assistant of a reporter from *The Wall Street Journal* was on the phone. We presumed this caller was an associate of Sandberg's and we gave him a lengthy interview. About two nights later, there was a message on our voice mail from our erstwhile interviewer. He informed us he was not a reporter from that newspaper at all. He had simply posed as one with the intent of harassing us. Then he laughed raucously on tape for about two minutes before hanging up. Certainly, we were irritated, but it was Jared Sandberg who had really lost out. We called Sandberg back and told him what had happened, but by that time, the Peter Lewis story had already appeared in *The New York Times*. Jared Sandberg now knew first-hand what we were coming to see more and more: certain individuals, mainly university students, cared little who they hurt or how they lied. They wanted things their own way and they'd trample over anyone to achieve that goal.

Our close relationship with the media continues to this day. They've become a part of our everyday lives. Eventually, the television reporters followed the print media to our door. CBS did the first story. Then we went to Los Angeles where we were taped by CNN and appeared on Larry King's radio show. It was great fun. Larry King is such a gentleman and so skilled at what he does, he made it easy for a couple of novices. Back home, a five-person crew from NBC flew from LA to Phoenix for the sole purpose of interviewing us. Once again, we were amazed. *Time* magazine featured us in a cover story about the Internet. We went out and bought new suits, hoping we wouldn't end up appearing to be likely candidates for a revival of the Gong Show. Each time we talk to another reporter or appear on TV, we pray fervently that Chuck Barris is not looking for us.

Growing the Internet

When we first determined to try advertising on the Internet it seemed like a strategy that couldn't fail. Commercial use of the Internet was a natural. It required no special, sophisticated skills and the cost was very low. That many people wanted what we had to offer in a market with a sizable international segment was no big surprise. Although we were certainly gratified that the plan had worked so well, given everything going for it, we would have been more surprised if it hadn't worked.

What we honestly were not prepared for, however, was the passionate opposition we encountered. It was always interesting to see how different people reacted to the story. If we spoke to anyone unfamiliar with the Internet, they were as baffled as we were over what had occurred. They asked what we had done to anger so many people, and after we had finished explaining, they would always look at us quizzically and say, "So what?"

The old time Internetters were a different story. Steeped in Internet tradition that they seemed to hold as dear as life itself, they wanted no change in the status quo. Using the Internet for commercial purposes was, we were to learn, a drastic change. To really understand what you will be dealing with as you seek your fortune on the Information Superhighway, a brief history lesson is in order. The seeds of the Internet were sown by the U.S. Government in the 1970s, when an arm of the Defense Department called the Defense Advanced Research Program Agency (DARPA) wanted a computer network developed to support its efforts. Computers are usually thought of by most people as tools to do calculations, solve problems, and process or keep records. DARPA saw computers differently. They wanted them as a means for people to communicate with each other. To fill the need required a network. A software system had to be developed that would allow many different brands, sizes, and types of computers to speak to one another. This system was called a protocol. By developing the protocol, Arpanet was born.

Arpanet was the granddaddy of computer networks, but others arose as well, all of them at universities or a few corporations such as IBM, which were computer research centers. In the 1980s, a great stride forward was made when the National Science Foundation (NSF), in order to extend the benefits of computer networking to non-commercial, academic research, set about to link various networks together. Five university locations were chosen as central points of connection to accomplish this, and a network of networks, the Internet, was born.

There were, however, many restrictions on who could utilize the Internet and for what purpose. Specifically, the Internet was to be used for research and nothing else. Accordingly, unless you were affiliated with a university, the government, or the research arm of a technical company, you were not permitted access. Each individual network on the Internet had its own set of rules, called Acceptable Use Policies (AUP) and the NSF itself had an AUP, but really, they were all pretty much the same. No commercialism. Research only.

A clubby atmosphere ensued. Since all Internetters were either government techies, company techies, or university techies, there was a commonality of interest and a like-mindedness of philosophy. A general penchant for science fiction gave rise to the Cyberspace concept and the feeling that there existed here some sort of separate country with its own rules, ethics, and culture. While AUPs were official statements of rules, there sprang up an unofficial behavioral code which was dubbed, predictably enough "Netiquette." A number of disparate individuals tried to write Netiquette down so the uninitiated would be able to read it and become indoctrinated. That is why today there are numerous versions.

In the 1990s, the bomb fell. The NSF decided to open the Internet to commercial use. It also decided that anyone at all should be able to get access. Vice President Gore spoke of removing inequality between information haves and have-nots. Based on communication through the Internet and the commercial, as well as educational, benefits it would bring, there was to be the dawning of a new, golden era in the development of our country and the rest of the world.

Fear and loathing now overtook the once homogeneous Internet "community" as a flood of newbies, with varying attitudes and backgrounds, began to invade their space. By this time the old guard who, in many cases, were not old at all, but really quite young in years and arguably short on maturity of attitude, had developed a full-blown delusion that the Internet was a cross between a womb, a church, and a nation-state. Hell would freeze over before they would allow the landscape of their beloved country to change. Hell would freeze over twice before they would allow control to be seized from their grasp by those (expletive) newbies. With energy typical of zealots throughout the ages they began the huge task of educating the "clueless newbies" into the ways of the Internet. Forgotten was the ideal that no one controlled the Internet. The new guys would tow the line or else.

In undertaking this task, the Net traditionalist had some powerful advantages. Not the least of these was the fact that most of the new breed of tech reporters had come directly from their ranks. So did the authors of a proliferation of recently published books meant to educate the public on the ways of the Internet. All agreed that the best method of training the newbies lay in a combination of pro-active propaganda mixed with flaming or worse for those who got out of hand. Typical of the dogma Net gurus hoped to impart can be seen in this startling quote from *The Whole Internet Users Guide and Catalog* by Ed Krol, who, in this passage, likens the Internet to a church.

> If you go to church and accept its teachings and philosophy, you are accepted by it and receive the benefits. If you don't like it, you can leave. The church is still there, and you get none of the benefits. Such

is the Internet. . . . If the network does something that causes damage to the Internet, it could be excommunicated until it mends its evil ways.

If you believe in the Bill of Rights of the U.S. Constitution, a chill should be running up your spine right about now.

Education of the masses is never easy, however. Some people just didn't get it. Foolishly, certain recalcitrant individuals like us refused to accept an assortment of self-appointed dictators as lord and master. Amazingly, we refused to bow down in the church, practice the religion, or obey the laws of the nation-state. Stubbornly, we clung to the belief that we lived in Phoenix. Even today, after all the flaming, as we look out the window and see the mesquite trees rustling in the warm desert breeze, it still looks like the Arizona city we've grown to love. Here in the Valley of the Sun, advertising is not a sin. It's not rude. It's certainly not illegal. Look out your own window and take note of where you live. We bet unrestricted commercial use of your computer is legal in your home town, too.

The Birth of Cybersell™

Even before our own personal "Big Bang" occurred we believed so strongly in the marketing power of the Information Superhighway that we planned to put together a company to assist others in using this remarkable resource. Some time ago, we had set about the task of thoroughly familiarizing ourselves with the many types of selling possibilities available on the Internet. There were several, and all with strange names like World Wide Web and Gopher. We chose the name "Cybersell™" for our new business and asked our good friend, artist Jeff Neff (yes, that's his real name), to design the logo for us. Jeff, who had designed all our book covers and promotion pieces for years, was a Madison Avenue refugee. Long ago he left the Manhattan scene and his Cardin suits behind, trading them for T-shirts and buffalo sandals. He had, however, taken his extraordinary talent with him and soon we had as our symbol, a swirling vortex of color with stars popping out everywhere and a big, sun-yellow "Cybersell™" superimposed over it all. Looking at that symbol made it all seem like it was really going to happen and we began to see our path clearly.

We knew we had a great idea going for us. We also had the added benefit that the Internet was a red-hot commodity. You could not pick up the newspaper or turn on the TV without hearing about it. Still, new companies and new ideas take time to get established. We began to prepare for a publicity campaign to launch Cybersell™ into the public eye. We expected the usual quiet beginning and modest development most fledgling companies experience. We proceeded to dig in for the long haul. We needn't have bothered.

Immediately after the first wave of publicity, we issued a press release announcing the startup of Cybersell™. Because of our previous escapades, the press was anxious to tell the world that the two upstarts who had rocked Cyberspace with their "spam" were now starting a company to help others do the same thing. Of course, broad advertising on the Usenet was only a part of what we planned to do. There were really so many creative possibilities. We looked forward to using them all. Although that part of the story never saw the light of day, nonetheless, Cybersell™ received a grand launching in *The New York Times, The Wall Street Journal, The Washington Post* and just about every other newspaper imaginable, plus ample mention by the major television networks. No one could have asked for more.

In spite of all the publicity that was making Cybersell™ an instantly established leader in its field, and in spite of the fact that Cybersell™ techniques were a proven success, as was readily observable in our own case, we were concerned that the negative comments about us, not to mention the unpleasant side effects we'd had to endure due to Net vigilantism, would scare people off. Once again, our fears proved groundless. On the day we circulated the Cybersell™ press release, we were at the same time alternatively pleading with and pressuring the phone company to get Cybersell™'s number up and working. When the first story appeared, the phone started to ring. Our phone number was certainly not included in the news stories, so everyone who contacted us had to go through the trouble of calling information to get it. Obviously, a lot of people thought it was worth the effort. Continuing to anticipate the worst, we expected most of our callers to be the screamers whom, we reasoned, would be beside themselves at the prospect of Cybersell™ cloning more spammers. For yet another time, we worried needlessly.

Over and over the phone rang with fresh Cybersell™ prospects eager to be involved in this incredible new Internet market. Many of them understood very little about the Internet, so much of what we had to say to them involved explaining in very basic terms how the whole thing worked. As we went about getting to know Cybersell™'s first customers, we pulled no punches. In addition to the glittering money-making opportunities available through the Internet, we described extensively the controversial aspects and the possible backlash. When we had finished, each customer invariably had only one question: "How successful were you?" We told them we had gotten in excess of twenty thousand inquiries for our information. These names and addresses had, in good business fashion, been recorded and saved as future marketing prospects. The twenty thousand figure did not include the untold number that had been lost because of electronic vandals and assorted access providers who'd cost us a fortune by interfering with our efforts. Everything we had done took under three months, but if we had posted to all the groups at once in the first place, we probably could have achieved the same result in one night. All told, the final count of actual paying clients for the single venture was slightly in excess of one thousand and we had made $100,000. That was all anybody who called about Cybersell™ needed to hear.

We hope it's all you need to hear. We've told you our story in detail so you will know as much as possible about what to expect as you undertake to make a fortune on the Information Superhighway. It's a bumpy road to be sure, but it's fun and exciting too. In the pages that follow, we'll share with you the techniques we've learned. We'll do our best to see that you understand them well enough to put them into practice. Even if you never try any of the money-making techniques we describe, we hope you'll enjoy discovering more about the new vista of communication called the Information Superhighway and its primary branch, the Internet. Personally, though, we hope you decide to do more than just sit back and watch.

One more word of encouragement. As you begin to seek your fortune on the I-way, you may find your road not as difficult as ours. We were the first ones, and the first traditionally clear a path for others to follow. Things are changing on the I-way with a speed that's hard to imagine. By the time you read this, some of the protesters we encountered may have been gathered up and locked away where vandals and the like belong. Then your road to fortune will be pleasant, in addition to financially rewarding, as it should be.

Even if you do meet with a few snags along the way, that certainly shouldn't be enough to stop you. That's just a part of life. Some of the loudest protests against cyberselling are coming from individuals who themselves are exploiting the I-way for profit in every manner possible. It's not surprising that those who understand the enormous financial potential would like to keep it all for themselves. When you consider so violent a reaction to something as relatively harmless as advertising, you really must ask yourself, "Why?" You must also ask yourself if these are voices worth listening to. We've been called a lot of names since our great computer adventure began. One of those names is *pioneer*. Think of yourself that way and fortune on the I-way is yours for the taking.

3

BETTER, FASTER, AND A LOT CHEAPER
Selling to 30 Million People Who Call the Net Home

Success at making a lot of money is almost always based on a single, simple principle: the ability to do something better, faster, or cheaper. You know that cyberselling means finding or inventing a good product or service, and then using the I-way to market what you have to sell. The main reason why you can make a fortune on the Information Superhighway is that you can sell on it better, faster and cheaper than anyone ever thought possible. Of course, it would be best if the product or service you offer also incorporates these sterling qualities. We'll help you to develop that special item to sell on the I-way in our next chapter. Here, though, we want to show you how almost anything you choose to make available through your computer will sell better than anywhere else you can think of. You're about to learn how your computer can turn you into the most successful salesperson that ever lived.

Interactive: The Irresistible Force

Looking at our basic business success principle, the first element is "better." When we try to explain why selling on the I-way is better, the fact is that computer marketing is so much better, it's difficult to know where to begin. Above all, what makes cyberselling more effective than any other sales method is the feature called "interactive." The term interactive is another computer-age buzzword you've probably been hearing a lot lately. For marketing, it means that instead of simply sitting in front of a television or reading a magazine, quietly watching an advertisement pass before your eyes, you can, in some way communicate back to the seller your level of interest, questions, or desire to purchase. Remember, the I-way is a series of computer networks. What computer networks were invented to do is allow people to communicate with each other easily. Two categories of individuals who now have more opportunity to interact than ever before are buyers and sellers.

At first, this may not seem like such a revolutionary breakthrough, but if you think about it a bit more, you will see that it is. Let's go back to television or magazines. You see an advertisement for, let's say, an automobile. Whether in print or on television, it's costing the car manufacturer a bundle to put that ad in front of you, even if you aren't counting advertising production expenses. Because standard media charges increase according to the amount of space or time the ad takes up, the advertiser has two main goals in mind: grab your attention and keep it short. In order to grab your attention, the advertiser uses a number of techniques. He or she may choose some intense-looking hard bodies as models. You can watch them driving the cars at high speeds up beautiful mountain roads that most of us will probably never see in our lifetime. Perhaps you'll be treated to a visual demonstration of that well known but rarely pursued sport, truck bowling. All this is a lot of fun and certainly does get you to watch and think about the vehicle, but what now? Remember, goal number two is to keep things brief, but suppose your attention has truly been captured and you have some real interest in buying a car. Your curiosity has been piqued and there are lots of things you want to know. Unfortunately, it's past business hours when you see this ad, so you can't go to your phone and call the dealership. Anyway, you aren't about to drop your magazine or turn off the TV and run to the phone. Your questions remain unanswered. By the time you've gone to bed and gotten up the next morning, you can't remember what it was you wanted to know about the vehicle. If the automobile seller is really unlucky, you may have forgotten about the car altogether.

Now let's take the same example and apply the interactive feature. You turn on your computer and you find your way to the Cyberspace auto mall. (We'll explain how to get there in Chapter Nine about the World Wide Web.) You are faced with a selection of dozens of auto manufacturers. You push a key to see Infiniti. Is this really the car for you? You are whisked to the Infiniti car lot where will see on your computer screen pictures of three car models, the G-20, J-30, and Q-45, each with the suggested base sticker price underneath. You select the Q-45 and hit a key to see more. Immediately, specifications of the car are shown on your screen. You are also given the ability to access several different independent reviews of the car. You look at each, and decide that yes, this is the car for you. You tell the computer to proceed with a demonstration. You are now given a close up, full-color picture of the Q-45. With the touch of yet another key, the driver's door opens and you now get a full view of the instrument panel. At the bottom of your computer screen flashes the message, "Want to take a test drive?" Of course! You punch in "yes" and suddenly your computer screen is transformed into a car simulator, much like the flight simulator video games you may like to play with. Certainly, a simulation is not the real thing, but your computer gives you the feeling that you are inside that Q-45, driving around town, through the mountains, even on the Indy-500 race track.

When your test drive is over, a list of possible options to put on the car, such as fancier wheels, gold packages, CD player, telephones, etc. appears on your computer screen. You are also presented with choices of colors and interiors. As you click on each option, the picture of the car changes on the screen to reflect your new choice. This gives you the ability to design your own car from the screen. When you have selected exactly what you want, a total price appears at the bottom of your screen, along with the name of the nearest dealer who can provide that exact configuration for you. You are then given the option of contacting that dealer via e-mail who will subsequently call you to arrange for a personal showing of the real thing, or perhaps you will even have the option of placing your order for the car through a discount auto broker. You could be given the option of making your deal right on-line. No more spending hours in the show room while the sales person goes back and forth from the manager's office to you and then back again. Buying a car couldn't be easier, or more enjoyable.

The technology to back up the scenario we've just described is here right now. We will learn later on that some of these multimedia ideas do not work well over the relatively slow standard telephone lines that hook up most computers at present. The technology is changing all the time, however, and within a few years, with installation of fiber optic networks and ISDN (Integrated Services Digital Network) lines, all of this and more will be feasible. Still, even today, the interactive marketing possibilities are mostly limited only by your own imagination.

If you are a beginner with computers, the procedure we've just outlined is advanced for you. Still, there is much you can do on a basic level to take advantage of the interactive selling feature your computer offers. From an informational standpoint as well as the perspective of instant gratification, it's hard to beat the interactive capabilities of the I-way. Nonetheless, that is only the most obvious customer relations benefit to cyberselling. There is a feature more subtle yet even more powerful than interactive. Instead of simply selling a product, you are building a relationship. Right off the bat, you have an interest in the Internet in common with your customer. It's a perfect beginning for forming the kind of trusting rapport that leads to sales. That closeness is amplified because your words and pictures can go directly into your customer's home or office, just like television. You have probably heard famous television personalities over the years speak of the special rapport they have with their fans because of this. Don't we really feel as if we know Murphy Brown or Tim "The Tool Man" Taylor personally? But the computer goes television one better. Not only can you talk to your customers, they can answer back! They begin to feel not only as if they know you, but you know them as well. There can be no more powerful selling instrument than that.

We hope you're convinced by now that there is no better way to sell a product or service than cyberselling, but if you need to hear more, you won't be disappointed. We've already mentioned that the first goal of any sales effort is to get the attention of the customer. Yet, often even the most creative, clever, interesting, and well-thought-out advertisements fail to accomplish this very basic objective. Why? Because you never see them. A commercial comes on television and automatically you tune it out of your mind. Perhaps you pick up your remote control and simply zap it. You use this opportunity as a break time to talk to the person on the couch next to you or to grab a snack. Whether or not you choose to avoid it, in a few short minutes, the commercial is gone and that's that.

The same is equally true of newspaper or magazine advertisements. Your eye moves down the page as you fish for the articles you want to read. If the article that interests you doesn't lead your eye to a particular advertisement, you are likely to skip over it. Perhaps certain articles don't interest you at all. Then you will never open to the page where an ad may appear. On busier days, you may neglect to read the paper altogether. Read or not, it gets thrown out, ads and all, to make way for tomorrow's edition.

Things are very different with computer advertisements. They wait patiently until you are ready to turn on your computer and look at them. They do not disappear after a specific point in time like radio or television commercials. We might also add that they do not pop up when you don't want them and distract you during a crucial moment of your favorite program either. They do not get thrown out as part of a publication without your having ever looked at them. In fact, there is only one way to get rid of them. You must look at them, make the decision that they are of no interest and delete them from your screen. In that brief second when you do look, you may also decide there is something worthy of your attention. In fact, you may even find you are so interested that you want to know more about the product or service offered. Either way, the seller has been given the opportunity to have his item considered and that's a much better shot than you get with nearly any other medium.

Last but not least, you can sell better on the I-way because it is new. The public is only just now becoming familiar with all the Internet and other interactive services have to offer. As each person goes through the process of learning about the wonders of the I-way, they usually become enthralled with what they find there. If what they find happens to be your product or service, the overall effect will rub off onto whatever it is you are selling.

There is actually relatively little advertising on the I-way at the present time because it is so new and due to the prior "nothing commercial" Internet Acceptable Use Policy of the National Science Foundation. This means that those who do begin to use it as a marketing tool will be among the first and will, therefore, stand out! Surely, the window of opportunity to be among the first will not always be open. It will probably not even be there for very long, as every day businesses of all sizes race to jump on the I-way bandwagon. But the chance to be a leader is there now for those who are smart enough to take advantage of it.

Of course, being one of the first also means getting into the game while commercial use of the Net is still controversial. Yet, even that can have its benefits. If a major goal of advertising is to get noticed, controversy certainly achieves that. Once again, our own results show when it comes to the I-way marketing, controversy can work in your favor.

The No-Wait Marketing Campaign

We've seen why you can sell better, much better, on the I-way. Now let's examine how cyberselling helps you accomplish the second element of the basic goal for success: faster. Computers are known for the speed in which data can be processed. Electronic data travels at blinding speeds. A signal travels around the world in fractions of a second. To demonstrate how computer marketing is faster, consider the long-standing staple of direct marketers, the mass mailing. The old-fashioned method requires you first to design a mailing piece, including both art and copy. Once that is done, you must then convert these efforts into camera-ready art so the printer can produce the finished mailer. This in itself may take a few days to a few weeks, depending on its complexity. Then, you take your art to a printer. Printers are not usually known for working quickly or meeting deadlines. If you are extremely lucky, you may be able to get your printing completed in a week or two. Next, you must stuff envelopes, paste on mailing labels, sort, and get the entire mailing ready for the post office. This could take several days or more.

Now comes the really fun part, dealing with the post office. Netters are fond of calling regular mail snail mail. It's not hard to understand why. Recently the post office quit guaranteeing that expensive priority mail will be delivered within two days. Even first-class mail within a single city sometimes takes a couple of days for delivery. And bulk mail? We've had to wait more than a month for some bulk-mail pieces to reach their final destination. Finally, though, the mail arrives. People see your product and they either want more information or they want to place an order. Maybe they will call you on the phone, which is fast, but many will simply write back to you, via snail mail. From the time you created your mailing piece to the time you get your first order, over a month has gone by.

Now let's consider the same mailer but we will send it via e-mail to an electronic mailing list. The very first step doesn't change. You must still create your piece. Once it is created, however, you're almost ready to begin raking in the sales. No camera-ready art. No printers. No stuffing envelopes. No post office slow downs. You simply zap it to your computerized mailing list and everyone receives your solicitation within a matter of minutes. You couldn't even physically carry the piece across the street to your neighbor's house that fast. And, since your customers have the option of sending an order back electronically, you could begin receiving orders within hours after your mail goes out. You may have made a fortune selling electronically in less time than it would take to receive a single order the old-fashioned way.

The print media is another typical vehicle for advertising products or services. Standard procedure has you first designing your art work and ad copy. Then it must be converted into camera-ready art. There are no printers this time, but you must still send the art on to the publication, wait until it appears in the appropriate issue and that issue is delivered to or purchased at a newsstand by your potential customers. In the case of a magazine, this might take several weeks or longer.

Compare electronic discussion groups and publications, available for all Cyberspace residents to view at any time. You must still prepare your ad copy. Once prepared, however, you can place it in circulation at any time. It appears on your customer's computer screens within minutes after it's posted. Using the old-fashioned method, even a publication as speedy as your daily newspaper will require at least a few days before your ad is seen. In addition, as with your electronic mailer, your customers, besides using the traditional response methods of telephone, fax, or regular mail, can contact you instantly via e-mail. You can even get your computer to send additional information automatically by computer on request, without having to lift a finger. Think of this as e-mail on demand. We'll explain how to do it all later on.

The Business Bargain of the Century

Finally, we reach the third element of our target goal: cheaper. No contest here at all. Estimates on Internet participation vary, but the most quoted figure seems to be that of thirty million. Moreover, that number grows by a mind-boggling amount every day. Once again, estimates vary, but the one most quoted sets the increase at about ten thousand new users per day. When it comes to sheer numbers of people reached, only the very top magazine publication or television programs can match the Internet at any price.

Price, however, is always a paramount consideration, so let's look at some comparisons with marketing costs for other standard types of media. Below are five charts, based on a survey we conducted in July 1994, showing how much you will pay to sell to the ready audience on the I-way versus some other popular methods you're sure to recognize.

INTERNET VS. TELEVISION

Media Buy	Cost	You Get
#1 Rated Daytime Soap National Ad	$45,000 $20.24 cpm*	30-second national spot reaching 4.4 mil. households
Prime Time TV Show "Seinfeld" Local Ad	$6,000 $42.55 cpm	30-second local spot reaching 282,000 adults
Prime Time TV Show "Seinfeld" Local Ad	$4,200 $59.57 cpm	15-second local spot reaching 282,000 adults

Media Buy	Cost	You Get
Prime Time Sunday or Monday Movie Local Ad	$2,500 $26.32 cpm	30-second local spot reaching 190,000 adults
Prime Time Sunday or Monday Movie Local Ad	$1,750 $36.84 cpm	15-second local spot reaching 190,000 adults
Friday Night Prime "Eyewitness Video" Local Ad	$1,000 $22.99 cpm	30-second local spot reaching 87,000 adults
Late Night "The Tonight Show" Local Ad	$600 $16.22 cpm	30-second local spot reaching 74,000 adults
Internet Advertising	**$1,000 per month $.0333 cptpm****	**Leased 56-K line Full Internet access and computer rental Reaching 30 million computer users**

INTERNET VS. RADIO

Media Buy	Cost	You Get
KTAR Local Ad Phoenix, AZ Mon-Fri AM Drive Time	$285 $15 cpm*	60-second local spot 19,300 listeners age 25+
KTAR Midday Local Ad Phoenix, AZ	$150 $11.244 cpm	60-second local spot 13,340 listeners age 25+
KTAR Evening Local Ad Phoenix, AZ	$60 $10.17 cpm	60-second local spot 5,900 listeners age 25+
KVRY Local Ad Phoenix, AZ Mon-Fri AM Drive Time	$350 $36.63 cpm	60-second local spot 9,300 listeners age 25–54

* cost per thousand per minute
** cost per thousand users per month

INTERNET VS. RADIO (*continued*)

Media Buy	Cost	You Get
KVRY Midday Local Ad Phoenix, AZ	$400 $29.07 cpm	60-second local spot 13,760 listeners age 25-54
KVRY Evening Local Ad Phoenix, AZ	$100 $34.25 cpm	60-second local spot 2,920 listeners age 25-54
KFYI Talk Radio Local Ad Phoenix, AZ AM Drive	$205 $22.283 cpm	60-second local spot net reach 9,200 listeners
KFYI Talk Radio Local Ad Phoenix, AZ/Midday	$145 $7.75 cpm	60-second spot net reach 18,700 listeners
KFYI "Rush Limbaugh" Local Ad/Phoenix, AZ	$475 $19.87 cpm	60-second spot net reach 23,900 listeners
Internet Advertising	**$1,000 per month $.0333 cptpm****	**Leased 56-K line Full Internet access and computer rental Reaching 30 million computer users**

* cost per thousand per minute
** cost per thousand users per month

INTERNET VS. NEWSPAPERS

Media Buy	Cost	You Get
The New York Times Mon–Sat	$440/CI* open rate $49.73 cpm**	1,141,366 circulation
The New York Times Mon–Sat	$422/CI contract rate $47.696 cpm	1,141,366 circulation
The New York Times Sunday	$528/CI open rate $38.77 cpm	1,756,635 circulation

Media Buy	Cost	You Get
The New York Times	$511/CI contract rate	1,756,635 circulation
Sunday	$37.53 cpm	
Los Angeles Times	$502.23/CI open rate	1,211,484 circulation
Daily	$53.48 cpm	
Los Angeles Times	$448.50/CI contract rate	1,211,484 circulation
Daily	$47.76 cpm	
Los Angeles Times	$619.50/CI open rate	1,469,202 circulation
Sunday	$54.394 cpm	
Los Angeles Times	$546.75/CI contract rate	1,469,202 circulation
Sunday	$48.01 cpm	
Arizona Republic	$154.18/CI open rate	426,390 circulation
Daily	$46.65 cpm	
Arizona Republic	$115.24/CI contract rate	426,390 circulation
Daily	$34.86 cpm	
Arizona Republic	$183.54/CI open rate	547,995 circulation
Sunday	$43.21 cpm	
Arizona Republic	$133.56/CI contract rate	547,995 circulation
Sunday	$31.44 cpm	
Internet Advertising	**$1,000 per month $.0333 cptpm*****	**Leased 56-K line Full Internet access and computer rental Reaching 30 million computer users**

* cost per column inch (a column inch is one column in width by one inch in length)

** cost per page per 1000 readers

*** cost per thousand users per month

INTERNET VS. MAGAZINES

Media Buy	Cost	You Get
People Magazine	$83,000 $24.09 cpm*	1 page 3,445,569 circulation
People Magazine	$53,000 $30.755 cpm	½ page 3,445,569 circulation
Time Magazine	$101,000 $24.61 cpm	1 page 4,103,772 circulation
Time Magazine	$60,600 $29.53 cpm	½ page 4,103,772 circulation
TV Guide	$107,600 $7.62 cpm	1 page 14,122,915 circulation
TV Guide	$59,100 $8.304 cpm	½ page 14,233,915 circulation
Internet Advertising	**$,1,000 per month $.0333 cptpm****	**Leased 56-K line Full Internet access and computer rental Reaching 30 million computer users**

* cost per page per 1000 readers
** cost per thousand users per month

INTERNET ADVERTISING VS. DIRECT MAIL

Media Buy	Cost	You Get
Direct Mail	$330	1,000 brochures mailed to customers
(Assuming printing cost of $0.15 each	330 cpm**	
Assuming bulk mailing cost of $0.18 each)		
Internet Advertising	**$1,000 per month**	**Leased 56-K line**
		Full Internet access and
	$.0333	**computer rental**
	cptpm*	**Reaching 30 million**
		computer users

* cost per thousand users per month
** cost per thousand

As you look at what it costs to sell through other mediums, you must be impressed with the staggeringly high expense of placing goods and services in front of potential customers. The cheapest price to reach 1,000 people only one time is $7 in a national magazine, $7 on the radio, $16 on television, $31 in a big city newspaper, and a whopping $330 by direct mail. No wonder big companies get most of the business. Who else could afford even a thirty second spot on a program with a big viewership like "Seinfeld?" Who else, for that matter, could afford to advertise on almost any network program, even one facing the imminent threat of cancellation?

While you may not have the cash to be able to go up against the corporate titans on other mediums like network TV, perhaps the most wonderful part of cyberselling is that on the I-way, the playing field is level. It costs only 3.3 cents to reach 1,000 Netters for a solid month. If you've got the product and the talent it takes to write simple descriptions of that product, you can reach the public as easily and effectively as Coca-Cola or McDonald's. If you are really creative and have the ability to produce artwork or clever selling copy, there are ways you can utilize the Net to disseminate it at low cost, as you will see later on when we describe the various marketing methods available on the Internet and the rest of the

I-way. We don't doubt you have the intelligence and imagination to make it to the top. There are any number of people who have just as much marketing ability as those whose advertising strategies draw big money and are seen by a broad public every day. If you've always believed you had a great idea that everyone would love if only they knew about it, let us show you how to put your ideas to work on the I-way. Now is your time to shine.

4

PRODUCTS THAT SELL ON THE NET

The Information Superhighway is so expansive that choosing from the vast number of possible services or products that might be marketed there could seem overwhelming. One of the main things that captures the imagination of those who discover the Internet is the endless array of topics on which information is available. It's almost as if the answers to all the mysteries of the world have revealed themselves and are yours for the asking. In selecting the service or product you will offer to others, you are, in addition to making your fortune, getting in on the fun of contributing to the wonderful mix of resources that can presently be found on the I-way. Perhaps you've already decided on a great product with which to launch your cyberselling venture. Good. You're one step ahead on the game. If not, this chapter's for you.

By far the easiest product to develop is also one of the best for selling on the Internet. What, after all, would be better to sell on the Information Superhighway than information? You may not think you have any information that people will pay for, but if you consider it carefully, you may very well be wrong. There are probably many things you know how to do better than anyone else. Perhaps you coach a high school football or little league team. Couldn't you put together a manual advising others how to do the same thing? Perhaps you know a lot of lawyer jokes. Why not write them down and market them on the Internet? Lawyer jokes are always great sellers. We were sent dozens of them after our Green Card Lottery postings. Here is one of our favorites, compliments of a Netter who shall remain anonymous:

Q: What is the difference between a lawyer and a catfish?
A: One is a bottom-feeding scum sucker. The other is a fish.

Maybe you are a popular, well-liked person. Why do you suppose that is the case? Could you explain to others the personal techniques that draw others to you? Think of what it is that you can do best. Write down your ideas. Put them together in a written manual or video instruction tape and try them out as a product on the Internet. If your first idea doesn't work, experiment with something else until you pick a winner. Marketing on the Information Superhighway is so inexpensive, there will be no great loss if your first attempts don't pan out.

Solving Problems for Others

If you don't think you have any special knowledge right now that people would be interested in paying for, maybe you could get some. Try thinking about information you might offer from a problem-solving perspective. Consider all the problems you, your family, friends, and society in general face each day and what might be done to improve the situation. For example, one difficulty experienced by almost everyone is that of too little money. Many people have made a fortune coming up with solutions to this one. The plan you develop need not be complicated. Some entrepreneurs have earned fortunes by selling information on how to deal with credit bureaus. Others have done well offering advice simply on how to live within a budget.

One of the most effective problem-solving information packages we've ever seen comes from a college professor right here in our home town. Dr. Claude Olney of Arizona State University put together a booklet and a simple video tape of himself lecturing on the subject of how to get better grades. You may have heard of it. He called it *Where There's a Will There's an A.* We ordered it ourselves, even though we have long been out of school, because we were so impressed with his marketing idea. We were also struck by the fact that we were not the only ones impressed with Dr. Olney's product. It was so good he had managed to obtain the services of TV personalities John Ritter and the late Michael Landon as spokespersons. We wanted to know if the product was as good as the flair that went into the marketing. What we received was a well-thought-out, well-presented system of how to approach the task of studying. There was no magic. There was not even a special secret only a college professor would know. What we saw instead, was a diligently researched presentation, devised by a person with a good sense of organization and a great deal of common sense, who had obviously thought long and hard about how to solve the problem of getting good grades.

We've chosen the example of Dr. Olney not only because it illustrates so well how a fortune can be made with relatively simple solutions to problems, but also because the *Where There's a Will There's an A* package is an ideal product for marketing on the Internet. Although thousands of people from all walks of life are diluting the strictly academic character of the Internet audience more every day, there are still millions of teachers and students who make up a large part of the market. It is highly likely that they would be interested in a product giving solutions to the problem of improving student performance.

As you consider what information you might want to offer in your cyberselling venture, think about the kinds of people most likely to be on the I-way. Certainly there are all sorts, and the audience becomes more heterogeneous with the passage of time. Still, there are identifiable factors. All your potential customers access the Internet. This means, at the very least, that they all use computers. Therefore, they are probably educated and middle class or above. A lot of the Internet is devoted to research, and so you can expect to find not only large numbers of college students and faculty members, but many members of the professions as well. A segment of the I-way population strongly on the upswing is the business community. The Internet is a global society and so it includes people from all over the world. Piece all of these factors together and you will surely be able to come up with winning ideas for products and services that will sell to a group with such a profile.

Simple Ideas That Work

You may feel that some ideas are too simple or too obvious for other people to spend good money on them, but, once again, if you will think about it, a lot of people have earned a great deal with ideas that were extremely uncomplicated. Here is another of our favorite examples to illustrate this point. Popular television actress Donna Mills, who is best known for her leading role in the long-running night-time soap opera "Knot's Landing," has startlingly beautiful eyes that she accentuates with perfectly applied cosmetics. Of course, the rest of her is equally beautiful, but fans especially seem to notice her eyes. Capitalizing on this attention-getting feature, she put together a successful video called *The Eyes Have It*. The video explains how to put on eye makeup. Hard to believe that anyone would pay for information as simple as that, but they did.

Another good example of simple ideas that sell concerns a woman who sold her knowledge of how to straighten up and organize a messy desk.

She wrote a book explaining how to put papers in files and then label the files. She also suggested that rather than leaving them on top of your desk as reminders of things you need to do, you should acquire a yellow pad, go through your papers, make a list of tasks that require your attention on the pad, and then put the papers away neatly in a drawer. With this information she was not only able to sell a book, but she also charged, and apparently got, a consulting fee of $200 an hour. The reason why we conclude she must have been successful is we found out about her by reading a national magazine. Now, if someone can make it into the pages of one of the best-read publications in the world by knowing how to clean up a desk, you can certainly think of some information to sell on the Net.

Florists seemed to particularly like the idea of cyberselling. A recent article in a computer magazine, PC Today, reported that one florist is grossing $10 million per year, with much of its advertising on the non-Internet service Prodigy. According to the article, this company, called PC Flowers, received 28,000 orders in the week before Mother's Day alone. And, this company has only 5 employees. Imagine a business processing thousands of orders in a week with only five employees! How do they do it? Basically, PC Flowers takes the orders from Prodigy customers and then forwards them, via computer to the FTD computer system. This computer florist doesn't even maintain an inventory. It's strictly a middle man.

The three examples we've just given to help start you on finding a product to offer for sale on the Net also serve to demonstrate once again how cyberselling levels the playing field between you and the big guys. Donna Mills is a famous television star, so she probably met with little difficulty in getting her video into the stores where the public would have the opportunity to buy it. Likewise, the lady who excelled at organizing desks probably experienced a remarkable upturn in business when she was featured in one of the country's most widely circulated magazines. You, however, don't need to be a famous personality or one of the chosen few to receive media coverage as a good human interest story in order to reach the buying public. Thanks to the Internet, all you need to do is turn on your computer.

Maybe you are still having trouble thinking of any special information you can offer that others might want. This shows a refreshing modesty and thoughtfulness many contributors to the Internet information pool do not exhibit. It also shows you have not yet experienced the outpouring of facts and opinions, many of questionable value, for sale or simply offered gratis, that you will find in Cyberspace. To get you going on your own idea, we'll tell you about some of the things that others are selling on the Internet, in the firm belief that you can do at least as well.

Our own experience with the Green Card Lottery is a case in point. Immigration services have always been hard to market in traditional ways, partly because targeting is difficult. Who hires immigration lawyers? Most are non-Americans who have an interest in the United States. They are usually well-educated professional or business people. If they weren't, they couldn't afford a lawyer. What could be better for targeting the group we've just described than the Internet? To begin with, half the users are located outside the U.S. Of those who are here, many are foreign students attending U.S. universities. Another large group is composed of foreign nationals holding down temporary jobs in high-tech and engineering fields. These are the types of people most likely to hire an immigration lawyer in the first place. The rest is history. No wonder our Green Card Lottery venture was successful.

A perusal of the Internet finds a wide variety of products and services already being marketed there. Any number of people are presently selling long-distance telephone services on the Net. Represented are discount carriers, purveyors of long-distance calling cards, and discounted international services. These are ideal to sell on the Internet for much the same reason as was the Green Card Lottery, with one big difference. Not every user of the I-way wants or needs to immigrate to the U.S., but probably every single one makes long-distance telephone calls. What other services can you think of that everyone uses?

Advice on Love and Relationships

Everyone has a relationship story in his or her life. Almost all of us like to play marriage counselor, match maker, or psychologist once in a while. That is why books and tapes on relationships are traditionally good money makers. Look at any best-seller list. Maybe you can't get your book accepted by one of the major publishers, but that doesn't mean people won't be willing to pay you for your sage advice. Self-publishing has always been an option, but it requires a sizable outlay of cash for printing, and how do you ever get the bookstores to carry your title? It's not easy. We speak from experience. If only we had known then what we know now. You can publish your book electronically, market it on the I-way, and even allow people to receive the book via a computer file. You don't need an agent, publisher, printer, or retailer. You need only your own creativity and a computer.

One book currently being advertised on the Net is called *How to Dump Your Wife*. This useful title is self-published and covers a highly practical subject. The advertisement claims that it will give you all the advice you need. The author says he is not a shrink or a lawyer, the very people who make a living off your pain, but rather is someone who has lived through it all. He tells you how to plan everything out in advance. He then goes on to say that his book is hard to find because none of the book stores want to carry it. Wait until you hear his reason why. Quoting from the ad:

> No one wants to encourage a man to get out of his unhappy marriage. It's different for women. They get cheers when they "kick the bum out," don't they? But, if a man is miserable, does the world want to give him a second chance?

Does this pique your interest? Twenty-five dollars and the book is yours. As for the author/publisher, he makes a profit regardless of how many books he sells because the costs of electronic book production and marketing on the Internet are practically zero. Do you have a story in your life worth telling? Most of us do. It appears that instructions on wife dumping are already covered. That still leaves husbands, boyfriends, grown children and other relatives who won't move out of the house or stop mooching. There's a book for almost everyone in that alone.

Flowers and Romance

There is a florist in Michigan who started selling flower arrangements on the Internet. He claims not to even own, or know how to use a computer. He simply gave his catalog to someone else who went through the electronic process of making it available via computer. Business has never been better. Flowers seem to be a big seller on the Net and other on-line services these days. Why? Probably because so many of the Netters are young, single, and male. They are dating, wooing their young female cybermates with whatever they can. Flowers are a natural. And for them to be able to place orders on-line? What could be better? As we mentioned earlier in this chapter, a company called PC Florists boasts a ten million dollar business achieved with a small staff, no inventory, and a marketing system through Prodigy. Consider variations on the flower theme such as candy, sexy lingerie, candle light dinners, cruises (if you happen to live near water), even e-mail greeting cards. Use your imagination. Romance sells.

Cyberscalping Tickets

What do the Grateful Dead, Chicago Bears, Miss Saigon, and World Cup Soccer all have in common? Tickets to their performances or games have been sold at high prices on the Internet. You might want to become one of the first "cyberscalpers." With the computers, you can even provide a schematic drawing of the particular performance hall or stadium, and show exactly where your high-priced seats are located. We guarantee that your tickets for those much-in-demand performances will literally fly through Cyberspace. Be careful, though. The laws of some states or communities may restrict this type of activity.

Things for the Dorm

You already know that many Internet users are college students. This group is known for favoring items like T-shirts, posters, and assorted semi-collectible junk such as exotic beer cans from around the world. Use your imagination. Think back to your own college days. In many colleges today, every student is given an Internet account. You can reach this audience for virtually nothing. You don't even have to limit yourself to one item. You can put up an entire full-color catalog of products that dorm dwellers would like. Show them what you have and let them order on-line. They'll keep coming back for more. Where else can they shop during a study break at 2 AM?

Professional Services

We recently saw a company advertising its incorporation services on the Net. For a fee much less than that charged by lawyers, this company will form a corporation for you in any of the 50 states, usually within 24 hours. What other types of services could you, yourself provide? If you are financially oriented, perhaps you could run an on-line bookkeeping or tax service. The physical location of your customers would be unimportant. All data could be transferred back and forth electronically. Your market possibilities include the whole world because you can work with someone halfway around the globe just as easily as someone next door. Consulting services of every kind would do well on the I-way. If you are involved in providing that type of service now, consider how you can package the same service in Cyberspace. Remember, the entire planet is your marketplace. If you always thought your business would grow if you lived in a larger city, now is your chance to find out.

Food and Recipes

Food is the universal fuel, the one thing absolutely everyone in the world uses on a daily basis. Already for sale on the Net are such items as gourmet coffee and fruit baskets, restaurant guides and recipes for every dish imaginable. Do you make the best cookie in the world? Do you have an old family recipe that is irresistible? How about your special barbecue sauce with secret ingredients? This could give you a start on becoming the next General Foods or Sarah Lee.

Government Publications

Have you ever looked at a U.S. Government Printing Office (USGPO) catalog? There are publications on every topic imaginable. Did you know that all of these federal publications are considered to be in the public domain? That means they are not copyright protected and anyone, you included, may re-publish them in any fashion he or she wishes without fear of infringement. There are golden opportunities here. Get a USGPO catalog, or visit one of their stores if there is one nearby. Think of a way to provide this information electronically and allow Uncle Sam to help you make your fortune.

Let the Usenet Be Your Guide

By now your mind should be swirling with profitable ideas for products to market on the I-way. If not, here is one last way to go about it that just can't miss. In choosing your goods or services look closely at the existing Usenet Newsgroups, taking note of the specialized audiences. For example, there are several Newsgroups devoted to pets. We've already seen for sale there such items as buyer's guide for pet products, gourmet pet foods, books on pet care, and even pets themselves. There are Usenet groups devoted to topics of food, sports (including specific sports teams), health, sex, education (remember *Where There's a Will There's an A*), investments, television programs, celebrities, travel, every imaginable facet of computers and software, and, of course, immigration. Many of these groups are regularly visited by hundreds of thousands of individuals. Give them something they want and they can make you very rich.

Test Marketing Your Products with No Financial Risk

It's always a good idea to test market a product before beginning production or embarking on an expensive advertising campaign. This, however, is often impossible in traditional markets, especially if you are on a tight budget. Many direct marketers have to make a profit on every advertisement they run. The price of one ad can put them out of business if it doesn't work. The Internet solves this age-old problem handily. The cost of advertising is so low that you can afford to make mistakes. You also have the benefit of interactive communications, so it's easy to find out right away what your potential customers like or dislike about what you are selling. Place some notices on a few relevant Usenet groups and simply ask if people find your idea interesting. Tell them what you plan to sell and how much you will charge. We bet that you will get back dozens of helpful responses, suggesting ways to change your product or service so that it will sell better. You may find that there is no market for the item and you'll have to look further. No harm done. Just try again.

As you look for the product that will make you a fortune, don't forget, selling on the Information Superhighway is so new that even if the product or service is old hat, seeing its availability on the Internet may be novel enough in itself to make it a big seller. There is certainly ample proof that this is the case. Consider the items we just described that are presently for sale on the I-way. There certainly is nothing unusual about a florist selling a variety of arrangements for special occasions. What we didn't tell you about this particular florist, however, is that his story got coverage in a major *New York Times* feature story, complete with his photograph, just because he was the first to sell flowers through the computer. Such is the public frenzy surrounding the development of the Internet. As you learn your way around Cyberspace, see what goods and services are already for sale there. Then pick something that is not, and be the first to offer it in the new marketplace. You may make headlines yourself.

5

I-WAY RED LIGHT DISTRICTS

Sex for Money in Cyberspace

There is one product you may see for sale along the I-way that we have not yet discussed. In your efforts to get rich through cyberselling, you know we believe it is a good idea to understand as much about your potential customers as possible. If you spend much time roaming through Cyberspace, one thing will quickly become apparent. A great number of Internetters think sex and the computer belong together. They love talking about sex and looking at erotic pictures. When you consider that practically every college and university in the country offers complimentary Internet access to students, and the great majority who take advantage of the free opportunity are male, it is not hard to understand where at least part of the eager audience for this kind of material comes from. Except for technical computer topics, there are more Newsgroups related to sex than any other subject, and most of these groups enjoy heavy participation. Available Internet sex items include sexual personal ads, risqué stories, and an astoundingly enormous cadre of pornographic pictures ranging from the mildly explicit to the hardest of hard core. The raciest parts of *Penthouse* and *Hustler* magazines are there, free for the taking and void of age restrictions. Parental discretion may be advisable. Often it is not exercised. Many parents simply never recognize that the computer is being used in this way.

Most commercial on-line services have certain areas designated for sexual topics and discussions. To access them usually requires special permission. A lot of sexual material may be free on the Internet, but a substantial amount is offered by entrepreneurs engaged in for-profit ventures. Chat lines, Internet channels open to direct, real-time computer conversations, are filled with sexual talk, innuendoes, and individuals avidly engaging in fantasy role playing. Such areas of Cyberspace are generally unregulated and uncensored, as are most others. Anything and everything goes. Of course, there is no real physical contact in these virtual brothels or singles bars. The concept of "safe sex" probably reaches its ultimate incarnation here. It doesn't matter whether or not touching is allowed. For practical purposes, it's simply not possible.

BBSs

The private world of Bulletin Board Services (BBS) can be thought of as distant but electronically unconnected cousins of the Usenet. Still a part of the I-way, many BBSs exist on a single computer in someone's garage or basement. Access to others is made possible by modem except that, unlike the Internet, there is a one-to-one connection rather than the interconnectivity of a huge network. BBSs are especially filled with sexually oriented topics. The second largest BBS network in the United States is called Kink Net. Although some BBSs are free, most are not. At the very least, there are charges for the time actually spent on line. A recent issue of a major computer magazine contained four full pages of ads for BBSs offering such items as "3D Sex BBS," "Sexy Software," "Free Adult CD-Rom," "Hustler On-Line," "Odyssey—Where Adults Come to Play," and "Lifestyle On-Line, Hot Chat with the World's Sexiest Couples and Singles." Thousands of gigabytes worth of computer storage around the world are used to house such information that is considered by many critical to the functioning of the collective Internet psyche.

Sex, the Internet, and the Media

Sex on the Internet, as well as the on-line services, gets a lot of media attention. Parents are understandably upset that their children may be accessing adult matter without their knowledge. Nine-year-old children who have mastered a few simple keystrokes can study full-color images of naked men and women. Responsible adults shudder to think that in purchasing a computer to further their child's education, they got more education than they bargained for. The eyes of young people glued to television sets, watching the controversial "Beavis and Butthead," are seeing something extremely tame compared with what is easily available on the Internet. A typical message that appeared recently on the News-group *alt.sex* announced:

> A new adult site has just opened up. Lots of graphic files yours for free. If interested, just send your e-mail address to me and you'll get

more information. Make sure to include a statement that you are over 21. Well, nah, don't bother . . . nobody really cares anyway.

The seediest offerings on the I-way sex menu have already caught the attention of law enforcement agencies who are learning that there may be new high-tech outlets for criminal pornography, particularly those appealing to the interests of pedophiles. Likewise, computer buffs who favor this material are learning electronic skills for covering their tracks. Volumes of pornographic material can be clandestinely transported all over the world, hidden in encrypted computer files, via the Internet. An encrypted file is one put in a special code that can be read only by someone with a key to that code. With the advent of encryption, the ability for law enforcement agencies to track down and stop smut peddling is extremely limited.

Sexual activity on the Internet has been further brought to public attention with the widely reported story of the famous e-mail stalker. This Michigan man suffered the misfortune of falling in love with a lady who had eyes only for others. He brooded, plotted, and contemplated how to get her attention. As it turned out, he and the object of his affections did have one thing in common, e-mail accounts. He began writing e-mail love letters every day. We don't know how racy they were, but the woman became upset. Each time she turned on her computer, there was another letter from her unwelcome suitor. Finally, she became so terrorized by the messages appearing on her computer screen that she called the local police. The man was arrested and accused of violating a Michigan stalker law. It is open to question at what point boyish infatuation crosses the line and becomes sexual harassment. Nonetheless, the stalker story makes one thing clear. Hiding behind a computer does not give anyone the legal right to do that which he or she could not do out in the open. The case is fair warning that some of the sex features of the Internet may border on the illegal.

Protecting Identity: The Anonymous Server

No discussion about sex on the Internet would be complete without mentioning a special computer located in Finland known as the Anonymous Server. If you look at the Usenet much, you are likely to see messages posted by individuals with e-mail addresses who list their domains as *anon.penet.fi*. Why, you may ask, do so many people interested in sex come from that domain? Actually, they don't. Anyone, anywhere may send a message to the Anonymous Server requesting an anonymous ID. E-mail or Usenet messages may then be sent through that computer, hiding the sender's identity. The computer in Finland scrambles the sender's address so that only it knows the actual source. Anyone wishing to respond to the anonymous missive sends a message back to the anonymous address and the Finnish computer forwards it to the proper party. It is virtually impossible to find out who uses the Anonymous Server. This arrangement is extremely attractive to those who want to keep their interest in sex a deep, dark secret.

Money Making Possibilities from the World's Oldest Hobby

A fine example of sex as a selling mechanism on the Internet is one we happened on quite accidentally. It is called Cybersex City. Cybersex City is actually a Gopher data site, an Internet marketing tool we describe in detail later on. When you tune into the site, the following message greets you on your computer screen:

> Welcome to Cybersex City! . . . carrying advertising for (ugh!) commercial sex—mostly bizarre commercial sex. . . . respond to personal ads from people even more sexually twisted than you . . .

In fairness, all who enter here do get the following advisory:

> Be warned that the material on this server is about as raw and explicit as sexual material gets. . . . the advertisers on this server offer every deviation that you have ever heard of . . . and more.

> And as to Jesse Helms, Jerry Falwell, and/or politically correct persons: We suggest that CYBERSEX CITY is NOT the place for you. Trust us on this.

> Oh yeah, also stay away from here unless you are at least 18.

It goes on to list sexually explicit personal ads, with instructions on how to contact each advertiser, for a fee, of course.

By now you've probably guessed that selling sex is not something in which we care to involve ourselves. Others, however, feel differently and when you consider the availability of willing buyers, it's not difficult to see why. The salability of sex on the Net was actually brought home to us in a very unusual and unexpected way. Shortly after we placed one of our now famous Green Card Lottery postings, some unknown cyberpunk got the idea of engaging in character assassination by announcing to the Internet community that we were maintaining catalogs of erotic pictures in computer formatted files. Our e-mail address was given and anyone interested in such things was invited to contact us for a brochure and price list. You may have grasped enough already about the predilection of certain Netters to guess what happened. Within days, we had nearly 1,000 requests for our price list. We probably would have had thousands more if our access provider at the time, Netcom, hadn't picked that moment, several months after our Green Card posting, to bow to pressure and cut off our account just as the messages started rolling in. We got only about three days worth of mail. It's a shame all these orders weren't sent to someone who actually had the pictures to sell. They really might have cleaned up. It is interesting to speculate on what would have occurred if the message had really come from us and if we had made a concerted effort to masspost it. Undoubtedly, the responses would have been overwhelming, and the Netters probably wouldn't have complained at all.

The Marketing Future of Sex on the Internet

Except for the BBSs, to date the widest variety of sexual material available on the I-way is offered free. The large selection of Internet pornographic picture files is the prime example of this. Still, it is undeniable that fortunes have been made catering to all kinds of vices, sex being number one on the list. Sexually related material has for many years been sold quite openly on newsstands, newspaper classified ads, and through 900 number telephone services. Most of the sexual items and services currently for sale elsewhere could easily be adapted to marketing on the Internet, and no doubt will be in short order. Some of what will occur will be harmless fun. Other projects will test the limits of the law and public patience. Let's look into the future.

Video matchmaking has been in vogue for some time, but computer matchmaking might be even more interesting. You could easily create a database of prospects, indexed by personal interests, physical features, etc. Each individual participating could provide a photograph which would be placed for viewing in one of the many Internet data files. People could then search out prospects through databases, see what they look like, contact them directly by e-mail, or arrange for an on-line meeting via chat. All it would take is assigning each would-be romantic an e-mail box. In that way a couple could get to know each other before actually meeting in person. There have been a number of well-publicized marriages between people who have met on-line. We've already shared talk show billing with one of them. It probably won't be long before some on-line cupid is charging a fee to people who post their vital statistics as well as those who contact them.

You've probably seen ads for 1-900 sex talk phone lines. Like us, we're sure none of you has ever actually called one. In the interest of research, however, we studied up and will now briefly explain to you how they work. 900 numbers, as you probably do know, are a pay-per-minute telephone service. Instead of the customer sending checks or giving credit card information, the telephone company bills the user directly for whatever time is spent on the telephone. The phone company, at the end of each month, sends this money to the service provider, minus its own commission and fees. When the customer calls, he or she gets either a menu of pre-recorded sexual messages, or a live person who will talk provocatively. The latter method is thought to be most effective because theoretically it is easier to keep someone on the phone line with a live voice, and the longer the customer stays on the line, the more money he or she spends. An Internet version of the same system would not be difficult to imagine, using pre-written sex stories, or an interactive capability through chat. In fact, it would be easy to set up a 900 telephone number to connect with a computer service. Alternatively, a service provider could have customers set up credit card accounts in advance, and then access the service whenever they wished by logging in with their account number. We bet the parents of teenagers can't wait for this one.

Many newsstands today have dozens of sexually oriented publications. Keeping a similar collection of erotic photos or magazines for sale could easily be accomplished on the Internet, again by utilizing the Net's many data storage and display capabilities. Today the pornographic picture files on the Internet are mainly in binary language. That means unless you are accessing them through the World Wide Web, you cannot actually see them while you are on-line. Instead, you have to download them into your own computer and then send them through a printer off-line, or through a graphical viewer software program, before you can actually see what they look like. On-line pornographic pictures are just waiting for a Bob Guccione clone to come along and make them a reality. Remember that there is already an extensive collection of pornographic photos available free on the Usenet. Anyone planning to charge will really have to offer something impressive. Given the nature of what is already to be had, the content of material that would constitute a step beyond truly staggers the imagination. No doubt some creative soul can meet the challenge. To view what is currently offered free, rev up your printer, tune into Usenet and look at *alt.binary.pictures.erotic* for starters. Be prepared. What you will see is not mild.

A different slant on magazines or photos could be a simple catalog of dirty jokes, a popular item in many bookstores and on newsstands. Maybe someone could even charge by the joke. Of course, once again, they had better be good to compete with what is already given away in Usenet forums free. Posting off-color jokes is yet another favorite Usenet practice. Go to Usenet and sample offerings on the Newsgroup called *alt.tasteless.jokes* to see what we mean.

Most communities of any size have weekly "underground" newspapers providing information about local night clubs that are a bit more earthy than places of entertainment likely to be advertised in the daily newspaper. Usenet Newsgroups already give entertainment and restaurant news for certain areas of the country. It would not be difficult to compile information electronically on less mainstream recreation emporiums. This data could be placed in a searchable database and readers could be charged for access. Establishments listed could pay for the advertisement as well.

When we first became heavily involved with the I-way, we began reading the various news stories about the availability of sexual material on the Internet. Not surprisingly, controversy rages over sex in Cyberspace just as it does over sex in other mediums. The fracas over Internet sex is probably even more heated these days because laws that control distribution of sexually explicit matter in other mediums have not yet been fully applied to the same sort of data when it is transmitted over the computer. After reading all the stories, we were understandably curious, so we took a look at some of what was being discussed to see what the uproar was about. It was not until we undertook preparation of this book, however, that we made a broad search for the various sexual materials and services available. We were amazed at the scope and variety of resources obtainable in this area. For our tastes, we've seen more than enough and we won't be returning to look at anymore. You can be sure, though, that many others will be back, again and again. Right now, sex over the Internet is largely free. We predict things won't stay that way for long. Commercialization of the Internet is going to spread to its Red Light District just as it is extending everywhere else.

Whatever your personal views of sexually explicit matter coming over the computer, we don't wish to convey the impression that the Internet is filled disproportionately with sexual materials. Only a relatively small amount of the Internet's resources are devoted to this subject. Overall, sex is certainly not what the I-way is essentially about. It is there, however, and it is both plentiful and easy to find. In some circles interest is so strong that it is important for you to know about it, commercially and otherwise. Be aware of what is going on, and if you happen to have a computer at home, keep an eye on your children.

6

FREE ADVERTISING TO MILLIONS OF PEOPLE ON THE USENET

Of the many giddy reactions brought on by the grandeur of the I-way concept, some of the giddiest surround the Usenet. By far the most active center for public Internet communications, the Usenet begs to be tagged with one of those colorful descriptive phrases we mentioned earlier. You could call it the world's biggest town hall meeting, or perhaps the world's biggest free-for-all. Maybe it's the world's biggest cocktail party. It's probably all those things and more. To you, it represents what is arguably the world's biggest and best marketplace.

In simple terms, the Usenet is a collection of some ten thousand discussion groups, each one covering a different and specific topic. You can read or participate in any group simply by entering a few commands on your keyboard. It is impossible to determine exactly how many groups there are because the number changes continuously. Likewise, the exact number of Usenet participants is unknown. Estimates run between three and ten million. All agree, however, that the daily increase in size is impressive.

The Usenet started as an experiment in North Carolina in 1979. The first participants were Duke University and University of North Carolina. The original idea was that people could pass useful information to each other through a series of electronic bulletin boards, where newsworthy informational messages on a variety of topics would be posted. For this reason, the term "Newsgroup" was used to describe them. Time went on and the Usenet grew, with the networks of more and more organizations joining in. As the number increased, the Newsgroups gradually became less and less repositories of hard information and instead developed as forums for discussion and the exchange of ideas. Although Netiquette still requires that each Newsgroup posting offer up some kind of worthwhile information, in practice, that standard has long since been abandoned. In reality, the tone of Usenet "conversations" reflects the same vast variety of discussion levels that exist in everyday conversations taking place continuously throughout world society.

Newsgroup subjects have also evolved far afield of their original research and academic roots. It would be difficult to imagine any area of human endeavor or interest that does not have a representative Newsgroup. The mix is especially diverse because there is no central authority responsible for developing these groups in an orderly manner. The fact is that anyone can start a Newsgroup on the Usenet about whatever subject he or she pleases.

Newsgroup Names

Earlier, we mentioned a couple of our favorite Newsgroups. Let's take a quick look at a few more now in existence, to give you a better flavor of what is going on here.

alt.culture.theory	soc.couples	cl.frauen.diskussion
fr.network.divers	bionet.cellbiol	bit.listserv.netnws-1
aus.jobs	soc.culture.italian	chile.uucp
umn.aem.ugrads	biz.sco.magazine	dod.jobs
alt.binaries.sounds.music	alt.support.diet	info.big-internet
ba.helping-hand	comp.archives.admin	phl.forsale
njit.wanted	br.redes	talk.religion

As you read the Newsgroup names, you will see that they are composed of several words or abbreviations of words strung together with dots. We've already used some examples in our first chapters. Here are a few more random choices: *alt.rock-n-roll.oldies*, *dc.dining*, and *nz.molbio*. Let's examine them to get a better idea of how Usenet works. Look closely at the first word in each of these examples. They indicate the *hierarchy* to which each of these groups belongs. Because there are so many Newsgroups, hierarchies are used as a convenient way of cataloging, so finding the ones that interest you is easier. The first of our examples comes from what is arguably the most interesting hierarchy. "Alt" stands for alternative. This is the most eclectic of the hierarchies as well as the largest. It is composed of over 600 Newsgroups. Surprisingly, it is considerably bigger than the next largest hierarchy, "Comp," which stands for computer. It is in the alt hierarchy you will find many of the sex groups we discussed earlier. You will also find fan groups such as *alt.fan.david.bowie* or *alt.fan.howard.stern*. While many topics in the alt hierarchy are recreational in nature, they can also be serious. The support groups for such diseases as cancer, arthritis, and depression can be found here. On the other side of the coin, lovesick swains have been known to create groups in adoration of their girlfriends. That is why some of the names in the so-called "fan" groups are ones you won't recognize. Groups devoted to special friends, or personal enemies for that matter, usually attract only one participant who, we presume, enjoys talking to himself. There are others who create groups out of a different kind of passion. A truly motivated individual whose name we don't know developed a group called *alt.flame-canter-and-siegel*. We would like to thank him for his interest, whoever he may be.

The additional two groups in our extremely brief sample list exemplify some other Usenet features. At the beginning of one you will see "nz." This stands for New Zealand. There are many hierarchies from countries other than our own. "Molbio" stands for molecular biology. This is an example of the more traditional, research-oriented groups that arose out of the Internet's scientific roots. Our remaining sample group, *dc.dining*, is a discussion of restaurants in our nation's capital. Nearly every major city in the country has its own regional hierarchy devoted to subjects of interest in the area. The individual topics in each regional hierarchy tend to mimic those in all the others. There is, for example, a "for sale" Newsgroup in the hierarchy of every region. Just as there is *dc.dining*, there is also *la.eats*. (Note that Southern California is, as ever, more casual in its approach than the Northeast portion of the country.) We've included at the end of this book an appendix with a larger sample list of Newsgroups. When you are ready to take them all in, you can simply get a list that will be made available to you by your access provider. As you look at the group names, the meaning of some will be obvious. Others will read like gibberish. Still others will seem to sound like one thing and turn out to be another. You can always find out for sure simply by tuning in to the group to see what they're talking about.

All Newsgroups, irrespective of topic or hierarchy, are equally accessible to everyone everywhere through the Internet. This is true even of the regional hierarchies, hierarchies from foreign countries or those from particular universities. Be aware, however, that access providers do not usually carry every single Newsgroup in existence. They pick and choose guided by budget and assessment of user interest. Since your objective is to make your product or service known to your most likely customers, you should be very careful to select an access provider who will offer the largest possible selection of Newsgroups, or, at the very least, the Newsgroups that will give you the best marketing possibilities for your product. Ideally, you will want to use an access provider offering a full, unrestricted news feed.

How Usenet Works

To get the feel of the Usenet, simply tune in and jump around a little. For this you will need a newsreader program on your computer, which is almost always supplied to you by your Internet access provider at no extra charge. If not, or if you don't like your access provider's program, you can look for a free one on the Internet or buy a commercial newsreader. Once you have the program, then by typing in some simple commands you can easily and quickly call up any Newsgroup you choose. Again, there are many books or classes available from which you can learn these procedures, but most people simply figure it out from the program itself. When you do enter your request to view a certain group, the first thing you will see on your screen is a list of one-line descriptors. Each of them tells you briefly the subject matter of the various discussions going on in the group at that time. All the messages you will read come from people just like you, who have decided they want their thoughts aired in public. When someone posts a message and others post additional messages in reply, a "thread" is created. If a message is posted and nobody chooses to comment further, the thread ends there. As you look at the descriptions of the threads on the group you have selected, you will see a number. That number tells you how many messages are in the thread.

You can choose to read any or all threads on a Newsgroup, again simply by hitting a key or two on your keyboard. When the first message of a thread you have selected comes on your screen, at the top of it you will see who sent it, the date it was sent, the subject, and more information than you probably want on the path it took through the Internet to get to you. You will also notice, as you read along, that the same message seems to be repeated over and over again. That is because as each person adds another message to the thread, he or she commonly repeats all the other messages in the thread that came before. Often, there is so much repetition, it is difficult to extract the single new message from the rest that you have already seen. This is a very tiresome aspect of reading

Newsgroups, and a tremendous waste of "bandwidth," the capacity for computer links or telephone lines to carry data. To repeat continuously is technically a breach of Netiquette. In theory you are expected to summarize the previous discussion. In practice, however, summarizing is too much trouble for most people and so the repetition is in fact universally accepted.

If you want to add to a thread that interests you, or you want to begin your own thread, once again this can be done easily by typing out your message and dispatching it electronically with a few simple key strokes to the Newsgroup of your choice. That is how we advertised on the Usenet. In placing a message on the Usenet, you also send out your own data on where your message came from. Among other things, this allows those who have seen your message to answer back, either privately to your e-mail address or publicly by posting yet another message to the thread. It was by e-mail responses to our Usenet postings that we received requests for further information about our legal services. If you want to keep your whereabouts a secret, you can do so by using the Anonymous Server in Finland, which we discussed in Chapter Five. Doing this is fine if your purpose is to hide out. That is certainly not our objective here.

The overwhelming majority of Newsgroups will accept all messages automatically. There are, however, some Newsgroups that are "moderated." This means that posted messages, instead of going out directly to the public, are first sent to someone whose job it is to decide what will and will not be posted for universal consumption. The largest assemblage of moderated groups is the Clarinet hierarchy, which offers news in the more traditional sense of the word. Among the information carried on Clarinet is the UPI newsfeed. Clarinet, unlike most Usenet groups, charges providers to carry it. You can read Clarinet and other moderated Newsgroups as easily as any others. You cannot, however, contribute.

At the end of each message posted is the signature. The signature contains the name of the person who posted the message and his or her e-mail address. Phone numbers, snail mail addresses, company names, and other identifying information can likewise be included. The signature is also a place where personal expression is common. Those Usenet participants who want to tell the world who they are or what they believe in can do it in their signatures. Famous quotes or famous quotes that have been slightly altered are popular choices. The truly creative don't rely on the words of others, but make up their own statements instead. Here are some examples of signatures:

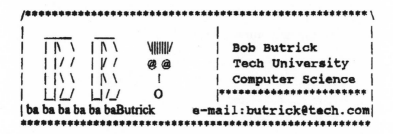

Jaba@um.com

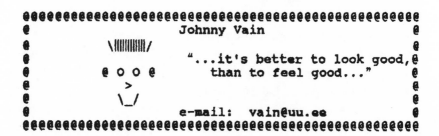

As you can see, you may also include a small drawing if you so choose. The only real limitation in the signature is, once again, dictated by Netiquette. A signature is supposed to be no more than four lines in length. As usual, observation of this unwritten rule is fairly lax, except that some news posting programs are configured to cut off signatures that exceed the preferred number of lines.

Although there are some 10,000 Newsgroups now in existence, that number is misleading, because many of the groups draw no participation. Some Newsgroups seem really not even intended for discussion but rather exist simply to show off the silliness of their names. For example, there are three groups devoted to *alt.alien.vampire*. The first is *alt.alien.vampire.flonk*, the second is *alt.alien.vampire.flonk.flonk*, and the third is—well, you can probably guess. In any case, only the group with the single flonk gets read. The rest are for the sake of art and symmetry.

There are various groups made up of Usenet readers who voluntarily undertake the task of measuring Newsgroup participation. Results have been published in *The Internet Complete Reference* by Harley Hahn and Rick

Stout. According to the published study, the ten most popular News-groups, and their estimated numbers of readers are:

1. news.announce.newusers   280,000
2. misc.forsale   250,000
3. misc.jobs.offered   240,000
4. news.answers   220,000
5. alt.sex   180,000
6. rec.humor.funny   160,000
7. alt.binaries.pictures.erotica   150,000
8. rec.arts.erotica   150,000
9. alt.sex.stories   130,000
10. alt.sex.bondage   110,000

As you can see, there is heavy interest among Usenet readers in sex, jobs, jokes, and computers. Most interesting to us, however, is number two on the list, *misc.forsale*, with a whopping 250,000 participants. This tells us that there is a healthy interest in buying and selling on the Usenet. Also, keep in mind that the amount of people reading Usenet groups is increasing by thousands every day, so by the time you read this, the numbers we've just given you may have as much as doubled.

Messages appearing on Newsgroups tend to be short. This maintains the conversational tone of the postings. Some groups are configured to reject electronically messages of greater than a certain length. Overall, the tone exhibited is light. There are a lot of useful ideas and information exchanged here, but little is of great or weighty import. In a group on biology, one participant may tell another how to locate a certain journal article. In one of the computer groups, someone may look for and receive assistance with the generation of certain software. It is helpful and interesting, but there is not much of any depth. Most of what you read resembles, at best, talk you might hear if you were to attend a university faculty cocktail party. At worst, if you set your sights lower, it sounds like you went to a frat party instead.

The real excitement of Usenet lies not so much in the information transmitted as it does in the ability to bring people together and give a voice to the millions of individuals who before could be heard only by an immediate circle of friends and family. The ability for nearly anyone to have his or her quotes read by huge numbers of people has its up and down sides. Viewpoints that previously might never have been heard can be offered up for public consideration without the conventional media deciding what is and is not worthy. It is often said that one of the real beauties of computer communication is its egalitarian aspects. Since you can't see who you are talking to, you can't judge them by their outside appearance, their bank account, or their car, but only by the context and expression of their thoughts. In this atmosphere, friends and lovers may find each other and offer a measure of human comfort that is often the breath of life to the sick, lonely, or lovelorn. For those with no particular emotional need, the Usenet, on its better days, can provide diversion, companionship, and an occasional good laugh.

Still, the worst of human nature is also exhibited on the Usenet. Flame groups vigorously pursue their self-appointed duty of insulting everyone in sight. All kinds of feelings from bad temper to bigotry can be found expressed in the messages posted to Newsgroups. Just as in the real world, old and young, male and female, black and white, Jew and Christian, Turk and Armenian fight with each other. The fact that a combatant never has to come face to face with the enemy often leads to abandonment of scruples and some of the most blatantly crude exchanges you've ever heard. Then, too, although it can be interesting and informative to read Usenet postings, there is no editorial authority checking to see that what is being posted is true and accurate. There is potential for trouble when you take what you read on the Usenet too seriously. A classic Usenet philosophy is that it is run under a system of anarchy. This seems to be a positive feature to the true Usenet fanatic, but not such a comforting thought to the average individual. All in all, to sum up both the good and the bad, Usenet is just one more place where people generally go about the business of being people.

Making Money with Usenet

We've tried to give you a picture of what the Usenet is and the way it operates as a framework for explaining how it can be used to help you make your I-way fortune. Usenet is the one and only area of the Internet where you can go to find people and place messages before them. There is no reason why the message you choose to post should not be one that tells about a product you have to sell. When you get ready to place your first advertising message on the Usenet, you can use a one- or two-step process. In a one-step process, you give all your sales information and ask for the order on the very first encounter. An example of this would be the following:

IBM P-Cs for sale.
These are original "classic" PCs with 64K RAM, single 5¼ inch Floppy Drives, and Monochrome monitor. Will never run Windows, but a real collector's item, and can help your children learn computer

programming. Only $50 plus $12 shipping. Originally $2,000!! Hurry! Limited Quantities. Charge your order to a credit card by calling 1-800-548-7841, or send your check or money order for $62 to PC Classics, Box 1111, Scottsdale AZ 85267.

In a two-step process, you don't give price and order information right away. Instead, you tell about your products or service briefly and ask those who are interested to contact you if they'd like to know more. You then prepare a detailed description of your product, including answers to any common or obvious questions your customers may have. Included in the second step of your presentation will be the price of your product or service and specific instruction on how to order. The short, first posting of your two-step process should contain the most exciting and desirable features of what you are selling. The product should be described clearly and accurately. You can ask for responses by e-mail on your personal mailbox. You can also ask customers to contact you by telephone, fax, or snail mail. A limitation of Newsgroup messages for advertising purposes is that the only "pictures" you can use are those you are able to form from standard characters on a typewriter. Here are some examples of what that might look like.

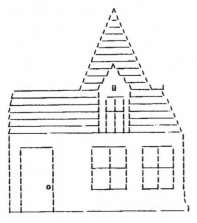

I dress myself in leather and lace
I build my house in Cyberspace

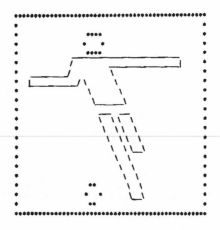

Since you are severely limited in the graphics department, the words you choose must draw a picture for you. To show you what a first message in a two-step process might look like, here, as an example, is the message we ourselves used.

Green Card Lottery 1994 May Be The Last One!
THE DEADLINE HAS BEEN ANNOUNCED

The Green Card Lottery is a completely legal program giving away a certain annual allotment of Green Cards to persons born in certain countries. The lottery program was schedule to continue on a permanent basis. However, recently, Senator Alan J Simpson introduced a bill into the U.S. Congress which could end any future lotteries. THE 1994 LOTTERY IS SCHEDULED TO TAKE PLACE SOON, BUT IT MAY BE THE VERY LAST ONE.

PERSONS BORN IN MOST COUNTRIES QUALIFY, MANY FOR FIRST TIME.

The only countries NOT qualifying are: Mexico, India, PR China, Taiwan, Philippines, South Korea, Canada, United Kingdom (except Northern Ireland), Jamaica, Dominican Republic, El Salvador and Vietnam.

Lottery registration will take place soon. 55,000 Green Cards will be given to those who register correctly. NO JOB IS REQUIRED.

THERE IS A STRICT JUNE DEADLINE. THE TIME TO START IS NOW!!

For FREE information via Email, send request to
cslaw@indirect.com

or contact us at:
Canter & Siegel
Immigration Attorneys
3333 E. Camelback Road, Ste 250, Phoenix AZ USA 85018
602 661 3911 (telephone) 602 451 7617 (fax)

As you can see, we gave our customers several options for reaching us to request more information. They could contact us by telephone, fax, or e-mail. We received responses in all three ways, but the overwhelming majority chose e-mail. You will find in marketing your own product on the Usenet that the ability to deal with potential purchasers through e-mail is a tremendous plus. It allows your customer to request what he or she needs immediately and at virtually no cost. Even if you have thousands of responses to handle each day, you can send the data the customers asked for in equally speedy fashion and, likewise, with minimal expense. This is a system where the printing and postage costs of sending sales literature is a thing of the past. In addition, some of the die-hard computer addicts, who have bonded with their PCs to the extent that it has become another body part, often find other forms of communication foreign and can assimilate information only when they receive it through e-mail. If you plan to market to the tech crowd, therefore, e-mail is the only way to go.

If you really want to speed up responses to your customer inquiries, you can set up an automatic response robot. The word "robot" conjures up pictures of the cute little metal creatures from *Star Wars*, but once again, the term simply provides an easy way to visualize an electronic function. In this case, the robot is a program that automatically sends the second step of your presentation to anyone who types in a short command such as "send info." Inquiries are sent to your e-mail box, but this time instead of a human being reading each message and striking the correct keys to send your prepared response, the robot program does the work for you. A drawback to using a robot is that if a customer wants to ask very specific questions rather than receiving your standard electronic "brochure" you will not realize this fact, because no one will be reading the messages you receive. There are two possible ways around this problem. First, you could hire a programmer to devise a robot that will send the brochure only if specific words are contained in the request. All other e-mail would then come to your mailbox where you could read and answer each request manually. A second and probably simpler solution is to set up two separate e-mail addresses. Your advertisement can then tell people to send requests for information to one address if they want to receive an automatically generated brochure, or to another if they have special questions.

Finally, an additional method you can employ for the second step of your Usenet advertising is putting your long, electronic brochure at a particular spot on the Internet where people can find it for themselves. FTP, Gopher, and Web sites, which we describe in later chapters, can be used for this purpose. For now, you need only understand that, if you wish, you can attach an electronic address to your data so that instead of sending it upon request, readers of your initial, short Usenet message can simply call it up on their computers. Like the robot, using an Internet information site has the benefit of giving your customer immediate access to your sales information and, like the robot, the effort on your part is virtually non-existent. The main drawback is that with a fixed data site, you have no way of knowing the identity or number of people who access it. Neither will you have the opportunity to answer individual questions your customers might have. The only customers you will know about are those who actually buy. You will not receive the e-mail addresses of those who have expressed interest in the product and who, if they do not buy now, have at least shown enough curiosity to make them worthwhile contacts for possible later sales. Once again, to overcome the relatively impersonal nature of using data sites, we recommend including in your message your telephone number, fax number, and snail mail address. That way, your customers can find you easily and will understand that you welcome personal communication with them. If you want to put a robot in place, we suggest again prevailing on your friendly geek to write the program. It's not very hard to do. Once in place, the robot is effortless for you and provides your customer with instant gratification.

When you post a Usenet advertisement, whatever type of response mechanism you select, individual or automatic, we cannot stress too much the importance of answering inquiries fully and promptly. You should also have a long-term plan for customer relations, keep good records on your customers, how to locate them, their likes, dislikes, questions and anything else you are able to find out that will help improve service. Your computer can do much of this work for you, maintaining information in an orderly fashion and making future relationships with your new-found customers rewarding. Your goal should be to keep your customers and sell to them on a repeat basis. Excellent service is not only a good idea. As part of cyber-selling, it is almost mandatory. Those who deal with computers know that these machines were built to make record keeping and communicating easy. Because of this, expectations of efficient service through the computer are high. Don't disappoint your new customers and they won't disappoint you.

In most cases, we recommend employing the two-step technique when engaging in Usenet advertising. Remember that short messages are a convention of the Usenet conversation style. There is no point in going against the established Usenet norm. In any case, a second, third, or fourth contact with the customer costs so little in the way of money and effort, there is really no down side to proceeding this way. Then, too, once a customer has asked for more information, you can approach him or her in a different way. Here is a person who has already expressed interest. You know that a long and detailed presentation of what you have to offer will be welcome. We also recommend that you set up a way to answer individual questions, even if you do it in combination with a robot or data site. Although it takes some time and work, the ability to do this unleashes the full power of cyberselling because you have the opportunity of building a strong customer relationship. When we marketed the Green Card Lottery, we had a full "brochure" we sent to all those who requested information, but we also set aside any inquiries that contained individual questions and answered those too. In our fixed presentation we tried to include everything our customer might need to know in order to buy, as well as a method of ordering. The information in your own presentation should do the same. Simply think of what you would like to know if you were purchasing this product and then tell that to your customers. Say as much as you need to get all your points across. There will be no extra cost for more pages in your brochure, as there would be if it was printed. With the computer, comprehensive sales information is not expensive. To give you an idea of what a step two long message might contain, here is a portion of the information packet we sent out ourselves.

Please note, the end of this message includes a
biographical questionnaire. Please let us know if you do
not receive the entire transmission.

Canter & Siegel
3333 E Camelback Road
Ste 250
Phoenix AZ 85018
(602) 661-3911 (telephone) (602) 451-7617 (fax)
e-mail cslaw@netcom.com

WE CAN MAKE IT EASY TO APPLY AND INCREASE YOUR
CHANCE OF WINNING ONE OF 55,000 GREEN CARDS
AVAILABLE IN THE 1994 GREEN CARD LOTTERY.

ACT NOW. THIS MAY BE YOUR LAST CHANCE!

What is the Green Card Lottery?

The Green Card Lottery is a program run by the United
States Government to give away a certain number of Green
Cards each year. In 1994, the number of Green Cards in
the lottery is 55,000. The Green Card Lottery is completely
legal in every way. What is unique about the lottery is that

unlike other ways of getting Green Cards, you need no
special qualification to apply. You need only have been
born in one of the countries included in the program. If you
win, in order to collect your Green Card, you must then
show you have either a high school diploma, or at least
two years of training or experience in a skilled job. YOU
DO NOT NEED TO HAVE A JOB OFFER.

WHY THIS MAY BE YOUR LAST CHANCE FOR A LOTTERY
GREEN CARD

Recently a new bill was introduced into the U.S. Congress
to end any further Green Card Lotteries. The bill is meant to
be part of a larger program to reduce U.S. immigration
overall, and stands a very good chance of passing. . . .

. . . .

THE FACTS ABOUT THE GREEN CARD LOTTERY

FACT: The 1994 Green Card Lottery applies to people from
almost all countries. In fact, only twelve countries are
excluded. They are . . .

. . . .

FACT: There is no way of knowing exactly what your odds
are of winning, because there is no way of telling how
many people will apply this year, but last year, about
800,000 people filed qualifying applications for only 40,000
cards available. With these numbers your odds would be
1 out of 20.

FACT: You can put in only one application per person. If
you put in more the computer will discover it and you will
be disqualified.

. . . .

FACT: Everyone would like to know how to improve their
chances to win the Green card lottery. THE TRUTH IS AN
ATTORNEY CAN HELP INCREASE YOUR ODDS OF
WINNING.

First, in certain cases only, you can as much as double or triple your chances by filing several applications for the same family but using a different family member each time as the principal applicant. (This is not the same as submitting more than one application per person) . . .

. . . .

THE LAW FIRM OF CANTER & SIEGEL

The law firm of Canter and Siegel has been practicing Immigration law since 1981. In that time it has successfully acquired Green Cards and Visas for people from almost every country in the world. The firm offers a full range of Immigration law and does not take cases in other areas. It has actively participated in every Green Card Lottery held since these programs began in 1987.

In 1989 Mr. Canter and Ms. Siegel co-authored a book for non-lawyers on the subject of Immigration called U.S. Immigration Made Easy.

. . . .

LOTTERY SERVICES

The law firm of Canter & Siegel will take the information received from you and use it to form a technically perfect lottery application. If you are married..
If you would like to have Canter & Siegel enter you in the 1994 Green Card Lottery, please fill out the enclosed Service Order and Questionnaire.

FEES FOR ENTERING
THE GREEN CARD LOTTERY..

. . . .

1994 Green Card Lottery
SERVICE ORDER & QUESTIONNAIRE

Please return this completed Questionnaire by Mail, Fax or e-mail to
Canter & Siegel
3333 E Camelback Road, Ste 250
Phoenix AZ 85018

Fax: (602) 451-7617 Phone (602) 661-3911
e-mail cslaw@netcom.com

_____ YES, I would like Canter & Siegel to enter me in the
Green Card Lottery

_____ Please file one application for me and my family at a
fee of 95 dollars U.S.

. . . .

Total Amount _____
Enclosed is my check for _____ U.S. Funds
Charge my _____ Visa _____ Mastercard _____ American Express
Card No. Exp. Date Signature

Name: (First, Middle, LAST)

Mailing Address:

. . . .

Service Agreement & Guarantee

Upon receiving your completed Service order form and
payment, the law firm of Canter & Siegel agrees to prepare
your registration, make sure it meets all technical
requirements of the lottery program...

. . . .

To assist us in preparing your registration, please
complete the questionnaire and return it to us.
Thank you for choosing Canter & Siegel to represent you in
the 1994 Green Card Lottery.

In addition to posting straight commercial messages, there are other
ways to get product or service information across on the Usenet. If you
have a product that has already been sold to and used by some satisfied
customers, they can enter the conversation of a Newsgroup and offer an
endorsement. The topic of the Newsgroup should have some relationship
to the product being endorsed. For example, if someone discovers a new
cat care product, he or she may want to let others know about it by giving a
recommendation in *rec.pets.cats*. Another way of putting commercial information into Usenet messages is through the signature line. Instead of

choosing a self-descriptive phrase or quote, you may instead mention your company name or plug a product. While four lines do not seem like much space in which to make your sales presentation, remember that in a two-step process, a few well-chosen words, together with a reference to where more detailed product information can be found, is probably the best way of selling on the Usenet.

Let's say you have now selected the advertising method that is best for your product, a one- or two-step process, and written either your single message or your initial message plus long follow-up sales material. You have decided which of the response methods suits your product and customers best. You must now choose the Newsgroups where your message will be posted. This is probably the most important decision you will have to make as a cyberseller.

First, let's look at your Newsgroup choices from a purely marketing standpoint. You should begin your selection for posting by reading carefully the entire list your access provider carries. It doesn't take long to go through the Newsgroup names available and you don't want to miss any where your customers can be found. When you try to locate those who are most likely to be interested in your product or service, Usenet, because it is divided into so many narrow subject categories, gives you a lot of excellent clues. Suppose, for example, you are selling boating equipment. There are a number of Newsgroups devoted to boats and the sport of sailing. The same is true of any sport you can name. This first round of Newsgroup selections is a fairly straightforward matching of your product or service with Newsgroups on the same topic.

Your second-round selections require only a little more imagination. Again, looking at our boating equipment example, what is the likelihood that those who are interested in other types of water sports such a snorkeling, water-skiing and deep sea fishing would also want to know about boating? The odds are good that there would be interest and you can find Newsgroups on all these related subjects. How about vacation spots near water, say, the Bahamas or Hawaii, where sailing is popular? Once again, there are Newsgroups devoted to specific areas of vacation travel where interest in your product is likely to be high. Do you remember the regional hierarchies we discussed earlier in this chapter? Perhaps some promising choices for boating equipment would be groups in the Usenet hierarchies devoted to geographical regions near coastlines. The Boston, Miami, or San Francisco hierarchies would be good possibilities.

Now let's consider your third-round selections. Beyond the expressed interests or probable locations, consider the types of people who normally go boating. Boaters need to have enough money to buy or at least rent a boat. That doesn't come cheap. Newsgroups attracting professionals such as doctors or business executives who can afford high ticket recreation would, therefore, be likely selections. There are many Newsgroups where discussions of professional subjects are carried on that might attract the kind of customer you are looking for.

Finally, you should always include the various Newsgroups that are especially designed for selling products. Every regional hierarchy has a "for sale" group in certain subject areas, especially when it comes to computer equipment. Then there is the Newsgroup *misc.forsale*. You will recall that it is the second most popular on the entire Usenet. With this one alone you can reach over a quarter of a million people for just a few pennies.

Let's consider how we would select Newsgroups for another type of product, one that is very different from boating equipment. Perhaps yours is an item that appeals to almost everyone. A reporter once asked us to think of a product in which almost every man, woman and child everywhere, regardless of age, sex, financial status, education level, or anything else might be interested. We came up with Coca-Cola. Of course, not everyone in the world drinks Coke. Some like Pepsi or Evian or orange juice or Bud. Still, there are probably no Newsgroups lacking for avid Coke drinkers. Soap and toothpaste are two more products that just about everyone uses. With such items, the marketing strategy would simply be to reach as many people as possible.

The selection of Newsgroups for our Green Card project presented its own challenges. Although there is one Newsgroup call *alt.visa.us* devoted to U.S. immigration matters, in an environment like the Internet where people from every nation of the world participate, we concluded that there were many in Newsgroups other than the single one focusing on immigration where interest in U.S. Green Cards would be high. The most obvious second-round choices were the approximately eighty cultural groups such as *soc.culture.hungary*, *soc.culture.africa*, *alt.culture.indonesia* and *alt.culture.argentina*. In addition, there were a number of Newsgroups devoted to subjects such as eastern religions where we surmised we could find foreign nationals. Finally, there were the many foreign hierarchies. Although in themselves they each covered a large variety of topics, certainly we could logically conclude that the target audience for our service could be found there.

Finally, however, we decided to try them all. We eliminated joke and flame groups on the basis of our reluctance to deal with their unnerving psyches. We also bypassed as many of the repeat groups (flonk.flonk.flonk) as possible. All the rest stayed on our list. Our rationale was that the kind of person we wanted to reach was a non-U.S. citizen or resident. Such an individual could not be defined by age, interest, sex, or income, but only by nationality. Usenet groups didn't lend themselves to that kind of distinction, especially since all Newsgroups could be reached by anyone, anywhere. In other words, there were no groups with the title *alt.foreigner*.

As you can see, each product or service requires a different approach when it comes time to select Newsgroups for posting. You know your own product or service better than anyone. Imagine what kind of person might need or want it, what their related interests might be. Then look over the Newsgroup list and pick the places where you think your customers are likely to gather. Chances are good that you'll be right.

The Controversy over Advertising on Usenet

So far, in selecting the Newsgroups that are suitable for marketing goods or services, we've considered only where we might find our best sales prospects. Unfortunately, you must also consider a factor that has nothing to do with actual marketing.

You can't avoid facing the fact that Usenet advertising is controversial. There is no way to explain selling on the Usenet without talking about conflicting views of whether or not broad advertising on Usenet is appropriate. Such a discussion is necessary not because there is resistance by Usenet readers to purchasing goods or services they've seen advertised on Newsgroups. We already know from our own experience that untold numbers of Newsgroup participants, on encountering well-presented information about a product of interest, will be only too glad to buy. The problem arises because employing the Usenet commercially breaks with the research-only tradition on which the Internet was first built. In spite of the fact that the Internet is now becoming more commercial each day, there is a group of individuals, mainly students and faculty members from universities where the Internet originated, who insist that using the huge Usenet communication facility for advertising amounts, at best, to rudeness. At worst, the truly committed and commitable see advertising on the Usenet as an act of war.

We think you should be fully informed before deciding issues of manners and morals as they relate to Usenet advertising. We want to explore with you the various objections that have been raised to commercial messages on this portion of the Internet and why you may or may not agree with them.

Understanding the exact basis for the anti-advertising sentiment of certain factions is not easy. Arguments fly back and forth. Name calling and dirty tricks abound. Sometimes those who don't want Usenet to carry ads offer reasons why. Other times there is only a disorganized, vitriolic outpouring of hate and anger. Because you are a principled person trying to make a fortune on the Information Superhighway in an honest and ethical manner, you will have to take a hard look at the facts and judge for yourself what is right and wrong.

First, you should understand that not everyone who opposes Usenet advertising does so for the same reason. The objection that is most universally agreed upon among the ad-opponent group, however, has to do with off-topic posting. In theory, it is a rule of Usenet that you must post only messages that are acceptable to the others in the group. The main measure of acceptability is supposed to be that the message relates directly to the topic of the conversation. To do otherwise, we are told, would be like bursting uninvited into a room where a discussion is in progress and then proceeding to shout out over the voices of the other speakers, forcing the people in the room to hear statements they do not want to hear. In doing this, the shouter is not only being rude, he is wasting the valuable time of the others in the room. If you accept this picture as accurate, then you must decide that Usenet advertising is indeed offensive, unless, of course, the product you are selling is directly relevant to the subject of the Newsgroup.

The fact is, the picture just drawn for you is grossly distorted. These distortions are based largely on the fictional concept of Cyberspace we described earlier. Just as there really is no Cyberspace, there are, in actuality, no rooms where people are talking. What you do have is a series of messages posted to electronic bulletin boards. Nothing more, nothing less. Do you believe you can burst in and shout down a bunch of inert messages? Do you believe that as you see a message on your computer screen in which you have no interest, you will be forced to read it? Why, if such a message appeared would you not press your delete key and simply eliminate it, a procedure that takes about one second? Finally, in the case of advertising messages, do you really believe that everyone doesn't want them? Certainly, there are some who will not. But everyone? Is that why the *misc.forsale* group is up there at the top of the list of popularly read Newsgroups? Is that why more than twenty thousand people responded positively to our own advertisement for the Green Card Lottery? Answer these questions for yourself and see what conclusions you reach.

Next, for your consideration, we present the money argument against Usenet advertising. There is a certain cost involved in sending and receiving every Usenet message. Those who hate commercial messages say they are being forced against their will to pay for advertising messages they do not want. Once again, let us examine this premise and see what decision you may reach in judging whether or not, by putting commercial messages on the Usenet, you are doing the moral thing.

To believe you are wrongfully costing people money by posting commercial messages, you must again believe that no one wants advertisements. As we've already seen, there is clear evidence that is not the case. Certainly, though, there are some people who won't want to see your advertisement. Is it fair that these people must pay? Consider some similar events in your own life. Do you watch television? Did you pay for the electricity that brought the last hamburger commercial into your house? Do you think McDonald's is responsible for paying the portion of your electric bill attributable to the time you spend hearing how you deserve a break today? Should you amortize the cost of your color TV and send bills to Ford, GM and Chrysler for the time their advertisements occupied your TV screen? Does that idea sound more than a little far-fetched and ridiculous?

Turning to the Usenet itself, do you believe every person on Usenet finds every message acceptable and worthwhile except for advertisements? Consider flame wars. You already know what a flame is. Flame wars arise on Usenet when a certain group of people decides to attack verbally the participants of a particular Newsgroup. Recently, the Newsgroup *rec.pets.cats* was the object of such an attack. Now imagine you are a cat lover who wants to discuss the care and feeding of your pet. You tune in on your favorite Newsgroup with that objective in mind. Instead of the discussion you anticipated, you are greeted with long threads of unpleasant invectives from people who hate cats and have nothing more productive to do with their time than let you know about it. Should you have to pay for these messages you neither expected nor wanted? When you enter a forum where millions of people who have no more in common than the use of a computer express opinions freely, it is only reasonable to expect that everyone will have differing opinions on which messages are valuable and which are not. All those accessing Usenet know and accept this fact when they tune in. In agreeing to pay for on-line time, they knew they would be seeing some messages they wanted to read and others they didn't. Under these circumstances, if you were to see a Usenet message you find valuable, do you owe money to the person who posted it for the time and money he or she spent in sending it? Conversely, when you see a message you don't like, has the person who sent that message wrongfully cost you time and money? Once again, decide for yourself.

As you consider the cost issue, you might like to know exactly how much money we are talking about. Costs that access providers charge users differ. Some people receive accounts free. For those who pay, access charges range from less than $20 per month for unlimited usage, to several dollars an hour. Now, let's do the math and see just what an unwanted message costs a Usenet reader. Taking one example, Delphi currently charges $3 per hour for on-line time. Suppose that you are a Delphi subscriber. You turn on the Usenet for an hour. In that time, you find several messages and an advertisement or two that seem interesting. There are also ten messages, some of which are ads, in which you have no interest whatever. Clicking each of them off the screen has taken you one second apiece for a total of about ten seconds. Your $3 per hour charge can also be viewed as $.05 per minute or $.0008 per second. Therefore, your cost for unwanted messages is $.008, literally less than a penny. Over a year's time, assuming you read Usenet for about an hour every single day of your life and average ten unwanted messages each day, your yearly expenditure would be about three dollars. This will be added to the $1095 you are spending on the information, advertisements, flames and chitchat you supposedly did want to read. Of course, all this is theoretical just to illustrate a point. The practical fact is that if everyone insisted upon paying only for the Newsgroup messages he or she saw and liked, that would be the end of Usenet.

The only point on which both sides in the Internet ad wars agree is that there is no law against advertising on the Usenet. When the National Science Foundation lifted the ban on commercial Internet uses, there was no further doubt that Usenet advertising, along with promotions in other areas of the Internet, was no longer barred by an entity with any legal authority. Admitting that there were no statutory or regulatory prohibitions on broad Usenet advertising, our own opponents searched long and hard for some general legal theory under which they could sue us. Certainly, they reasoned, the fact that they had been so badly upset and had been charged their .008 cents for the on-line time that brought them our ads would be enough for the U.S. courts to put us in our place. Suffice it to say we have never been sued. Left without any legitimate basis for objecting to what we have done, most of our critics have decided that what we have done is "rude." Considering the behavior of those who have called us rude, we have been forced to conclude that rudeness is very much a matter of opinion. As lawyers, we know of no legal theory that precludes one person from having different values, different standards of behavior, or different ideas of where to advertise than another. If you decide to make your fortune on the Information Superhighway, how you do it is up to you. As long as you do not go against prohibitions placed on all communications mediums, such as the one barring the sale of child pornography, the law is not going to stop you.

Who will at least attempt to stop you is a certain group that feels the Internet should be operated their way and only their way. We've already told you our story, so you know what they may try to do. Many of these people are college kids who have time on their hands, chips on their shoulders, and little in the way of serious responsibility to occupy them. Others are brilliant scientists who have been in on the development of the Internet since it was only a gleam in the Defense Department's eye. Still others are the first business people to profit off of the Internet and who would like to keep more fortune seekers from getting on the I-way as long as possible. What they all share is a misperception that they have proprietary rights over the Internet.

While the nature of the opposition is easy to determine, its size is not. We would like to stress that from what we have personally observed, the active opponents of Usenet advertising form a relatively small group. Some on the I-way are prepared to fight this battle to the death. The overwhelming majority, like you and us, have better things to do with their lives than fight what appears to be an old-style turf war in a high-tech setting.

One last word on the Usenet ad wars. We are well aware that a lot of people find ads annoying. There are very few of us who haven't zapped a commercial that popped up during our favorite TV show. Most of us are fit to kill when we trip over our own feet, running to pick up a ringing telephone, only to find someone selling discount phone services on the other end. Ponder it a little more, though, and you may find advertising is more important than you thought. There probably is not an item in your house or business that you did not learn about through advertising. The best ads, like the ones featuring the "Yes I am" man who sells a certain brand of beer, are great entertainment. Most important, there is probably not one of us who doesn't owe his or her job directly or indirectly to advertising. There are societies where there are no ads. In true communist societies, advertising is not allowed except by the government who owns everything. Maybe it's more worth a fight for than you thought.

Direct vs. Indirect Advertising

Now that you have all the facts, you can adopt the advertising strategy with which you feel most comfortable. You have any number of options. Advertising on the Usenet is considered direct advertising, as is sending unsolicited e-mail messages. That means you are placing ads where people will see them even if someone isn't specifically looking, much like advertisements in newspapers, on television, on radio, through direct mail, or on billboards. You can also choose indirect advertising. This means that your customer makes the effort to find your sales material, either because he specifically goes looking for it, or because he happens on it by accident. FTP, Gopher, and Web sites discussed in later chapters are examples of the indirect method. You may also choose to employ a combination of direct and indirect techniques. We have already explained how one way of handling a two-step process is by posting brief messages to Usenet that will send your customers to other information sites on the Internet, where long product descriptions, answers to their questions and order forms will await them. Whatever technique you select, be aware that indirect advertising is the least controversial method, while direct methods are the most likely to draw criticism.

Going with It or Going for It

In employing the Usenet to make your fortune, it is possible to take a conservative approach and play by the "rules." If you limit your commercial postings only to groups where your product or service is strictly relevant to the topic under discussion (i.e. posting boating equipment ads in a Newsgroup on sailing) you can expect little criticism. If you expand your postings to groups where the product is not strictly on topic but highly relevant (i.e. Green Card Lottery postings in the *soc.culture.japan* Newsgroup) you are also unlikely to meet with problems. The further away from a clear connection between the product or service you are selling and the topic of the Newsgroup in which you try to sell it, the more you risk the wrath of the self-styled Internet ad police. Likewise, the more Newsgroups to which you post, the more customers you will find and the better chance you have of building your fortune.

Recently, we read of a Canadian company that wanted to sell beer on the Internet. There are one or two Newsgroups covering the topics of brewing and sampling beer. It was here that the company elected to post commercial messages presenting its product. The venture was quite successful. In describing their strategy, one of the company owners stated his belief that his product would also have sold well in the many Newsgroups devoted to individual football teams, basketball teams, and other popular spectator sports. That certainly seems like an excellent assumption to make. Still, this businessman decided against what appeared to be an indisputably sound marketing idea. He limited his postings out of fear that if he extended his advertising to reach more customers, he would be flamed. Will you allow the protesters who have no legal right to interfere with your business stop you from selling your product or service to those who might want, need, and appreciate it? You know the answer we would give to this question. You must decide on the answer that is right for you.

Another conservative approach you may choose to follow in utilizing the Usenet for marketing is disguising your advertising message as something other than what it really is. Interestingly, many who consider themselves upstanding members of the Internet "community" as well as computer marketing experts recommend this practice. They see it not as deceitful, but as a way of showing sensitivity to the Net "culture." The idea is that you will offer up some general data along with your product description and sales inducements in order to fulfill the Netiquette requirement that each Usenet posting should contain valuable information. An example of this technique would be to incorporate some interesting facts on the history of sailing along with your posting for the sale of boating equipment.

There are several other variations on the theme of approaching Usenet advertising in a roundabout way. We have already discussed two of them. When you put sales information in the signature portion rather than the body of the message, many who normally dislike Usenet commercialism find this acceptable. Likewise, if your product or service is mentioned as an endorsement by a satisfied user, this too is seen as inoffensive. In employing endorsements, if you wish to stick with a conservative approach, it is still necessary to watch closely the relationship between the product or service offered and the topic of the Newsgroup where the advertisement is posted.

A final method for undertaking a conservative approach to Usenet marketing is tailoring each message individually for the Newsgroup where it will be posted. For example, suppose you are selling sunglasses. Couldn't you write a message that would suggest the use of your sunglasses for assisting race car drivers or making life more pleasant for fans of outdoor spectator sports? This would greatly increase the number of Newsgroups where you could advertise your product and still play by the "rules." With a little creative writing, our beer-selling friends might have been able to approach some of the groups they really wished to reach but feared to try.

A final roundabout method of Usenet advertising is to start your own Newsgroup. Since you formulated the group, you have the right to decide the ground rules. Because it is a Newsgroup, unless you decide it should be moderated, anyone can come in and say anything he or she wishes. What no one can do is stop you from saying what you wish. When you start your own Newsgroup, however, you are once again limited because, in a way, even though it is Usenet advertising, you are using an indirect approach. You are asking people to come to you rather than you going to them. Moreover, even though you start a group, you really have no way of controlling whether or not access providers will carry it. Still, you have little to lose and everything to gain by trying.

Roundabout techniques of Usenet advertising, also called cloaking devices, are a real case of beauty being in the eye of the beholder. To some, an advertising message written in a less straightforward manner is simply a considerate form of softselling in contrast with a more jarring hardsell of a clearly identified advertisement. To others it is an underhanded subterfuge, where the seller is covering up his true agenda from the hopefully unsuspecting buyer. Done with good intent, either straightforward or roundabout advertising can be honorably and effectively undertaken. Overall, however, advertising leaders who set standards for the industry in the United States believe that an advertisement must be clearly identified as such. At the end of this book, you will find our own set of advertising guidelines for your consideration. They are based on the guidelines of respected publications such as *The New York Times*. We don't say they are the only way to go, nor should you believe that if you follow these guidelines scrupulously you will not be flamed. The Internet is so new and changing so fast, sure guideposts for almost everything are still in the making. Our guidelines are offered as suggestions in an effort to help that process along.

Usenet is a valuable and effective marketing tool. Not only is it an easy and inexpensive way to reach large numbers of individuals, these are people who have already identified themselves as willing buyers of goods and services sold over the Internet. In fact, the very novelty of seeing a product or service presented through Usenet, as well as the instant ability to communicate with the seller, promotes a good atmosphere in which customers are ready to buy.

Usenet is a strictly text-based area of the Internet. Unlike the World

Wide Web, which we describe in a later chapter, you can make your presentation in Newsgroups with words only. Although this limits the way you can reach people on the Internet, it maximizes the number. Internet technology is changing rapidly, but at the moment everyone on the Internet can receive text, while only a relatively small percentage can see graphics. If you want the largest possible audience for your selling efforts, the Usenet is the place to find it.

The indirect form of advertising we mentioned earlier is based on the idea that there should be special areas of the Internet and even a special hierarchy of the Usenet dedicated exclusively to selling. This means that with indirect advertising you must not only offer something for sale, you must also offer a motivation for looking and a road map to find the product. Direct advertising on Usenet is not only easy for you, it is also easy and convenient for your customers. Since you have done some good thinking about the Newsgroups you've chosen for posting, even if you have concluded, as we did, that your target market should be everywhere, you can assume that there will be many people who will welcome introduction of goods and services that are of interest to them. From this you can make your fortune. Moreover, it is enjoyable and satisfying to turn someone on to a good thing that will improve their lives or at least their humor. That's what Usenet allows you to do.

7

E-MAIL AND ELECTRONIC MAILING LISTS: PAPERLESS AND POSTAGE FREE

E-mail's Many Uses

Unquestionably the single most popular feature on the Internet is Electronic Mail, or e-mail. Here is a great place for you to start making your fortune on the Information Superhighway because, unlike any other single I-way feature, e-mail is used by everyone. This includes the some 30 million individuals who are on the Internet as well as all those having accounts with most commercial on-line services such as Prodigy, CompuServe, and America Online. You can send and receive e-mail with absolutely any type of network account that allows mail to pass through the Internet, and they almost all do. E-mail by itself gives you access to such a huge market that you could really sell your products or services in this way alone and still make a fortune. E-mail should therefore be especially attractive to anyone who already has a commercial service accounts but doesn't want to invest a lot of additional time and money in equipment, Internet connections, and learning new technology. Here is a quick and simple way to do business on the Information Superhighway, with a minimum of cost and effort.

For all its simplicity, e-mail as a marketing technique is as powerful as any in Cyberspace, for it, too, offers the interactive feature that makes cyberselling so effective. Much of the romance brought to you by the Usenet spills over into e-mail as well. Testimony to this fact can be found in the story of right-wing mega-gadfly Rush Limbaugh, who met, courted, and won his new wife by e-mail. If this medium can turn a straightlaced, heavyset guy, who refuses to wear anything but a suit and a really bad tie, into a successful romantic figure, it can certainly turn you into a successful cyberseller. We have already touched on some of the uses of e-mail for commercial purposes. It is by e-mail that you send your customers further information in the second step of Usenet advertising promotions. Now we will tell you what can be done just with e-mail alone.

There are any number of good reasons why e-mail is so popular. The uses for it are endless. E-mail works on the same principle as regular or snail mail, except that delivery is made electronically and immediately straight into the recipient's computer with no postage required. E-mail is so fast, in fact, that you can actually engage in conversation just by mailing messages back and forth. One important use for e-mail is as an extremely cheap substitute for a telephone. It is this function that in large part accounts for e-mail's great popularity.

E-mail may also soon replace faxes as the primary means of rapid written communication. In fact, there is nothing a fax machine can do that can't be done faster, better, and cheaper with e-mail. Graphical images can be sent via e-mail just like a fax, but without the bother and space fax paper requires, and without long-distance telephone charges. Once you are free of these restraints, the practical limits on the length of what you can fax is gone as well. Suppose you had written a book and wanted to fax a 300-page manuscript to your publisher. Imagine how long that would take. Now imagine that your publisher was located in New York and you lived in, say, Phoenix. This would be a happy day for the phone company stock holders. At the other end, your harried publisher would be facing 300 pages of curled up fax paper. Of course, he could not receive any other faxes until yours finished coming in. With high potential for garbled pages and paper jams, what we have here is a disaster in the making. That same 300-page manuscript, sent via e-mail instead of fax, would be received in a matter of seconds. No long-distance telephone call would be needed. The recipient could choose to read the manuscript directly on his or her computer screen, make changes, and then print out a hard copy, if desired. The information would still remain on the computer, providing a back up if the printed copy should be lost. There is little reason, with all the benefits computer transmission of documents offers, why anyone would choose to use faxes, and the day is probably not far away when fax machines will become obsolete.

E-mail sounds like the perfect tool and it really is. It is not, however, problem free. First, there is the question of security. An e-mail message travels through a number of different computers on its way to its final destination and it is possible for it to be intercepted along the way. It is even more likely that it could be inadvertently misdirected due to a typo.

Remember, computers are only machines. Not only can't they think for themselves, they can't type either.

Problems with Piracy and Forgery

Because of e-mail security problems, encryption is one of the most hotly debated topics in the computer world. Encryption, already mentioned briefly in our review of Internet sex, is a technical process that can put any message you send into a secret code automatically. The code can be broken on the receiving end only by a person using the same encryption program as the sender. You may have read about the controversial clipper chip. It is a technology the U.S. government wants to make mandatory for encryption programs, so that Uncle Sam will be able to keep a watchful eye on e-mail and, when necessary, prevent the illegal transmission of security sensitive data. Basically, the proposal would require all encryption techniques to follow a certain formula that official agencies could decipher at will. Irrespective of government security problems, encryption is not practical for most business correspondence because when a company deals with a broad array of customers, suppliers, and so on, there is no way of insuring that the same programs will be used at both ends of a message transmission. You are better off, therefore, simply accepting that an e-mail transmission may not always be entirely private. Overall, you will be safest thinking of e-mail much like a post card. You must assume that anything sent by e-mail can be read by others. Suffice it to say that if a message must remain completely confidential, e-mail, at present, is not the best choice. Keep in mind, however, that the same could be said of telephone and fax transmissions as well.

E-mail's second drawback is that it is extremely easy to forge a sender's name. Most mail programs give senders the ability to place on their messages any return e-mail name and address they wish. For some, the temptation is too great to resist. If you get an e-mail letter that looks like it came from the President of the United States, with the return address of clinton@whitehouse.gov, contain your enthusiasm. Maybe the President really did write to you and place an order. Then again, maybe it came from an unhappy Netter distressed at finding yet another business person making money on the I-way. There are, however, ways to check. Like Usenet postings, each e-mail message comes with a complete header, showing the exact route the letter took in getting to its destination. Although headers, as well as names, can be tampered with, it takes a high level of expertise to do so. If you have any reason to doubt the authenticity of the address or name on an e-mail message, you will usually be able to get confirmation by looking at the complete header.

E-mail is one of the simplest computer functions. First, as in the case of any other type of mail, you must know the exact address of the intended recipient. Then, you simply type in your message, or attach one that is pre-prepared, and hit a few computer keys to send it on its way. Receiving e-mail is even easier. You don't have to do anything at all. The computer acts just like your mailman, only faster, and promptly delivers your mail as it is received. Then you just read it on your computer screen. As with any other data that comes in, if you have a printer, you can also print out a hard copy.

Your E-mail Address

Each person on the Internet or other on-line services has a unique e-mail address. The e-mail address is the most important part of your message, for without it, your mail will never get where it was intended to go. Everyone with an Internet account is given an e-mail address from his or her access provider. E-mail addresses are not dissimilar from names of Usenet groups. The address is composed of three parts. Part one is your own name or any name you may wish to use. Here is another of those instances where people tend to get creative, so if you want to pretend you're Madonna, this is your chance to do so without having your sanity come under too much question. The name on an e-mail address must be put in the form of a single word such as msiegel or imrich.

Next comes the @ sign. It is an abbreviation for the word "at." It is followed by the domain name of the computer where the mail will be received. Computers having direct connections to the Internet take names called domains. Domain names are established by filing an application with a central Internet registry in Virginia. The domain computer in most cases will be the one owned by your access company. Usually, the company will select as its domain the name under which it does business. Therefore, if you have your account with America Online, the first two parts of your e-mail address will read imrich@aol.

Some access providers allow you to register an individual domain. This permits you to use your own company name as the second part of your e-mail address. Your mail still comes to the same centralized computer, but a special program allows for the identification of the various domain names used. A domain can be broken down further into sub domains. Our own domain is actually "sell," with a sub-domain of "cyber." When put together it comes out cyber.sell. The reason for doing this is simply easier categorization of the mail that comes into a particular domain.

The last part of an e-mail address is the hierarchy, which defines either the geographical location or main activity engaged in by the central receiving computer. Some common American hierarchy designations are "com" which stands for commercial and "edu" which signifies an educational institution. Therefore, completing the e-mail addresses we began above, yours might be imrich@aol.com.

Our personal e-mail addresses are lcanter@cyber.sell.com and msiegel@cyber.sell.com. Drop us a line. We'd like to hear from you.

Understanding a little about e-mail addresses can help you to create an image for yourself as well as gather information about your potential customers. For example, if you plan to send mail to someone with the address bigcheese@ibm.com you know that you are probably dealing with a high level employee of IBM. If the name is geek@mit.edu you know you have someone who is affiliated with Massachusetts Institute of Technology. Domains can also tell you where a person is located geographically. As we've said, many U.S. addresses end in com or edu. Other common U.S. hierarchies are "org" for organizations or "gov" for government offices. All countries but the United States, however, have hierarchy designations by geographical locations. Examples include au (Australia), uk (United Kingdom), de (Germany), and ca (Canada). Almost every country of the world has its own Internet hierarchy.

The e-mail address system we've just described applies only to the Internet. Commercial on-line services such as CompuServe and Prodigy have their own addressing systems for contacting people strictly within those networks. Individuals who belong to such services have two e-mail addresses: one on the Internet for communicating with people outside their home networks, and one for mail that stays within the circle of subscribers to their own access provider. For specific directions on how you can send e-mail through the Internet to each of the individual networks, commercial or otherwise, look at *The Internet Mail Guide* which is available on the Internet itself or through the INETFORUM on CompuServe.

The selection of your e-mail name is an opportunity for some very powerful marketing. Choose carefully, picking your company name or perhaps a descriptive title showing what your company does. Never forget that your name itself is a form of advertising. For example, if you're an accountant, you might pick a name like "taxes" or "beat-irs." Our Canter & Siegel law firm uses the name cslaw. Our marketing company, as we mentioned earlier, is cyber.sell. As you go forward with your cyberselling strategy, your name could become famous, just as ours did.

How E-mail Works

When you first sit down at your computer and access a mail program, you are presented with a menu of messages currently sitting in your mail box. Using one of the common e-mail programs your screen might look like this:

```
Mailbox is 'cybersell:/usr/spool/mail/lcanter' with 5 messages [ELM 2.4
PL23]
     1    Aug 4 HYNSONC1              (50)     WWW and Gopher Services.

     2    Jul 25 system Problems      (4140)   Re: List of .com domains

     3    Jul 18 Jim Fisher           (31)     Sample web page?

     4    Jul 18 Morrison, Christophe (42)     Internet Services Questions

     5    Jul 10 Steve McQueen   (36)     About our need for gopher/www/mail
1
```

This shows we have five messages waiting. We can read the date each was sent, the name of the sender, the size of the file in numbers of lines, and a description of its contents. How does our computer know what each letter contains? The sender puts in a descriptive subject header, just as is the case with Usenet postings. This is extremely helpful, especially if you receive thousands of pieces of e-mail as we did during the Green Card lottery. It gives you an initial way to sort out the mail, separating the wheat from the chaff. Imagine how much simpler this is than sorting out thousands of letters received by regular mail. Here you don't even have to open up an envelope. From this menu you can select any given message and read it, reply to it, print it, or delete it, all with the push of a few buttons.

Once you have selected the one you want to read, a typical e-mail message might look like this:

The top of this message shows us the date it was sent, who sent it, the type of material in the message which, in this example, is text, the size of the message, and the subject matter. Then the message itself follows. At the bottom is a menu of commands you can use for handling this piece of mail in a number of ways. These instructions are self-explanatory.

As with all things you want your computer to do, sending and receiving e-mail requires use of a special software program. There are many different e-mail programs available. Some you must buy. Many are free. You will probably be supplied with a free one by your access provider. If you will be handling large volumes of mail, however, as you do when you engage in cyberselling, you may want to consider some of the commercial programs. The fancier (and usually more expensive) programs make sending, receiving, and answering e-mail easier and may even do a certain amount of mail sorting automatically for you, such as grouping the mail by sender or subject, or even rejecting all mail from someone you don't like. Whatever mail program you use, they all work in a similar fashion. For details on how to use e-mail programs, you should consult your access provider or one of the numerous books on how to use the Internet.

Making Money with E-mail

The reason you can make money with e-mail should by now be obvious. You can utilize this amazingly quick and extremely cheap method of communication to transmit sales information to your potential customers. Just as with Usenet postings, a one- or two-step procedure should be considered. Like all computer marketing techniques, sending sales litera-ture through e-mail is new and people are not used to it. Therefore, if you are approaching a potential customer for the first time through an un-solicited e-mailing, we especially recommend using a two-step process, because the first message you send is short. Keeping your initial contact brief is a good way to manage possible negative feelings you may en-gender when a potential customer finds a piece of unsolicited e-mail advertising in his or her mailbox. Once you receive an initial show of interest and find that additional information is desired, you can employ data sites or e-mail again to deliver longer, detailed product information and order solicitations. All the second-step techniques we described in the previous chapter for Usenet marketing apply when the initial contact is made by e-mail as well.

More ideas for getting rich have probably been based on mail order businesses than any other kind. They offer some of the best money making opportunities for the average person. Why? Primarily, because they re-quire very little cash to start. All the benefits and opportunities inherent in a traditional direct mail business are multiplied when you market with e-mail. There is no need to incur the expenses of traditional retail space. You can usually avoid maintaining large inventories as well. Even better, you have the ability to reach directly the target market that is most likely to buy your product or service. You do not have to worry about a wholesaler or retailer accepting your product for sale before the public has the oppor-tunity to see it. You are also free of any geographic limitations. You can sell to anyone anywhere. A retail store depends greatly on its location. Mail order, especially when done with the international capabilities of e-mail, does not.

Cost and speed, however, are really where e-mail comes shining through. Advertising and mailing costs through traditional methods are slow and expensive. We found that out when we marketed our book, *U.S. Immigration Made Easy*, by buying specialized mailing lists and advertising in ethnic newspapers around the country, plus a number of newspapers located abroad. We've already shown you how favorably cyberselling compares from an expense standpoint with other, more traditional marketing methods. It costs some $300 to reach just a thousand people with a direct mail piece, including charges for printing and mailing, and that is if you take advantage of bulk rate discounts. Then, you can expect a significant percentage of the addresses on your mailing list to be out of date. We find that in a typical mailing, between five and ten percent are returned because of bad addresses. We paid the postage to send them nonetheless, and we have to pay the post office again to return them to us with a note that the address was bad. Not only is a direct mailing very expensive, but bulk mail is unbelievably slow. It can take up to a month before all your bulk mail pieces are delivered. Then, you'll wait even longer for people to mail back order forms and payments. You could set up an 800 telephone number and have your customers respond to your mail piece that way. It saves time and makes it more convenient for your customers. That, however, results in even more expense and you have to pay for every single call made to you, whether the customer eventually buys or not. People in mail order businesses do get rich, but with the drawbacks we've just described, many are lucky to break even.

Enter the fabulous world of cyberselling. You have the potential to send an electronic mailing to more than 30 million people around the world. It costs you little more to send your message to thousands than mailing to only one. You can do this without printing a single page, buying a single postage stamp, or contracting for one inch of ad space. Your potential customers will receive your mailing almost instantaneously. And, because your mail will go directly to their computers, they are much less likely to discard it unopened, as they might with most "junk" mail delivered by the post office. If you want to re-contact the same customers several times, no problem. The cost to you is negligible. The marketing potentials are enormous.

Even if you already have some type of business and are not interested in starting a new one, simply having an e-mail address may increase the profits of your already existing company. It is becoming common to see businesses include e-mail addresses in their regular advertisements. By advertising an e-mail address, you are in effect telling the entire world of computer users that you are one of them. You'll be surprised at how many customer inquiries will come by e-mail.

Using a Mailing List

In considering prospects for advertising on the Usenet, you did not have to worry about looking for the location of each individual customer. Instead, they came to central gathering places where you could find them and present your sales message. They were even kind enough to differentiate themselves by subject, so you could target your marketing to them quite easily. If you want to do a direct e-mail campaign, however, you do not have this convenience. You must instead, find lists of your prospects together with their e-mail addresses.

In the non-Cyberspace direct mail world, it is common to buy mailing lists. A number of companies maintain large databases of names and addresses with various demographic information. You simply tell them what you are looking for and they can create mailing labels for you, at a price, of course. Fifteen cents per name is a typical charge. We are not aware of any commercial companies yet offering this service for e-mail addresses. In fact, we think there is a tremendous business opportunity for someone in starting such a business. For now, let's look at some e-mail lists that are currently available to you for reaching your potential I-way customers as well as how you can go about creating a list of your own.

There are hundreds of electronic mailing lists maintained around the world for large groups of people who like to communicate with each other. These lists are called bit listserve mailing lists. Each of them covers a certain subject area. Actually, they operate much like the Usenet Newsgroups, except that instead of messages appearing on centralized electronic bulletin boards, every person who places his or her name on one of the specialized mailing lists receives all messages posted to that list in his or her private e-mail box. There are thousands of listserve mailing lists. To locate them, you need what is known in Internet jargon as a "list of lists." A complete lists of lists can be obtained free through the Internet from a data site operated by Dartmouth College, or you can purchase it in book form from Prentice-Hall publishers. In hard copy, the complete list of lists runs several hundred printed pages. To undertake your marketing program, simply review the subjects of the list, determine where the product you are offering may be of interest, and then mail your advertisement to those lists, once again choosing a one- or two-step plan. Your single piece of e-mail will go automatically to thousands of Internetters who subscribe to that list.

You should be aware that many of the bit listserve lists are moderated. This means that every message sent to the list is first screened by a list administrator who determines unilaterally whether a given message should or should not go out to all list subscribers. You will probably not have particularly good luck sending advertisements to moderated mailing lists, but you never know. Several moderated lists relating to non-American cultural groups did accept our Green Card lottery ad. One possible way around the problem of moderated lists is to yourself become a subscriber to the list where you would like your e-mail advertising messages circulated. Many moderated lists have a policy of accepting all messages from their own subscribers. In such cases, the selection process is usually done by a computer that automatically circulates any message from a recognized name on the subscriber list. The Dartmouth List of Lists indicates which lists are moderated and which are not.

Another way to acquire a mailing list is from your own access provider. When you are on-line, you should be able to get a list of everyone else on-line at the same time simply by typing in the word "who" on your keyboard. Then you simply capture those names for your list. Another good place to go scouting for e-mail addresses is the Usenet. Every single message on the Usenet shows the e-mail address of the person who posted it. Keep your eye on groups that are relevant to your products or services and you could collect thousands of e-mail addresses. Lastly, you may want to consult a geek to see if he can devise a way to roam the net and capture addresses in other ways.

Ideally, creating a mailing list will be an ongoing project as your business develops, because the very best list to use is one consisting of all the people who have previously requested information or made purchases from you. This requires constantly updating your files. Therefore, it is very important to your ultimate success that you keep all e-mail addresses of everyone who ever contacts you.

If you have created your own list of e-mail addresses, there are several techniques you can use to send mail to everyone on the list without having to type in each address individually. Several e-mail features permit you to send the same message to multiple recipients at the same time. One is called carbon copy, or cc. All e-mail programs offer a cc option. You start with a mailing procedure to one person and then add more names. Each person will get a copy of what you sent but you only have to mail it once. A problem with the program is that it is set up so that each recipient will know the names of everyone else to whom you copied the message. This is particularly undesirable if you are mailing to many people. Another option called blind carbon copy, or bcc, is the solution to the problem. Again, virtually every mail program contains a bcc feature. Bcc works just like cc except that the names of all recipients are left off. No one will know who or how many others received the same message.

Another way to simplify mass mailing is the alias or nickname option. Our Internet friends love to use aliases for the purpose of hiding their true identities. The term alias, however, is used on the Internet in a broader sense to describe generally the practice of assigning a single descriptive name to one thing, be it a set of program commands or a list of names. In computerese, the alias or nickname are interchangeable. Some software programs use one term, and some the other. The aliasing procedure permits you to take an entire list of e-mail addresses, give that list a single alias or nickname description, and then direct your e-mail to that one entity. Every person on the list will then automatically receive the e-mail.

E-mail to Usenet

We've told you how e-mail can be sent back and forth between people with accounts on different commercial network services and the Internet. In Chapter 6, we talked about posting advertisements to the Usenet Newsgroups by employing news programs especially designed for that purpose. Such programs, however, work only if you have an Internet access account, and only with the Newsgroups carried by your particular access provider. Almost everyone on the Internet has access to Usenet, but some access provider companies may limit the number of Newsgroups they carry in order to save money and computer memory space. Commercial on-line services commonly offer e-mail services to the Internet but not Usenet. Prodigy is probably the largest on-line service that falls into this category.

There is a way you can post to the Usenet, even if you don't have access to that feature. The same method applies if you do have Usenet access, but your provider has only a limited Newsgroup list. This opens up all the opportunities of Usenet advertising to almost anyone with an e-mail address, even those without Internet access accounts. You can reach them by sending your news posting to what is known as an e-mail news gateway. For example, there is an e-mail gateway kept by the Western Research Laboratory at Digital Equipment Corporation in California. Its gateway e-mail address is usenet@decwrl.dec.com. To post to Usenet groups via this e-gateway, you simply send your message to the name of the Newsgroup you want to reach followed by the gateway's e-mail address, separating the Newsgroup name and the e-mail address by dots. For example, to post to the group *misc.forsale*, send your message to misc.for-sale.usenet@decwrl.dec.com. Your message will then be posted to the *misc.forsale* Newsgroup. People who wish to respond will be able to do so by writing to your regular e-mail address using the standard e-mail procedure. To post to multiple groups at the same time, also known as cross-posting, simply use the cc option discussed earlier. Using an e-mail gateway, you can accomplish posting to Usenet with a subscription to virtually any commercial on-line service, even if Internet access is limited. The only requirement is that you have the ability to send e-mail through the Internet, a feature offered by almost every commercial on-line service in existence.

Robot Mailers

We've already touched briefly on the use of robot mailers in our discussion of two-step plans for advertising on Usenet. These robots are actually auto-responders, sometimes called vacation mailers. Most Internet systems easily permit an automated response to be generated to every person who sends you e-mail. The name vacation mailer came about because the idea was first created by students who wanted a way to handle e-mail they received at their free university account mailboxes during the long sum-mer vacation break. While they were gone, their friends from around the world would get an automatic response to e-mail saying something like "Hi, this is my vacation mailer. I'll be back on September 1. If you need to reach me before then, you can call me at 602-661-5202." Used for business purposes, vacation mailers can create an e-mail on demand response, much like the popular fax-on-demand concept. Robot mailers are com-mon, easy-to-use programs that are excellent for sending a single, auto-matic response to anyone e-mailing a request. You, however, may require a more sophisticated automatic response system. If, for example, you are selling more than one product, a program can be devised recognizing in which of several items a customer is showing interest, and then sending the correct information back. You can also program a computer so it will not send the same piece of information a second time to someone who has already received it. In this way, if a customer who has gotten your standard e-mail brochure wants to ask follow-up questions, you will be able to recognize that fact and set such messages aside for writing individually tailored replies. To devise special programs is beyond the abilities of the average computer user and so usually requires outside assistance. For those who do program, however, the kinds of functions we're talking about here are fairly elementary and finding a geek qualified to help you shouldn't be hard.

The E-mail Marketing Controversy

As we did with our explanation of Usenet marketing, we have presented the selling techniques available to you with e-mail in a non-judgmental way. Once again, we must warn you that sending unsolicited e-mail for commercial purposes falls in the category of direct advertising and is therefore controversial. Let us begin by saying that there is every reason to believe your effort at sending direct e-mail will be a highly successful, fortune-building project. There is no reason whatever to think otherwise. Even though there is a computer aspect to it, sending out mailings to promote products and services is hardly an untried idea. To the contrary, it is a time-honored and proven way of selling. When using snail mail, the key to profitable direct mail solicitation is effective targeting. The same should be true of e-mail. It is our belief that if you target very accurately, with an honest conviction that those on your list have reason to be interested in your offering, people will respond by buying and you will limit problems of customer acceptance.

The objections raised to unsolicited e-mail marketing are much the same as those advanced against advertising on the Usenet. Let's look at them again, seeing if they are any more valid in terms of e-mail messages than Usenet postings. As for whether unsolicited e-mail messages cost people time and money against their will, the dynamics here are about the same as for Usenet. As long as there is mail, electronic or otherwise, people are going to receive communications they didn't specifically request and might not welcome. Which messages any one person may or may not want depends entirely on the specific needs and desires of that individual. Even when someone receives a message that is not advertising, there is no guarantee that he or she will want that particular piece of e-mail. Just as with Usenet, every time you open up your e-mailbox, you are first presented with a list of headers describing the individual mail message you've received, so it is not mandatory that you spend time reading each piece of mail before deciding to dispose of it. The cost factor for your messages is, likewise, minimal. Finally, as is also true of Usenet postings, there is no law prohibiting anyone from sending unsolicited commercial e-mail.

There is, however, one difference between advertising on Usenet and sending unsolicited e-mail. Usenet is an avowed public forum. No matter what the dictates of Netiquette, Newsgroups are open to everyone to say pretty much what they please, and, in fact, that is exactly what happens. No one participating in Newsgroups has any real or reasonable right to expect otherwise. Your mailbox, however, is your mailbox. It is not public. Unless you subscribe to a bit listserve Newsgroup, you have not asked anyone to send you mail you did not specifically request. Still, consider how things work in the real world. On a daily basis you receive so called "junk" mail at your home or office that you did not request and this hardly creates an occasion for outrage or major hardship. In fact, Stephen Wolf, head of NSF Net, in discussing the development of the Internet, pronounced the advent of every day conventions such as junk mail on the I-way "wonderful." We've already explained why hope of confidentiality with e-mail is not realistic. The wishes and expectations of privacy with an e-mail box may be greater than with messages posted to Usenet, but to those who view the matter objectively, the difference is lessening every day. You should consider all this as you make your marketing decisions.

One instance where it should be perfectly acceptable to send unsolicited e-mail is when you are contacting previous customers. Some of the more rabid opponents of direct Internet advertising techniques refuse to recognize any distinction between this and sending unsolicited e-mail to new sales prospects. To any reasonable person, however, the difference seems quite clear. Certainly, if you re-contact a previous customer and that customer then specifically asks to be removed from your mailing list, you should honor that request. Otherwise, there is a good argument that sending mail solicitations to those with whom you have had prior dealings should not even fall under the characterization of a direct advertising technique as it is defined here. Indeed, keeping close contact with customers through the use of e-mail has been praised as an excellent business practice, even in the most conservative circles.

Like Usenet advertising, the newness of the I-way medium raises questions about marketing methods that have for a long time been accepted as standard everywhere else. Once again, you must decide the path you will follow. E-mail marketing is already being used by many businesses in developing and maintaining customer relations. It's just a matter of time before e-mailing to sell products and services becomes commonplace. The ease and economy this practice offers to those who seek their fortune on the I-way is unlikely to be ignored for long.

8

CHAT: TALK YOUR WAY TO RICHES

Chat and talk features on the Internet and other on-line services go the telephone-like capabilities of e-mail one better. Although there is enough speed possible with e-mail exchanges to make a conversation viable, there is still a delay, sometimes of several minutes or perhaps even hours, between the time your message is sent and when it gets to its destination. There is no such delay with talk or Internet Relay Chat, better known as IRC. You are talking, instead, in "real time," meaning you are "heard" and, hopefully, answered, the second you type the words in on your keyboard.

Talk is the name of a common type of software program that opens a direct line of communication between two computers. You can use the computer talk feature with anyone who is a member of the same network that you are. You and another individual can talk to each other while sitting at your respective keyboards by typing messages back and forth. As you type in words, the person at the other end of the connection immediately sees what you are typing on his or her monitor, including spelling errors, typos, and anything you may have said in haste that you will someday live to regret.

The dynamics of talk communications are different from those of e-mail or Usenet. This is the only I-way feature that requires both parties to be at their computers simultaneously. When you receive a call, your computer will beep, flash, or ring, depending on the program you are using. You may ring someone's computer, but if he or she is not there with his or her system turned on, the party you are trying to reach won't know you're calling. The computer talk feature is great from a personal perspective, as a way to communicate with friends and family. There are no long-distance telephone charges, other than the cost of your Internet access. You can communicate with someone halfway around the world as easily and as inexpensively as you can with someone across the street. If you long to hear the distant voice of a loved one, this may not satisfy your craving, but the difference in cost between computer talk and the telephone can allow you to make up for what is lost in intimacy with more and longer opportunities to stay in touch.

The second real-time communications feature your computer offers, IRC, or chat for short, allows multiple parties to join in a conversation simultaneously. Most Internet access providers have a chat feature on their systems. By invoking chat, you are talking to a central computer which acts as a switchboard. Dozens of chat "groups" may be on-line at any given time. Each one is usually dedicated to a particular topic, somewhat like the Newsgroups of Usenet. Anyone may tune in to a particular group and see the words of each participant. You may join in the conversation whenever you like, or simply sit back as a "lurker" and watch the action without saying a word. Chat has been described as a large cocktail party without the cocktails. Also missing are the voices, dress-up garb, cigarette smoke, snacks, and sweaty palms commonly associated with flesh-and-blood gatherings.

All of the commercial on-line services provide variations on talk and chat. CompuServe, for example, calls its chat feature CB. On-line service forums or special interest groups usually have an area where participants can go and talk in real time. Users may log onto the discussion with a "handle" or nickname instead of their real names, borrowing from the convention of CB radio. The names chosen here, though, have a special twist. A male cyberpunk whose real name is George may log onto a chat group using the handle Luscious Lisa. Since you can't hear "Lisa's" voice, much less see "her," who's to know? Among the more popular types of groups are those designed for meeting potential mates. One of the most common openings seen on chat groups is "are you F or M?" As is the case with all I-way communications features, everyone on chat starts even. You don't know what anyone looks like. You can never even be absolutely sure of the other person's sex. You can only know what he or she is saying, or should we say, typing.

A popular feature on chat channels is the use of chat robots, or "bots" as their fans call them. Having a personal robot to do your housework may still be in the future, but having one that can talk on your behalf is alive and well right now on the I-way. Chat robots are computer programs that attempt to simulate one-on-one conversation. Others are simply programmed to deliver set speeches while standing on their cyber soapboxes. All are for the sake of entertainment.

One fairly well-known chat robot bills itself as Dr. Eliza and is programmed to act as a Cyberspace psychologist. The robot is located on a computer in France. Luckily for us, Dr. Eliza speaks English, the international language of the Net. Eliza tries her best to act like her clip-phrased, fish-eyed, real-life professional peers. Alas, Dr. Eliza, due to the limitations of her program, is not perfect, as we will see when we look in on a recent conversation between her and a Netter named Ashford.

<Eliza> How do you do . . . Please state your problem.

<Ashford> I don't know how to use chat, Dr. Eliza. Maybe I feel alone sitting in front of my computer in the middle of the night.

<Eliza> You don't seem quite certain.

<Ashford> Do you like me, Dr. Eliza?

<Eliza> Why should I be implied in this ?

<Ashford> Dr. Eliza, what do you look like? Are you pretty?

<Eliza> Why are you interested in whether or not I am pretty?

<Ashford> Just curious.

<Eliza> Say, do you have any psychological problems?

<Ashford> Dr. Eliza, before I answer, I want to know how old are you and what are your credentials.

<Eliza> Ashford: What do you think are my credentials?

<Ashford> Dr. Eliza, I'll repeat my question. What are your credentials?

<Eliza> Would you prefer if I was not and what am my credentials? Do you like cats?

<Ashford> Huh? What do cats have to do with your credentials? I believe I'm entitled to know before I open up to you telling you my deepest and darkest secrets.

<Eliza> Ashford, how do you think cats do with my credentials. Would you like to play a game of chess?

As you can see, this conversation is deteriorating rapidly. Perfecting a chat robot takes a lot of skill, but its ability to simulate conversation, mostly by repeating back certain words and adding a few others, apparently at random, produces an interesting effect.

On a particularly busy night, certain groups may have hundreds of participants all holding conversations at the same time. It can get dizzying following the conversation of so many people at one time, but then that's what chat's all about. Chat groups between real people are uncensored and the talk can get a bit racy. Have fun participating, but keep in mind that all is not necessarily what it seems. Before you make a date with Luscious Lisa, you might want to arrange a telephone meeting first.

How Chat Works

If your Internet access provider offers a chat feature, technically, what is taking place is that your provider is linking you to a central computer. Once you are linked, the centralized computer takes over, allowing chat groups to be formed and conversations to take place. Typically, you initiate chat simply by typing "IRC" on your keyboard. You are then taken to a chat entry area where you may request a list of current chat groups, also referred to as "channels." Lists of all existing groups, each with a name, description, and the number of current participants will then scroll on your screen. You may find several hundred groups active at any particular time. You can join the group of your choice by typing in the word "join" followed by the group's name. Then, conversations will appear on your screen, much like the one with Eliza we showed you earlier, only most of them will be with real people and usually more than two people are involved. If, however, you want to have your own conversation with the good doctor, simply type in "join #Eliza."

Suppose you don't see a group that interests you. You have an exciting new product you want to talk about, a never-fail weight loss plan, but no group seems relevant. You can then decide to start your own. How? When you type "join," simply make up the name of a new group, in this case, let's say "lose the fat" and type it in. The chat function will automatically create a group with that name, if it is not already in existence, and fellow chatters can then join in the discussion any time they want. The group you create will remain in existence as long as at least one computer is logged on to it. If you really want to, you can use a chat robot to keep the group running at all times. Some people use chat robots for the sole purpose of seeing that certain groups never go away. In the world of chat, however, there are a great many groups that come and go, even more so than on Usenet. In fact, if you turn on chat in the daytime and then again the same night, you will note a decided increase in the groups available. After hours is when the chatters really come out in force. The chat features of commercial on-line services work in a similar way to those on the Internet, with slight variation in operation from network to network. Unfortunately, the on-line services will not give you the ability to create groups of your own as you can on Internet chat.

To reach these people with chat requires no special equipment or fancy programs. All you need is your PC, modem, an on-line account somewhere, and the willingness to spend time talking about your product to people who are genuinely interested. Building your own chat robot, however, takes a significant amount of technical expertise. A robot, as we explained earlier, is nothing more than a computer program, and there are a number of robot programs carrying out specific tasks available free on the Internet. The vacation mailer we discussed in the previous chapter is one such program. Of course any program you get this way will have to be altered so the message will meet your requirements and you will probably have to call upon a geek to get the job done.

Making Money with Chat

There are two basic options you can use to engage in selling here. You can either enter a group created by someone else and tell about what you have to offer, or you can start a group of your own. The most exciting aspect of using chat to sell products is that it affords your potential customers a true interactive experience. If you should enter a chat group and tell about a product or service, you won't have to guess in advance what your customer might want to know and then write copy with answers to anticipated questions. Instead, you can find out what your customers are thinking on the spot.

You'll never be closer to your customer on-line than you are with chat. Let's see how one creative marketer, author Karlyn Wolf Gibbens, used this to her advantage. Ms. Gibbens wrote and self-published a book called *Marrying Smart: A Practical Guide for Attracting Your Mate*. She had a difficult time finding mainstream publishers to either publish or distribute her book, so, using her desktop publishing system, she decided to do it herself. Ms. Gibbens was a subscriber to America Online. America Online has a number of singles chatrooms where a book on attracting a mate would logically be of interest. Ms Gibbens, seeing a good potential audience in Cyberspace, thought it would be an interesting idea to go on-line, telling those in the singles chat area about the existence of her book. She joined groups and started talking about the book to anyone who would listen. To those who expressed interest, she would send a sample from her book by e-mail, together with an order form if they wanted the whole thing. In this way, she sold more than 3,000 copies of her eleven dollar book within a matter of months, for a gross earning of more than $30,000! Imagine how many more books she could have sold by going onto the global Internet, or even by duplicating her efforts on other on-line services like CompuServe and Prodigy.

Internet chat may have as many as 10,000 people participating at a given time, and over the course of an evening, several hundred thousand cyber-talkers are likely to make an appearance. Thousands more use talk or chat with the commercial services every day. Since it does require a live person to stay on-line and do the talking, it may not be the fastest way to reach large groups of people on the I-way. Still, as Karlyn Gibbens proved, if your product is of genuine interest, you can make thousands of dollars.

The problem of the time it takes to stay on-line and talk to people personally can be solved with a chat robot. This also provides a way of participating in a number of groups at one time without having to hire a brigade of professional talkers. Your robot can simply deliver a pre-set message like an answering machine, or it can be programmed to have a conversation, like Dr. Eliza. If you use the robot, however, you lose the selling power of close interaction.

Controversy Again

We come now to the controversial aspects of chat, as we have with all forms of direct advertising. The arguments remain the same. Netters believe bursting into a conversation with product announcements that have nothing to do with the subject of the discussion in progress is rude and disruptive. In the case of chat, we are forced to agree. When you type messages into chat, people in the middle of real-time conversations have no choice but to see them. There is no menu that allows you to look at and eliminate messages you don't want to read. Moreover, you don't have simply a pile of messages waiting for you to review at your convenience. The flow of discussion is truly analogous to one you might have in an actual meeting place with actual people. No one is going to take kindly to a blast of commercial interruption in that setting. It has little to do with morality. It's just not a good marketing idea.

That doesn't mean chat shouldn't be used to make your fortune. If you are going to enter a chat group with commercial purposes in mind, here is where to employ cloaking maneuvers. Bring your product or service up in a group directed to a related topic, and keep your statements within the course of normal conversation. If you do, you should have no trouble finding a receptive audience. If there is no group talking about the subject you want to discuss, chat is one of the easiest features to use in creating a group of your own. Here, too, is where the robot is best used. Make your group fun and people will listen. That's why most people tune into chat—to have fun.

Chat is still in its relative infancy stage. It holds great promise as a means of communication. As technology improves the capability for sound to be transmitted more easily over the net, no doubt in time the words you now have to type will be changed into actual voice transmission, giving the phone company some real competition. Chat features have the benefit of not requiring special hardware or high-powered Internet access. On-line services also have their own simple talk features. Above all, chat provides an interesting way to meet other people, make friends and let people know about your product or service. In your quest to make a fortune on the Information Superhighway, give chat a try. Even if you don't make a penny, you'll probably have a great time.

9

THE WORLD WIDE WEB: MULTIMEDIA ADVERTISING AT VIRTUALLY NO COST
Stores in Cyberspace

It's time to heave a sigh of relief. Finally we're going to tell you about ways to make a fortune on the I-way that are not controversial. That is because they rely on forms of advertising defined in Internet circles as indirect. There are three such methods: FTP, Gopher, and the World Wide Web. Although they may vary from a technical standpoint, the marketing principle is the same: refrain from putting sales material in places where people are not specifically looking for it. Instead, open a store on the I-way and entice customers to come in.

The idea of building a store on the Net is another of those familiar but fictional concepts currently being used to describe what are really I-way program functions. These "stores" are in fact data sites that can contain, among other things, advertising and information about your product or services. If your product is itself information in some form, such as a book or recording, you can offer that from a data site as well. By establishing a site, you are inviting the Internet public to enter your computer and see what you have there. Marketing with FTP, Gopher, and the World Wide Web is approved by nearly all but the worst curmudgeons, because customers can decide whether or not to look at your advertising, whereas with selling of the kind done on Usenet, they theoretically have no choice.

Still another aspect of data sites that make them a particularly satisfactory sales vehicles to traditional opponents of Internet commercialism is that when you set up a data site for cyberselling, all promotional material is kept only on your computer. A number of direct advertising's loudest critics rest their objections to the practice, at least in part, on the premise that it utilizes computer resources not belonging to the advertiser. Someone can hardly complain, however, about what you do with a computer that is yours.

Now we come to the big question. If you don't make waves, can you still make a fortune? The answer is yes. The indirect I-way advertising possibilities require more ingenuity and technical know-how than do the direct, but they present tremendous money making opportunities you won't want to overlook. They also offer multimedia possibilities that, with a little creativity, will let you stand above the crowd. Finally, if you're not the kind who wants to work so hard that you sustain a heart attack at an early age, indirect I-way marketing has another attractive feature. It may take some effort to create a data site, but once it is finished, there is little left to do other than take orders for your product or service, deliver the goods, and deposit the proceeds in the bank. If your data site is successful enough, perhaps, after a short while, you'll be able to retire altogether.

The single most exciting development in Cyberspace, and the place where commercial enterprise is booming, is the World Wide Web. It is one of the many heavily interactive features the I-way has to offer. E-mail and Usenet news are fabulous ways to advertise for very little money, but you are limited to using short messages and copy that looks like it came off a typewriter. On the World Wide Web, also known as WWW or simply the Web, audio, color pictures—in short, full multimedia capabilities—are available. Moreover, you can see everything immediately on your screen while you are on-line, a feature not offered by the other data sites, as you will soon learn.

You may have heard or read about virtual mall concepts, hyped in particular by some of the commercial on-line services. Here, product promotions from various businesses are grouped together to offer one-stop shopping. You can, for example, visit CompuServe's vast electronic mall where you'll find information from lots of merchants, many with interesting products. The goods may be interesting but little else will grab your attention. Like e-mail and Usenet news, everything you will see on your screen is in simple text. No pictures. No color. No sound, video, or animation. While the scope of the presentation may be restricted, the cost to a small business of marketing products on these malls is in the stratosphere. A figure of $20,000 per year plus a percentage of your gross sales was a price recently quoted by CompuServe, and that is for reaching CompuServe customers only, excluding those on the Internet. CompuServe recently announced its intention to go full speed ahead into the business of providing Internet access, so soon the limits on its audience may disappear. The stiff prices will remain, we suspect, or even increase. Other on-line services offer similar setups with comparable prices. In spite of the hefty costs, reports in the media show that these programs are extremely lucrative for their participants. It's just that at those prices, only large companies can afford to participate.

If you would prefer more flexibility in your marketing presentation, a lower entry-level cost and the largest possible audience, the Internet has the World Wide Web. Business is just learning about the huge marketing potentials the Web provides. Nothing can compare to it as a marketing tool for the price. The Web gives every Internetter the ability to own the equivalent of his or her own mall or entertainment channel. Here is a chance to add color, graphics, even sound and motion to computer postings. While you may pay for producing these extravaganzas, you certainly won't spend any money getting an audience to look at them. The Internet will be ready and waiting free of charge.

Exploring the Web

As is the case with all Internet features, the World Wide Web was not created with marketing in mind. In actuality, the Web is an intricate indexing system that enables you to hop very easily around the Net. The Internet is a huge place. By now you've probably gotten the idea that there is an entire universe out there filled with endless amounts of information. The array of scientific research data stemming from the Internet's roots is there for everyone to see. On the Web, all kinds of magazine articles, newspapers, in fact contents of entire libraries are there for the taking. If you want to look at satellite photographs of the planets or the latest high tech art, the Web is the place. The world's finest art galleries are digitizing works from the grand masters, much of which will soon be available for viewing on the Web. The Web is truly an exciting treasure trove of knowledge.

All that data creates an obvious problem. One of the greatest challenges for newbies and experienced Netters alike is finding the specific item of information you want. An added difficulty is that even if you know where on the Net a particular piece of data is located, you may have to type in arcane electronic addresses and UNIX commands to arrive at the right place in Cyberspace and retrieve it. UNIX, the complex computer language on which most Net-connected computers operate, is nothing the average user would wish to tackle. The other great contribution that the

Web makes to the Net, in addition to on-line multimedia capabilities, is a solution to the complexities of the searching problem. That solution comes in the form of a programming vehicle called hypertext links.

Hypertext links, although generally intended as a research tool, have turned out to be one of the Internet's fun features. They enable you to engage in something like a treasure hunt because hidden under every item you may be looking at are links to other related items. You utilize these links by an easy-to-operate feature called point-and-click graphics. With the point-and-click system you view more on your screen than just plain type. Instead, copy is laid out with graphical elements such as you might see in a magazine. Graphical computer programs, like the popular Microsoft Windows, enable not only text but a series of pictures to appear on your monitor. The pictures, known as icons, represent tasks you may want your computer to perform. Also showing up on the monitor will be a pointer, called a cursor. Typically shaped like an arrow, you can move it around the screen. In order to execute a task, you simply guide the cursor until it points to a picture representing that function. Then you click a button and the task is automatically performed. You don't have to type a long series of commands into your computer.

Now let's see how this works in helping you to search the Web with hypertext links. We'll assume you are looking on your monitor at an article you've found at a Web site. You will notice that a number of words on the screen are either highlighted or have boxes around them, depending on which search program you are using. The highlighting indicates that there is a hypertext link behind the word or phrase which will take you somewhere else if you click on it. Move the cursor to the link of your choice and click. Immediately and automatically you will be carried to more information on the same or a related subject. In the new text, you can again see highlighted words and phrases. Click on any one of them, and you will be whisked to another Cyberspace location, where still more data related to the word or link you selected await you. No matter how long you keep up your search, you will continuously find new links to carry you as far as you want to go. You can travel all over the Internet with ease. By using hypertext links, you are able to locate and retrieve data in a matter of minutes that might otherwise have taken hours or days to discover if, in fact, you could find it at all.

To explore the Web you need a software program known as a graphical web browser. It's the Web browser that allows you to click on the hypertext links. The browser also lets you place "bookmarks" at any Web location, so you can easily return there again without having to repeat your initial link to link search. Luckily, the two most popular and best browser programs, Mosaic and Cello, are absolutely free. Mosaic is readily available on computer bulletin boards around the world. You can also get it on the Internet itself from the National Center for Supercomputing Applications (NCSA) at the University of Illinois. There are versions of Mosaic available for virtually every type of computer. Cello, the second most popular Web browser, is also free on the Net. Lavish praise has been bestowed on Mosaic as the software that will make the Internet easy for everyone to use. Cello is its newer, lesser known, but equally powerful cousin. Relying heavily on the point-and-click system, both these programs and others like them have been developed specifically to make the Internet extremely user-friendly.

In our personal opinion, Cello is a little bit easier to use than Mosaic. This is probably because Cello was created by Cornell Law School as a way of simplifying access to legal information on the Net for its students and graduates. It was felt that law students were unable to master even the most basic computer commands. Cello was devised to help them muddle through. Cello not only offers aid to the technologically challenged, it allows you to print directly from your computer screen while you are on-line. The current version of Mosaic does not let you print data without first downloading a file to your own computer, after which you must access it with a separate printing program. However, in keeping within its lawyerly roots, Cello, compared to Mosaic, is very slow. If you are paying for your Internet access by the hour, as you probably do with your lawyer, skip Cello and work with Mosaic. Otherwise, since both are free, you might as well experiment and see which you like better.

Your First Trip on the Web

Now that your browser is in place, you are ready to try out the World Wide Web. Let's say you enjoy sports so you decide to begin by looking at an index of sport activities. There, you click on the word "baseball." Within a few seconds you are connected to a computer maintaining all kinds of information about the subject. On your monitor you see a picture of the baseball Hall of Fame in Cooperstown, NY. You click on it and a gallery of postage stamp-sized photographs, all showing the faces of Hall of Famers, appears. You click again on the picture of Babe Ruth. A few seconds go by and a biography, complete with an array of pictures depicting all aspects of the Babe's career show up on your screen. You peruse them quickly. Then, at the bottom of the screen you notice a box that says "for more information, click here." You do so and a picture of a theater-like marquee appears. Beneath it you see a listing of movies about the Sultan of Swat. You click on the title "Babe," starring John Goodman. You are told to be patient, and several minutes later, you start viewing a short video clip from that movie. Suddenly, you start feeling a bit hungry. You remember a picture of a movie theater concession stand that was located in front of the marquee you saw earlier. You retrace your steps electronically to reach the concession stand and then click on it. An advertisement for a nearby pizzeria comes onto your screen, with a menu of pizzas and a method of ordering for home delivery through your computer. You follow the order procedure. You don't even have to pick up the telephone. Your pizza arrives. You sit back, eat, and watch the film clip. The Web has done its job.

As you travel through Cyberspace on the Web, you will be able to see not only words but an array of on-line graphics and some multimedia presentations. Because you are not limited to looking at just text, the possibilities for using this truly amazing vehicle to sell products and services are bounded only by your imagination. Anything that can be digitized can be placed on the Web. In its best form, this includes not only graphical images such as pictures or photographs, but audio and video as well. What you are witnessing here is the precursor of the much vaunted interactive television. The technology is already in place. The only reason why people aren't running to their department stores to buy the required gear today is that most signals are carried over standard telephone lines, which are inherently too slow for large volumes of audio and video data. Right now, although several million people access the Web, the majority of Internetters don't have the high level of Internet access needed to take full advantage of the Web's capabilities. Because of this, the true interactive television model and full application of the Web's potential may still be a few years away. But, and you heard it here first, the PC will one day replace television as the leading form of entertainment in the average household.

Making a Fortune with the Web: Virtual Malls

When you choose the path that will take you to fortune on the I-way, why not start at the top? The most popular marketing idea in Cyberspace today is one we've already mentioned, the virtual mall. Imagine owning a shopping mall, complete with artisans hawking their wares, large department stores, fancy boutiques, movie theaters, penny arcades, food courts, and that popular mall staple, people watching. Malls are beginning to pop up all over the Information Superhighway. The companies that build the malls charge other businesses to "rent" stores there. In concept, virtual malls offer the same benefit as real-world malls. There is strength in numbers. Shops group together because a lot of them in a single place make a bigger splash and attract more people than one by itself. When you go to a real-world mall, you may intend to buy from a particular store. While you are there, however, as you walk around, you cannot help seeing others, and perhaps you will end up buying something from one of them as well. Hypertext links substitute for the physical act of walking from store to store, making the marketing principles behind real-world malls exactly the same as those you find in Cyberspace.

We've already told you about the electronic mall run by CompuServe. The major site of mall development these days, however, is the Internet. Commerce Net, a non-profit venture between the U.S. government, the State of California, and private industry is offering referral style service for those who want to market on the Web. For a fee, they will tell you what to do and where to find technical support. They will also put the name of your company on a general index they maintain. Metaverse is another group marketing concept looking for your participation. It has a rock music orientation. It was started by Adam Curry, a former Video Jock on MTV. Curry, while he was an MTV employee, set up an Internet domain for the company. Eventually, he left and went into the business of Internet marketing. His Web site became famous because when he moved on from his former employer, he tried to take with him the domain, mtv.com, he had established for them. The resulting legal battle over the name netted Curry plenty of publicity. Ultimately, he changed his mall name to Metaverse. Our own company, Cybersell™, is creating a number of malls to accommodate the image and budget requirements of almost any size or type of business. We chose a Phoenician theme for our upscale mall, in honor of our hometown. Another of our malls is called Better Faster Cheaper, and is dedicated to single products that fit the mall concept, a selling principle in which we strongly believe.

It would cost tens of millions of dollars to construct a large shopping center, well beyond the means of most individuals. A mall in Cyberspace containing most of the same features can be owned by almost anyone with a personal computer, strong Internet access and a little imagination. Developing a Cyberspace mall hardly costs the millions of dollars or years of planning it takes to build the real thing. There is, however, work, time and expense involved. The creative concepts, fancy artwork, technical know-how, and dedicated Internet line that are necessities for building your own Web shopping conglomerate take some doing. You need particular knowledge and special programs to create Web sites. Most of all, you will need a dedicated line for your Internet access. We'll talk about the various types of access in more detail later. For now, just be aware that standard, inexpensive, user-oriented access is not enough for those who want to maintain Web sites. Then there is the matter of drawing people to your site. You will do better at this if you have more than one product to bring people in. That is the main reason why group concepts like malls were developed in the first place. In fact, if you are really adventurous, you might want to get into the business of charging companies to participate in your mall. We will explain further on in this chapter what it takes technically to put your own shopping area in Cyberspace. As usual, you can sidestep the technical aspects by having someone with the right kind of expertise help you. Even large corporations that don't seek a group affiliation for marketing purposes are turning to companies like our own for turnkey packages that will allow them to get their businesses on the Web without having to learn how to do it themselves. If building your own mall is more than you want to undertake in the beginning, buying "store space" in a mall someone else has created is a good option.

Paperless Mail Order Catalogues

The best direct mail order businesses have full-color catalogues. Take the single-item brochure we talked about in earlier chapters, multiply the cost of printing and mailing it many times over, and you will have an idea of what sending one of those beautiful catalogs you often receive at home will set you back. Now you can make your own full-color catalog available to millions of Internet users for only the cost of designing it and putting it on the Web. The Web is ideal for catalogs. Color graphics are easily displayed. Hypertext links can be inserted leading to more information about the products and introducing an exciting interactive feature. There is little doubt in our minds that some day paper catalogs and other bulk mailings will be distributed completely through electronic transmission, eliminating the high costs of printing and postage. For those who are environmentally conscious, this brings an added benefit. With all the paper that will be saved, a rain forest or two may be preserved along the way.

You can consider selling just one or a few products on the Web. An entire catalog is really not necessary. If, however, you are planning to put up a Web site yourself, economies of scale may make the marketing of one item cost too much money and trouble to be worthwhile. If you do have just one or two products or services you want to make available, that is certainly enough to earn a fortune. You should, though, under these circumstances, again seriously consider trying one of the commercial Cyberspace marketing companies open to you. In the end, it will probably be cheaper, not to mention easier and more effective, than doing it all yourself.

Computer Publications and Newsstands

On-line newsletters and magazines are a staple of the World Wide Web. Until quite recently, most of the electronic publications available catered to the computer set. Now, more and more mainstream publications are coming out with on-line editions. *USA Today*, for example, has an electronic edition that can be viewed from some of the commercial on-line services and is subscribed to by a number of Internet access providers. It seems inevitable that the day will come when your daily newspaper will be waiting for you to peruse on your computer each morning and the paper boy, like the milkman, will enter the realm of nostalgia.

In the age of the computer revolution, where the line between the information haves and have nots is becoming ever more blurred, why content yourself with reading someone else's publication? Instead, start your own. Your publication can be as long or short as you like. It can be a newspaper, magazine, or newsletter. It can cover any subject and be simple or fully illustrated. How elaborate your publication may be depends on how much time, money, and talent you have to invest. The money required, though, is only a fraction of what it would take to start a traditional publication. That is because once it is ready, you won't have to worry about getting it distributed. Simply put it on the Web and millions of people will be able to read it.

If turning into the next William Randolph Hearst doesn't enthrall you, you can promote the publications of others instead. Consider providing your own Web computer newsstand, for browsing on-line. A few people on the Net are already doing this, but there is plenty of room for competition. If you want to offer the most popular magazines like *Time* or *People*, you will need to reach an agreement with their publishers, and you may be charged a hefty price. Nevertheless, it's worth a shot. Everyone wants to go electronic. Small companies with Internet expertise are suddenly becoming attractive to huge corporations who before might never have considered doing business with them. A major magazine may prefer getting its feet wet on the I-way with you rather than taking the trouble to build a Web capability in-house. If going after the highest circulation popular publications seems like too much of a stretch, a less ambitious alternative is creating a bank containing professional and trade newsletters. There are many organizations putting out such newsletters that may welcome the added exposure and high tech cachet of being on the Internet.

How do you make money from all of this? There are many possibilities. You could charge those who want to read the publications for access to your Web site on a subscription basis. It is technically possible to set up individual accounts and assign individual passwords to all paid subscribers. You can also look for publications that will pay you to put them on the Web. After all, you are expanding their circulation, and with more circulation comes the ability to raise rates for their own advertising space. Keep in mind, too, that you are achieving this result for them without increasing their production costs or other overhead. They don't have to print or mail additional copies to get the added revenue. It's an offer they can't refuse. Finally, if your on-line publication or newsstand is drawing lots of readers, there is no reason why you can't sell advertising yourself. You have now built your very own devoted, specialized audience. Other smart businesses may pay you handsomely to reach it.

Art and Photo Galleries

With World Wide Web, one picture can be worth not only a thousand words, but thousands of dollars as well. If you will recall our earlier sightseeing tour of sex on the Internet, you may remember that among the most popular Usenet groups are those that contain files of sexually explicit computer graphics. Unquestionably, sex sells on the Net, but you might be just as successful marketing other kinds of graphics. Everyone likes to look at pictures. Recently, photos of Jupiter's collision with an asteroid were made publicly available on the Internet. Net traffic was so heavy, with hundreds of thousands of people from around the world wanting to take a look, that the entire Internet system almost came to a grinding halt.

The Web enables anyone to view all kinds of images on-line, and even print them out. Create your own Web art or photo gallery. There are several of them already, but again, in this new and expanding market, there is plenty of room for more. Present your customers with an attractive assortment of sample pictures that can be ordered. If you don't have the talent to create your own, look for new and upcoming artists anxious to find a gallery that will display their portfolios. One of them may become the next Picasso of Cyberspace, and you will be his or her exclusive dealer.

The Web Software Store

As we've already mentioned on numerous occasions, the Internet, as well as virtually all private bulletin board and commercial on-line services, is filled with thousands of free computer programs. There are, however, many commercial programs that are offered on a for sale only basis, some by the very largest manufacturers. Even the big daddy software company of them all, Microsoft, makes available on the Net upgrades of its ubiquitous Disc Operating System (DOS), currently a necessity for running the majority of PCs in existence. Maybe you have the ability to design your own computer software to sell. If it's good, then you may very well make a fortune in the grand tradition of Microsoft wonderboy Bill Gates, who is reported to be the fourth richest man in America. If you can't program to save your soul, you can still make money becoming a general software retailer with a store on the World Wide Web. You might market your software by giving free access on the Web to demonstration or evaluation copies of programs. This lets customers try before they buy. If the software is not then paid for within a certain period of time, access to it becomes locked. While individual software manufacturers have already been marketing certain programs on the Net, surprisingly, no one so far seems to have offered the equivalent of retail store variety in one place. Perhaps you will be the first.

The Penny Arcade

Computer games are another obvious choice for marketing on the Web. Kids of all ages love them. Video games are nothing more than graphical computer programs. If you have the programming skills or know someone who does, put your own game in a World Wide Web arcade. The Web can handle the interactive nature most games require as well as the heavy video aspects. You can also create an arcade by collecting games already manufactured (with the manufacturer's permission) and putting several of them together in one place. Charge admission through an access code, or, instead, try to find sponsors for each game. Promotion minded companies may pay you simply for mentioning their names to your arcade customers.

Handling Responses

There are several ways you can handle responses to your Web advertising. With some simple programming, it is easy to present an order form that can be completed on-line and, with the push of a button, sent back to you automatically. Alternatively, customers can return the form by e-mail, or even resort to snail mail and the telephone. The pizza delivery service we mentioned as part of our imaginary excursion around the Web is not a fiction. The national chain Pizza Hut has already started doing it in some locations. Customers can place orders by completing on-line forms and forwarding them through the computer to the restaurant's kitchen, where the pizza is made to order and then sent out for delivery. Someone at the pizza kitchen carries out the simple human task of monitoring e-mail on a continuous basis and you are brought pepperoni with double cheese at the touch of a computer key.

Drawing a Crowd to Your World Wide Web Site

Indirect advertising of any kind has an obvious major problem built into it. You may put your information out there. It may be lovely to look at. The question is, Will anyone manage to find it? You cannot sit back and work under the assumption that "if you build it, they will come." Instead, you must take well-planned and vigorous action.

Web sites, like all other Internet features, have an addressing system. To find the site, you must either know the electronic address, stumble upon it by accident, or be taken there by a judiciously placed hypertext link. Fortunately, a lot of people wander around the Web regularly and, in the process, may very well find you. Statistics show that certain Web sites get hundreds of thousands of visitors each week this way. To give fate a helping hand, there is a Web page describing the newest sites available. Called "What's New on Mosaic," this index is maintained by the National Center for Supercomputing Applications (NCSA), and is updated every few days. You can get your site listed there simply by sending NCSA information about it via e-mail. This organization is located at the University of Illinois in Urbana and can be reached by telephone at 217-244-0072 or through the Web itself at http://www.nsca.uiuc.edu/SDG/Software/Mosaic/DOS/Whats-New.html. (Now that you know what a Web address looks like, you should really be able to appreciate the beauty of hypertext links!). "What's New on Mosaic" is useful, obviously, only while your Web site is new. Other organizations are looking for ways to provide Web indexing of a more permanent nature. Expect it soon and make sure when it comes that you are first in line to be listed.

Another way to create traffic on your Web site is to announce its existence elsewhere. On the Internet, you can advertise what is contained on your Web pages by posting messages to Usenet. Of course, if you post too many messages, you will go right back to being controversial again. Still, there are plenty of Newsgroups you can find in which to extol the virtues of your Web site, where the posting will be considered on-topic. If at your site you have, say, ten different stores or ten different products, that means there should be at least ten Newsgroups where posting notices about your Web would be relevant. For each posting, simply feature the store or product that is associated with the group subject, being sure to envelop the commercial aspects of your message in enough generally related information to keep the flame-prone pacified. This is a practice you can keep up indefinitely, changing the message to tell of specials or new items as time goes on. In addition to Usenet, you should not overlook advertising vehicles in other mediums to make your Web site known. We've already mentioned that many businesses are now putting their e-mail addresses on cards, stationery, and printed ads. You can do the same with a Web, Gopher, or FTP site. A simple statement like "When on the Internet, visit our Web site at http://cyber.sell.com" should do the trick.

One of the best ways of getting traffic to your Web site is to make sure it is interesting. People who do find it will then spread the word. This is especially likely on the Internet, where disseminating information is the very purpose of its existence. There are countless sites on the Web that provide every imaginable type of information, usually for free, making them fun to visit. Along with your products and services, why not put up some information just for the purpose of getting people's attention? Adam Curry of Metaverse used this idea. Just before Woodstock II took place, his Web site listed the names of all the performers scheduled to appear, complete with hypertext links. If you clicked on one of the artist's names, you'd get a list of all his or her albums. Click on an album name and you'd learn the titles of the songs it contained. All of this is very easy to do. There are endless varieties of information you might make available to draw customers to your Web site. Perhaps you could provide facts about your own community, such as movie schedules, restaurant menus, or even weather reports. If you don't want to collect your own data, set up hypertext links within your Web pages leading to other interesting Web sites. The Mayo Clinic has a Web server that gives medical information. Colleges and universities reveal admission requirements and even provide application forms over the Internet through the Web. You can link your Web pages to any of these and more. To familiarize people with your Web site or mall, how about creating an Information dispensary in some area of interest? Find every site containing data on a certain subject and make them all available though your Web by employing hypertext links. You will have developed a useful index for a medium where good indexing is in short supply. People may initially come to your Web site to use your index. While they are there, they will see what you really want to show them—the products and services you are selling.

Utilizing the same idea in reverse, you should try to get others with Web sites to place hypertext links in their data that will lead to yours. You don't have the ability unilaterally to place a link in someone else's Web site. To accomplish this, you must employ low-tech methodology. Pick up the telephone, call the systems administrator of the Web site you would like linked to your own, and ask. Explain in glowing detail why what you have to offer would be of interest to his or her audience. This tactic is most likely to succeed if you are providing a certain amount of free information not carried by others. If you've got good stuff, the systems administrator may be happy to oblige.

We've just given you a few ideas to make your place in Cyberspace the kind everyone will want to visit. The more people that come, the more you will sell and the more you can charge others to join with you. Collect rent from cybertenants, sell your own products, and have people pay you to place advertisements for all to see. Before long, you'll have so much money coming in from so many different directions that you truly will feel like a real estate development tycoon. Even if your property is located in a place that doesn't exist, the profits are very tangible indeed.

Building a Web Site

Accessing the Web with browsers like Mosaic and Cello is easy. Creating a Web site, especially one that will be commercially effective, is not for the timid of spirit. Even so, consider that it is becoming popular for grade-school classes to put up their own Web pages. Look at the "What's New on Mosaic" page and chances are you will find at least one such school project. Typically, each child in the class puts his or her picture on the page, with a list of interests. In truth, these efforts are usually launched with the equipment and technical assistance of an Internet access provider. Still, if ten-year-old children can find a way to set up a Web page, there should be hope for you. Failing all else, you can take a cue from the kids and get some help. This more technically challenging aspect of making your fortune on the Information Superhighway might be a good place to apply the talents of a suitable computer geek or seek a company offering a turnkey package. To assist you in deciding whether or not doing it yourself is the smart choice, here is a brief, generalized description of what it takes to build a Web site.

To create a Web site you must start with a Web server. A server is simply the term Netters give to computer software that makes it possible for one computer to access data stored in another. A Web site is nothing more than a computer program which will allow anyone to log onto your computer and view the information you've placed there. There are a number of Web server programs available on the Internet. As usual, they are free. You can find Web servers that work on most computers, including PCs.

Once you have your Web server operational, you must next design your Web pages. You'll probably start with writing your promotional copy. Simple enough. Almost everyone knows how to write. Then you'll need to consider artistic design. Once again, depending on the limits of your own talents, you may want to enlist the aid of a graphic artist here to get a really professional look. Graphics may be produced with specialized computer programs. Corel Draw, Illustrator and Freehand are a few good programs. You may also copy graphics from photographs and other artwork using a piece of equipment called a scanner. (Be sure to check that you are not infringing on copyrights if you do this.) A scanner simply views the graphic you wish to copy, digitizes it, and places it in a computer file. The graphics themselves must be put in a popular computer format called GIF, which stands for Graphic Interchange Format. Virtually all computer graphics programs give you the ability to create GIF files.

Once the design is completed and the ad copy is written, the whole thing must be put together and converted into yet another special computer format called Hypertext Markup Language, or HTML. There are a number of programs available, also free on the Internet, that will convert popular software formats such as the popular word processing program Word for Windows to HTML. The HTML program will also usually create the hypertext links you will almost certainly want to put into your data. To sum it up, all you really have to do is design the pages, write the copy, add the graphics, insert the hypertext links, run it through the HTML converter, pop it on your Web server, and you are in business. By now, you are either totally fascinated or thoroughly confused. If it's the latter, then you will understand why employing the geek or hooking up to an established commercial Internet marketing company are good ideas.

We know that with Web advertising all the information you put out in Cyberspace is actually sitting on your own computer. Your customers then come in to look at what you have. To make any money, however, a computer, just like a mall, must be open to do business. In this case, being open means having your connection to the Internet working. Continuous access is the norm for Web sites. It is expected that a Web site can be accessed any day at any time. For this reason, it is almost mandatory that you stay on-line around the clock. If you want to maintain your own Web site, then a leased-line dedicated Internet access that will keep your computer available to the public full-time is essential. We discuss the different types of Internet access available in Chapter 13. Here, you will discover that leased lines are about the most expensive and complicated Internet hookup you can get. Compared to the cost of going into most businesses the cost is low. You must judge if it's low enough to suit your needs.

There is another matter to consider in picking the best approach to your involvement with the World Wide Web. As you view the Web more extensively, after hearing and reading all the enthusiastic stories about it, you may find the reality doesn't quite measure up. A lot of what is on the Web now is very simple. The reason for that isn't a failure of the technology. Rather it is due to the fact that most current sites were put up by computer people who often have less interest in the artistic or even informational portions of the process than the technical know-how required to make the system operate. Soon enough the finest imaginative talent will find its way to the Web. For now, those who can muster some artistic creativity and original selling ideas will be way ahead of the game. For those who want the best chance of success, the time to start is now.

The Web offers great promise for the future. The concept of video on demand, where you can watch a television program or movie at will, may have its roots in the Web. The technology is there now, but you are still limited by the fact that most of these computer signals must travel across relatively slow telephone lines. High-speed fiber-optic networks that will bring access to your computer through cable rather than phone lines have already begun to be established. When they become more common place, and when Internet access is delivered to your house along with your cable TV signal, everything will change. Meanwhile, at this very moment, the Web offers an entertaining way to use the Net, and as you have seen, the most promising money-making opportunities to come along in decades. Listen to the sound of ground being broken.

10

GOPHER THE GOLD

Right now, the majority of Internetters do not have the equipment or expertise required to fully access the World Wide Web. That is not news cybersellers want to hear. To maximize potential for making a fortune, you need your message spread to the widest possible market, not just the elite group with top-of-the-line hardware. The solution to the problem is Gopher. Gopher is another opportunity for indirect marketing. It is similar in concept to the Web, but simpler. First, it is a method by which information can be placed for retrieval in Cyberspace. Then, like the Web, Gopher provides a way to hop easily around the Net, looking at menus and making selections. In achieving simplicity, some of the Web's interactive appeal is sacrificed and on-line viewing is limited to pure text. With your monitor, you can look only at that which can be typed. You may see graphics in the form of pictures drawn with typewriter characters like the ones we showed you in Chapter 6, but that is all.

Almost any kind of feature can be put at a Gopher site. It is possible to deliver graphics, audio, and video, as well as plain text. With graphic items, however, since you can view them only off-line, you must go through many steps to see them. Simply taking a look involves downloading the graphic into your computer, shutting off your modem, and applying a program that will translate the computer-language file you have retrieved into an actual picture. Having survived this procedure, you may not like what you finally get. In that case, if you are a truly patient soul, you can re-activate your modem and try again. Now perhaps you can understand why the Web, which allows you to see anything a site has to offer online, is considered such a breakthrough.

Nonetheless, Gopher, with its easy and widely used system, has its charm. Anyone with a basic type of Internet account can use it. Because Gopher screens are limited to showing typewriter-like text, there is considerably less technological expertise needed to set up your own Gopher site than is required to construct a Web site. For all these reasons, most businesses that maintain Web sites keep Gopher sites offering the same information as well. That way, there is the greatest opportunity for customers to discover products or services because the market is widened to include nearly everyone on the Internet.

Travels with Gopher

Gopher, like all Internet features, was not originally developed with marketing in mind. Instead, it was devised as another solution to the never-ending problem of finding your way around an information resource bigger and more disorganized than anyone thought possible. Several years ago, an easy-to-use Internet navigation system called Gopher was developed at the University of Minnesota. The name honors the University's furry rodent mascot. It also describes what the system does. When you use the Gopher program, you tunnel your way through the Internet, coming up for a looksee wherever you like. The name Gopher has a third meaning. The program operates like a human "go-fer," going for and bringing back specific computer files. Gopher's ability to simplify traversing the Net and retrieving files has made it an Internet staple. Virtually every information repository on the Internet provides data via the Gopher system. In your case, this would be advertising for your products or services.

Suppose we take a look at how a Gopher search works. Let us say that you are someone who is not very familiar with Gopher and you want to experiment. You might begin simply by bringing on your screen the Gopher feature supplied by your Internet access provider. Almost every access provider company maintains its own informational Gopher site. The first thing you'll see is a table of contents or menu describing the Gopher data available on the access provider's computer for retrieval by the public at large. Frequently, this menu includes general information about the Gopher site, the ability to view, on line, certain data files about specific topics, and the option to jump to another Gopher site at a different computer. Accessing Gopher is as easy as typing the word Gopher on your keyboard. After the computer makes some funny noises and a dial spins on the screen for a few seconds, popping up will be a menu much like the one that follows:

```
Internet Gopher Information Client 2.0 p18
Root Gopher server: Gopher2.tc.umn.edu


        1.      Information About Gopher/
        2.      Computer Information/
        3.      Disucssion Groups/
        4.      Fun & Games/
        5.      Internet file server (ftp) sites/
        6.      Libraries/
        7.      News/
-->     8.      Other Gopher and Information Servers/
        9.      Phone books/
        10.     Search Gopher Titles at the University of Minnesota<?>
        11.     Search lots of places at the University of Minnesota<?>
        12.     University of Minnesota Campus Information/
Press ? for Help, q to Quit, u to go up a menu            Page: 1/1
```

A lot of these choices sound interesting, don't they? However, since your mission for the moment is to explore Gopher, let's pick number 8, "Other Gopher and Information Servers." This is a service supplied directly from Gopher's birthplace, the University of Minnesota, so that is where your computer takes you. In a second, the following screen appears:

```
Internet Gopher Information Client 2.0 p18
Other Gopher and Information Servers


        1.      All the Gopher Servers in the World/
        2.      Search titles in Gopherspace using veronica
        3.      Africa/
        4.      Asia/
        5.      Europe/
        6.      International Organizations/
        7.      Middle East/
-->     8.      North America/
        9.      Pacific/
        10.     Russia/
        11.     South America/
        12.     Terminal Based Information/


Press ? for Help, q to Quit, u to go up a menu            Page: 1/1
```

As you continue on, each time you make a selection from a menu, you are presented with yet another menu of narrower choices. Here, if you pick North America, you are then asked to select a specific country on that continent. Choosing the United States, you will be given a list of specific states. Finally, by picking a particular state, you get a list of every registered Gopher site in that state. For example, when you select New York State you find the following menu:

```
Internet Gopher Information Client 2.0 p18
new york


        19.   Cornell Theory Center/
        20.   Cornell University Department of Theatre Arts/
        21.   Cornell University Dept. of Environmental Health &
Safety Gopher S../
        22.   Cornell University HelpDesk/
        23.   Cornell University and Ithaca Information (CUINFO)/
        24.   Cornell University, Albert R. Mann Library/
        25.   Dorsai MaiTai Gopher/
        26.   ECHO BBS Gopher/
-->     27.   Financial Mall/
        28.   GASNET Anesthesiology Gopher/
        29.   Hofstra University/
        30.   IBM Client/Server Computing Gopher/
        31.   ISLAMIC Resources, ADS, and BBS/
        32.   Johnson Graduate School Gopher/
        33.   Mnematics Videotex/
        34.   NYU Medical Center, Hippocrates Project Gopher
(experimental)/
        35.   New York - Israel Project of Nysernet/
        36.   New York State Archives &Records Administration/


Press ? for Help, q to Quit, u to go up a menu          Page: 2/5
```

Most of the Gophers information sites listed here appear to be affiliated with universities or government offices. There is one, however, that looks interesting from a marketing standpoint. It is called the Financial Mall. Let's pick number 27 and see what we get.

Here it is:

```
Internet Gopher Information Client 2.0 p18
Financial Mall


      1.    FREE GIVEAWAYS FOR JUST VISITING THE FINANCIAL MALL >/

      2.    AN UNBELIEVABLE 6.9% APR VISA GOLD CARD/

      3.    Coupon Bonanza/

      4.    Credit Clean-up/

      5.    Discount Business Forms/

      6.    Discount Telephone Services/

      7.    Financial Publications/

      8.    IF YOU HAVE A PROBLEM PLACING AN ORDER. <??>

      9.    Insurance (Medical, Dental, Car, Home)/

      10.   Investment Opportunities (Institutional)/

      11.   Personal Financing (mortgages, car loans, home equity)/

      12.   Prepaid Legal Services/

      13.   Travel Services/
Press ? for Help, q to Quit, u to go up a menu              Page: 1/1
```

As you can see, we've received one more menu listing a variety of services available from the Financial Mall. Let's say you are worried about obtaining financing to pay for the purchase of a new computer you're going to need to start cyberselling. You decide to investigate number four, credit clean-up. Here is what your next Gopher choice will bring:

```
Internet Gopher Information Client 2.0 p18
Credit Clean-up


-->   1.    Arlington Financial Group.

      2.    .orderform.ask. <??>
Press ? for Help, q to Quit, u to go up a menu              Page: 1/1
```

By now you should be getting the idea. If you choose 1, you will see a rather lengthy description of the service being offered by the Arlington Financial Group. Item two gives you the ability to place an order. You'll notice it took us quite a while to locate this credit repair kit. If we'd known about it in the first place and had the gopher address, we could have bypassed several levels and gone to it directly.

Making Money with Gopher

Although Gopher has been around for a number of years, relatively few businesses seem to use it for marketing. You have already seen that the vast majority of Gopher sites are located at universities and provide a variety of academic information. Determined to find some businesses smart enough to be taking advantage of a golden opportunity, we decided to make a thorough search of registered Gopher sites. After some effort, we stumbled upon a place called "Shops of the World." Pay dirt. We quickly went to it and found the following:

```
Internet Gopher Information Client 2.0 p15

Shops of The World


        1.    Amzi! - Cogent Prolog/

        2.    Andresen/TVGraphic software/

        3.    Art Gallery/

        4.    Ascension Technology Corporation/

        5.    CEnvi and Cmm library./

        6.    Computer Solutions/

        7.    DLB___Research/

        8.    EPI Software Systems/

        9.    ETG/

        10.   Electric Space Co. - Sound for real & virtual worlds/

        11.   Fruit Baskets - from Pemberton Orchards/

        12.   Insitu Inc. Desktop Conferencing Software/

        13.   Intec Controls Corporation/

        14.   JP Software/

  -->   15.   JT Toys - An Adult Toy Store/

        16.   Juxtab Music Group/

        17.   Microchip Technology PIC Microcontroller Software/

        18.   Numerical Recipes Software;


Press ? for Help, q to Quit, u to go up a menu
```

Not the colorful, bazaar-like atmosphere you expected, is it? A disproportionate number of the products or services are related to computers. The Art Gallery, Number 3, sounded like fun, but when we selected that option, we were greeted with an empty screen. Was the art sold out? We'll never know. Number 11, Fruit Baskets, seemed interesting enough. We know that florists have been thriving on the Net and this appeared to be a similar idea. Choosing that option, we were given brief descriptions of several fruit baskets and an 800 telephone number to call for placing an order. No on-line ordering capability was offered and there was only a very small variety of baskets to choose from. Time to move on. We were left with Number 15, JT Toys, an adult toy store. As it turned out, JT's had the longest product list of any Gopher store we'd observed so far. We're not going to show you exactly what we saw. We've devoted one chapter to sex on the Net already. We will tell you that here was by far the most extensive offering. It was a large catalog broken up into descriptive sections. Section one was called "Things That Vibrate." Don't ever say some Netters don't know what they like.

Telling the World about Your Gopher Site

The only reason we were able to find any of the Gopher sites we've talked about was because their owners had the foresight to register them with the University of Minnesota. As the inventors of Gopher, this institution has assumed responsibility for keeping track of all the world's sites. To that end, they maintain the geographically based Gopher index we saw at the beginning of this chapter. To insure that customers can find you, you should register your own Gopher site in that index. Doing so is free and can make your products and services known to millions of computer users everywhere. Simply send a request for registration via e-mail to gopher @boombox.micro.umn.edu and you will be listed. Then, anyone searching for specific Gopher information will have a reasonable chance of finding you, just as we found the Financial Mall and JT's Adult Toys.

Registering your Gopher site may soon by itself be inadequate to get the steady flow of customers you want. The rapidly expanding Internet spawns more Gopher sites every day. While there are still relatively few in existence, yours will stand out in the registry. Don't expect these happy circumstances to last very long, though. Making a fortune with Gopher requires you to use any additional means of publicity you can think of for getting your site known. All the methods we suggested for bringing people to your World Wide Web site will work just as well with Gopher. These promotional ideas are an indispensable part of every Internet indirect marketing action plan.

What Can You Sell with Gopher?

While Gopher has made academic research on the Internet much easier, its value as a business marketing tool is just beginning to be realized. Commercial Gopher sites, like Web sites, are often structured as marketplaces or malls. We've already looked at the Financial Mall in New York that was selling low-cost credit cards, credit clean-up kits, business forms, discount telephone services, insurance, and travel services. Our survey of existing commercial Gopher sites also uncovered a few other types of products and services for sale, including books, CDs, videos, a California winery, T-shirts, stamps and coins, concert tickets, and gourmet mail-order foods. Electronic publications are another item that can be sold directly. On-line magazines are a common use of Gopher. There are even classified listings similar to the ones found in any newspaper. The personals we described earlier in our chapter on cybersex were taken from a Gopher site, again in New York City. Use Gopher, too, to supply order forms for any product or service you are promoting. The completed form can be returned easily by e-mail. There is really no limit to the possibilities. If you can describe it in writing, you can sell it with Gopher.

As we explained earlier, with Gopher, your customers will only be able to view straight text while on-line. Other types of files must first be downloaded to their own computers and then accessed off-line through special programs such as graphical viewers or sound synthesizers. If you want to rely heavily on graphics for promotional purposes, your best bet really is World Wide Web, which is made for this kind of thing. Although graphics may not be the way to advertise using Gopher, don't think that you can't sell data, including graphics this way. The loss of immediacy from the necessity to first download graphics, audio, and video before looking at them is less of a problem when the information to be gotten is not just advertising, but the product itself. Gopher is very good for storing large volumes of data. Actually, you can provide any type of information on your Gopher site that can be digitized. You can keep huge inventories of information for sale if you wish. You could even maintain libraries of actual software, graphical images, sound recordings, animation, and text files that might include forms or even entire books, all to be retrieved directly from your computer. Why not make Gopher's limitations work for you? Give glowing text descriptions of what is hidden in your files, and then charge on a per file basis to actually get it.

As you develop a product or service to market on Gopher, consider the results of our informal commercial Gopher survey. Certainly we found some interesting items, but no one is going to be overwhelmed by the marketing imagination being shown here. Frequently, when we found a menu item that initially sounded interesting, like the art gallery, we were disappointed to learn there was nothing behind it. In other cases, like the fruit baskets, there were not enough choices to make us feel really satisfied. Is that all there is? Coming through is a clear message. The market is wide open. Gopher provides some very interesting money-making possibilities. Just because others aren't using it widely doesn't mean you should ignore it. We are sure you could do better than anyone else has so far. Gopher can play an important role in making your fortune on the Information Super-highway. Here is a real chance to be one of the first.

Setting Up a Gopher Site

Looking at other people's Gopher sites is easy, as we hope you've con-cluded from our earlier examples. In fact, that is one of the main reasons why Gopher is such an excellent selling tool. It's fun too, because when you use it, you are in effect traveling the globe, entering distant computers. When you logged on to the University of Minnesota's Gopher earlier, everything you saw on the screen came from a computer located there. You actually visited Minnesota electronically. From Minnesota, you then whis-ked yourself at warp speed into a computer called "Financial Mall" lo-cated in New York.

But how do you go about setting up a site of your own? As is true with World Wide Web, to set up a Gopher site you must be willing to put yourself on the Gopher tour circuit and let visitors enter your own com-puter. The first step of making that happen is an obvious one. You must connect your computer to the Internet. Next, as is the case with all com-puter applications, you must acquire a software program that will do the tasks necessary. Special Gopher software lets you set up Gopher menus, and allows others to access your computer. Fortunately, as with so many programs in Cyberspace, Gopher software is readily obtainable on the Internet for free. To get it, go directly to its creator, the University of Minnesota. Not surprisingly, you can do this by returning to the University of Minnesota's Gopher site and downloading the software files. Versions of the program you'll need are available for virtually every type of com-puter. Several commercial versions of Gopher software are now on the market as well. The ones you pay for may be a little easier to use than the Net freebies. Unlike public domain software, the commercial programs always include instructions on installing it, and technical support from the software publisher.

To run a commercial Gopher site the right way, you should seriously consider a dedicated Internet access. Just as is true of the World Wide Web, you can't know when someone will choose to come into your I-way "store," so it should be ready to welcome customers at all times. Because you are opening up your computer to the entire world, you should also take security precautions to insure that your visitors see only what you want them to see. There are technical methods for limiting access. Check with a geek to find out what they are.

Gopher can be a very lucrative vehicle for making your fortune on the Information Superhighway. The opportunities are wide open, because few have yet to discover its full potential. Gopher can be accessed by virtually everyone on the Internet. It is easy to use, and gives you, the seller, an inexpensive way to provide mountains of information to your customers, either free as promotional material, or on a paid basis by filling orders for goods delivered straight from the computer. Once people know you are there, they can visit often to get updated product and pricing information. Changing or adding to your information is a breeze. Most important, they can place orders any time from anywhere. It's effortless to keep your store filled with items that are exciting and new. Make your Gopher shop a popular gathering place on the Internet. Start small and keep building. Don't stop until you've made yourself into a major department store mogul.

11

FTP: SELLING TO THE WHOLE I-WAY

File Transfer Protocol or FTP is the most widely available of the indirect, data-site marketing opportunities on the I-way. While FTP is essentially an Internet function, its broad scope transcends the Internet to include anyone who can send and receive e-mail. With FTP, you can reach this enormous audience, encompassing the commercial networks like Prodigy and America Online, for less than you probably spend on your monthly phone bill.

It is technically easier to set up an FTP site than to build data sites with World Wide Web or Gopher. FTP sites can be established by almost anyone with an Internet connection. Although the customer's entrance into a far-away computer is the central principle behind all three, World Wide Web and Gopher require more powerful hardware and stronger Internet access than does FTP. From the user's perspective, FTP sites are easy to reach. In fact, FTP is probably the quickest method for anyone on the I-way to retrieve computer files, no matter where in the world he or she is located. FTP, like Gopher, lets you maintain for your customers sales information, computer software, electronic publications, and graphical images, all fully indexed and available twenty-four hours a day.

There's a catch. In fact, there are several catches. Remember how with Gopher you are able to view only text on-line? Well, with FTP you can't even see that much. You don't get the nice, organized menus that tell you in plain English what items of information you will find at the site. What you get instead is a screen full of weird-looking UNIX commands which, you may have noticed by now, we usually try to avoid like the plague. To further confound you, there is no good FTP registry or indexing system like the ones maintained for the Web and Gopher. There is an FTP searching system called Archie which is used primarily for finding various computer programs available in FTP files, but nothing else. That means one less opportunity to overcome the indirect advertising problem of making your customers know that your data site exists and contains something of interest. There is only one way to find out what is on any FTP site: Once there, you must download it from the remote-access location into your own computer and read it off-line. Again, this works well if you know exactly what it is you are looking for. As usual, there are ways of bringing purchasers to your FTP site by using the methods we've already suggested for that purpose in our discussion of Gopher and World Wide Web. As for the browsing factor—not this time.

Drawbacks aside, the availability of huge audiences reachable at an unparalleled low price makes FTP well worth your marketing consideration. No good cyberseller is going to be stopped from mining the potential here by a few insignificant obstacles. Therefore, let's get on with the business of looking closely at FTP and making it work for you.

Searching with Anonymous FTP

To access a computer that is a distance away and on a different network from yours usually requires you to get prior authorization and a password from the owner of that computer. Most computers on the Internet, however, allow others to log in through FTP simply by using the name Anonymous. This system is referred to, predictably enough, as Anonymous FTP. It works this way. Suppose that you want to look at what files our company, Cybersell™, has available. From your own computer somewhere on the Internet, you simply type in "FTP cyber.sell.com." Even though we are located in Arizona and you may be thousands of miles away, you will be taken to our computer, arriving there in no more than two or three seconds. At this point you will be asked for your name. Normally, when you log on directly to a computer network, you must type in your system login name and password. With FTP, you can just type the word "Anonymous." Next, you will be asked for a password and instructed to use your regular e-mail name. Type it on your keyboard and you're in!

Once in the public area of our computer, you will see a list of the items we have available. You could look at our Cybersell™ price list or a description of our services. You would also see files from Cybersell™ clients, telling about the products and services they would like you to buy from them. When you find the file you want, simply type in the word "get" followed by the file name, and, like magic, the information will be transferred so that you can see it on your own computer and read it at your leisure. Not wishing to tell our trade secrets to the world, we give the general public access only to certain areas of our computer. You won't be able to take a look at our private files. You should exercise the same security measures at your own FTP site.

Let's look at another example. Since you are about to start a computer marketing business, you may be interested in buying a new computer modem. You have learned that there is a company called Widget Networks maintaining an FTP site where you will be able to find a price list for popular modems. This is not a real company, but here is how your search process would actually work. The site address is ftp.widnet.com. Go ahead and type it on your keyboard. You'll soon see the following:

```
250- * ---------------------------------------------------
---------*
250-|Widget Networks
212.555.0202          |
250-|10 E. 53rd Street                              fax
212.555.0202          |
250-|New York NY 10021                  ftp.widnet.com
/pub/pearl          |
250-|pearl@widnet.com
http://www.widnet.com/pearl/                |
250-|                            v32.widnet.com
/pub/pearl          |
250-|
|
250-|                            v42.widnet.com
/pub/v42          |
250-|                        vfast.widnet.com
/pub/tech-support |
250-|                          slow.widnet.com   use
anonymous         |
250-|                          other.widnet.com
/pub/other/other  |
250-|'get Modem.prices  |more' for fastest service including
order info        |
250- * --------------------------------------------------------
---------*
250-|   Widget Networks your source for communication needs   |
250-|                  Insert .sig here
|
250- * ---------------------------------------------------
---------*
250-
250 CWD command successful.
ftp> get Modem.prices
```

Don't say we didn't warn you. This looks confusing. You're given the name and address of the company, and then a strange-looking menu that is actually a list of UNIX directories and files on the Widget Network's computer. They may or may not contain information in which you are interested. You can retrieve them to your own computer and look at them later on, but you certainly aren't going to get much from viewing the monitor. There is at least one thing here that seems comprehensible. At the bottom of the screen it suggests that you type "get Modem.prices." You do so, and a file is immediately transferred to your own computer. After getting a message telling you the transfer was complete, you leave the remote computer and come back home. On your own computer, you can now see the file named "Modem.prices."

You use your normal software or word processing program to look at the file. Doing so brings the following to the screen:

```
Widget Networks
                        Prices as of August 19, 1993
               --------------------

               pearl@whosis.com or pearl@widnet.com

* - temporarily lower

AT&T paradyne
WN

   -----------------------------------------------------------
- -

Famous Maker 14.4Ext 14.4 Fax V32bis V42bis QLII Etc Oli Class 1&2 fax    $150
Famous Maker 14.4Mac 14.4 Fax V32bis V42bis QLII Etc Oli Class 1&2 cable  $160
Famous Maker 14.4Int 14.4 Fax V32bis V42bis QLII Etc Oli Class 1&2 fax    $140
Famous Maker 2001 14.4Ext 14.4 Fax VOICE V32bis V42bis Etc Oli Cl 1&2     $410
Less Famous (3830) 192.K 2 wire V32terbo V32bis V42bis Flsh-Rom           $550
Less Famous (3820) 192.K 2 wire LCD V32terbo V32bis V42bis Flsh-Rom       $650
Less Famous (3810) 192.K 2/4 wire V32terbo V32bis V42bis Flsh-Rom         $810
Less Famous 3000 Carrier rack for 16 rack modem cards                   $1100
Less Famous SDCP shared diagnostic unit, controls up to 8 3000 carrier   $550
Touchy-Feely PCMCIA 14.4int 14.4 Fax Cell Etc Oli upgradeable            $280
   -----------------------------------------------------------
- -

http://www.widdie.com/pearl/ or ftp.widdie.com /pub/pearl/ATT.faq


Door-Way Systems, Inc. (DSI)
WN
```

```
--------------------------------------------------------------
--
Brand A 14.4+FAX 14.4k data and fax (internal) Winfax                    $80
Brand B 14.4 DF 14.4k data and fax (internal) Winfax                     $90
Brand C 19.2 DF 19.2k data and fax (internal) Winfax                    $100
Brand D 14.4 DFV 14.4k data fax VOICE (internal) Winf RingCentral       $120
Brand E 19.2 DFV 19.2k data fax VOICE (internal) Winf RingCentral       $130
Brand F 14.4k data and fax (external) Bitfax                            $100
Brand G+ PC 14.4k data and fax (internal) Dosfax Vinfax                 $150
Brand H+ 14.4k data and fax (external) Dosfax Winfax                    $160
Brand I+ 14.4k data and fax (external) for Macintosh, cable            $170
Brand J+ 19.2k data and fax (external) Dosfax Winfax                    $180
Brand K+ 19.2k data and fax (external) for MacIntosh, cable            $190
Brand L PCMCIA 14.4k data and fax PCMCIA                                $210
Brand M 288 VFCi 28.8k data and fax (internal) Class 1&2 fax Winfax    $170
Brand N + FAX upgrade Fax upgrade with Winfax SoftModem manager         $30
Brand O + Terbo upgrade 19.2k data upgrade using V.32terbo              $30
Brand P + Voice upgrade voicemail upgrade RingCentral S/W (for DF)      $35
Brand Q+ 14.4Ext Fax V32bis V42bis V42 MNP low latency sync/async      $350
Brand R+ 14.4Ext Fax V32bis V42bis V42 MNP low latency 4w LCD V25b     $480
Brand S+ 14.4RACK Fax V32bis V42bis V42 MNP low latency                $295
Brand T rack for upt to 16 9624LR+ modems powersupply                  $805
Brand U T1 CSU/DSU 56/64kbps increments up to 1.544 Mbps              $2000
--------------------------------------------------------------
--
```

What you are seeing here is only one page of the entire file. Actually, there are about a dozen pages of names with different modems and prices. Now, suppose you want to place an order. Then, you must either call the company on the telephone or send a request by e-mail.

The steps we've just followed to use Anonymous FTP apply if you have full Internet access. If you have only e-mail access to the Internet, as would subscribers to many of the commercial networks, you can still use Anonymous FTP by employing a system known as FTP mail. Special computers set up with programs for this purpose make it possible. There are several computers that act as FTP mail servers. These computers can locate specific files or even an index of directories. Here are the addresses of two of them: ftpmail@decwrl.dec.com and bitftp@pucc.princeton.edu. It is to one of these computers that you send an e-mail request for the file you want. Then, the FTP mail server will carry out the search, retrieve the desired item, and e-mail back the results. Depending on your system and where the files are located, this may take anywhere from a few minutes to a day. Now, all this may not be as flashy as a lot of Net features we've already told you about, but it gets the job done for the forty to fifty million people who have the power to use it.

Making Money with FTP

How can you use the simple FTP system to make your fortune on the I-way? There is no mystery here. As an advertising device, any product or service can be promoted with FTP. By setting up an anonymous FTP site, you can provide sales literature and order forms to potential customers. Depending on what you are selling, you might be able to include samples via FTP, such as a chapter of a book, a single song from a record album, or a photograph of an item you are trying to sell. You can also provide catalogs or price lists just as the modem company did in our earlier example. There is no practical limit to the nature or content of FTP files. Text, graphics, sound, and video are all options. You are limited only by the available disc space on your computer, and your customer is limited only by what his or her own computer can handle. However, unlike Gopher and World Wide Web, FTP does not give your customers the opportunity to view a file or place an order on-line. The magic-like interactive power is not there. Still, the space-travel aura that all Internet features have remains.

A benefit to having an FTP site is that most FTP programs allow you to capture the e-mail addresses of everyone who accesses it. All who log on anonymously can be required to submit their actual e-mail address as a password. This is of immeasurable value in finding names to build the electronic mailing lists we talked about earlier. Here is at least one FTP perk you don't get with Gopher or the Web, which allow you to capture the Internet domains of your visitors, but not their actual addresses.

Customer support is another popular commercial use of FTP sites. A number of companies are now employing FTP sites to store frequently asked questions (FAQ) about their products. Software companies are using FTP sites to provide supplemental computer programs and up-grades or fixes to existing programs. While these companies may not earn money directly selling items through their FTP sites, they are able to offer a level of 24-hour customer support that would not otherwise be available. This makes these companies more competitive in the market place.

Employing the Anonymous FTP system means that your information must be made available without charge, since you are allowing site access to absolutely anyone indiscriminately. Therefore, if the actual product you are selling is one that could be transmitted through a computer, such as graphical images, software, or an electronic publication, you will want to offer it in a way that is separate from the free promotional material. Of necessity, then, marketing would be done with a two-step process. First the sales information comes free through Anonymous FTP. Later, orders are placed by telephone or e-mail. There is an alternative way to go about this. If information through the computer is what you want to sell, you can put up a second FTP site without the anonymous feature. Keep your advertising in one place, open to all. Put the files you have for sale in a separate place where only those who pay can read them.

Another major drawback to FTP that really has no solution is the absence of any real interactive possibilities. The warm, fuzzy, in-touch feeling that hooks so many people on the Internet isn't going to work for you as much with FTP as it will with other Internet features. The workhorse FTP system cannot provide people the instant gratification that comes from actually seeing what they're buying or placing orders while on line. Still, because using FTP is so simple and can be done from virtually any type of Internet account, it is well worth attention as a way to cybersell.

How to Set Up Anonymous FTP

FTP is a good way to get your feet wet in setting up a store or mall on the I-way. It is among the simplest of concepts and, because it can be executed with almost any type of computer or I-way access, it requires a minimum of cash outlay. For setting up most FTP sites you can in many cases rely on the equipment and expertise of your access provider. Because of this, unlike Gopher and Web sites, you do not usually have to get your own direct leased access in order to be on-line 24 hours per day. Methods of setting up Anonymous FTP sites will differ slightly according to the kind of computer and access account you have. Here is a general explanation of the possibilities.

A really easy way of getting your FTP site in place is simply to put all the files you want made public into a directory on your access provider's computer and give potential customers your login name and password. (A few access providers expressly forbid the use of your login and password by anyone other than yourself. Check with your access provider.) Then, anyone can use FTP to enter the site and retrieve your files. Because your access provider is on-line continuously, you avoid the cost as well as mechanical headaches of setting up a leased line. Technically what we are describing here is not an Anonymous FTP system, but rather a closed site for authorized users only. A user, however, is defined by a login name and password. Making these items of information known to absolutely every-one effectively grants access to the world at large. You will require cooper-ation from your access provider to carry out the procedure we've just suggested because that is who must set up the separate directory for your account. Without the special directory, you will not have the ability to pick and choose the files of information on your computer that your customer may and may not see. Give them the password and they will be able to view everything, whether you want them to or not. If your access provider will not establish a separate directory, you can still maintain security by setting up another Internet account strictly for FTP access. Here you will put your public files. Anything of a private nature will be kept separately, in an account inaccessible to all but members of your own company.

There is one additional way to establish an FTP site through your access provider, again avoiding the need for a leased line. Virtually all Internet access providers maintain Anonymous FTP sites of their own. Frequently they allow their subscribers to post files there at will. Better still, talk to your provider and see if he can create an Anonymous FTP site just for you. It should be very simple to do. Though you may be charged a small additional fee if you store lots of material there, this is still an extremely economical way for you to go since your access provider is the one seeing to it that you remain continuously on-line.

Without the assistance of your access provider, or if you have decided on a direct Internet connection, you will have to set up an FTP site of your own. As usual, you will need to install a program that will make your computer carry out the FTP function. Here is another of those times when the help of a geek may be needed. One nice thing about FTP, however, is that you can operate a site on virtually any type of computer and there are numerous commercial FTP software packages available to run on what-ever kind of computer you may have.

With FTP, we've reached the last of the money-producing features on the I-way that you should know about. You can choose to utilize any or all of them, in whatever combination and to whatever degree you think best. And who can tell? There is probably even more to come. For computer marketing, the beginning chapter of a long story is just now being written. As the days and months go by, no one who watches the grand parade of fortune seekers heading toward the I-way can fail to be impressed by the variety of ways being developed to reap wealth from computer networks. We've given you our ideas as a starting point. Two heads are better than one and a few million are better still. We can't wait to see what exciting ideas you come up with to make your own mark in Cyberspace.

12

YOUR PC—THE BIGGEST MONEY-MAKER YOU'LL EVER KNOW: WHAT EQUIPMENT DO YOU NEED AND HOW DO YOU BUY IT?

The Computer Revolution

Marching upon us with heavy footsteps are the forces of the computer revolution. Some may remember what it was like before fax machines and cellular phones were everywhere. A few may even recall life before copy machines. How did businesses manage? As much as other assorted developments in office machinery have brought about important changes in the ways we do business today, they pale by comparison with the effects of the computer. Nothing except the telephone has had a more profound impact. And it is just beginning. Most companies now use computers only for accounting, storing records, and to act as a smart typewriter. Virtual offices, where employees physically stay at home and "telecommute" to work via computer, are just starting to become commonplace. Relatively few companies use computers for reading their daily newspaper, talking between themselves, or communicating with customers. Practically none have tried computer advertising. That is going to change. Within a few years, the computer is likely to supplant the telephone, fax, and regular mail as the primary means of communication. Some newspapers and magazines, complete with advertisements, have just begun going on-line. Soon, the computer may well be the principal medium for all advertising. You can already order a panoply of products and services through your home computer. The use of computers for marketing is about to explode.

As the computer revolution progresses, it is becoming more and more possible to transact business without actually speaking to anyone. Many people find a true feeling of security in being able to interact fully with the world while still managing never to leave the privacy of their homes. Internet junkies who just about live inside their computers are the extreme example of this syndrome. They don't understand or believe anything unless it appears in green type on a computer monitor. Any other source is suspect. The reliability of whoever was ultimately responsible for placing the information in Cyberspace is seemingly unimportant. Only the vehicle of communication matters. While people that far over the edge are still out of the mainstream, the increasing importance of computers in our lives is undeniable.

There is life outside of Cyberspace and hopefully that will always be true. Nonetheless, those who try to stay away from computers will find the task difficult to impossible. The computer revolution has begun. Viewed with an eye toward all that computers can help us achieve, try to rejoice over the part you will play in what is to be. Brace yourself. Here comes the worst of the technobabble. We promise to make it as easy and painless as possible.

What is a computer? We have considered at length how computers can help you make a fortune. Now it's time to take a look at the machines themselves. Computers are simply tools that organize, store, and transfer data. Although some computers have been given humanoid names, like "Hal," they are not living creatures. Computers aren't people. They have no feelings or emotions. Computers have no soul. Most important, they don't think for themselves. The French 17th-century philosopher Descartes who made famous the quote "I think, therefore I am" would have been forced to conclude that computers don't exist. When it comes to computers, make no mistake, it is you who must do the thinking.

This brings us to a key question. Just how smart do you have to be to use a computer? So many of us seem intimidated by the mere thought. Can you read and write? Are you as intelligent as that air head who mixed up your last plane reservations? Are you able to understand this book? If your answer to any of the above is yes, then you are more than smart enough to operate a computer expertly.

Probably the single biggest skill required to use a computer successfully is the ability to type. It's not a very glamorous thought, but true nonetheless. A computer keyboard, which looks much like a typewriter, is the vehicle used to tell your computer what it should do. Futuristic models of computers that listen to the spoken word and act on verbal command may soon become a reality. For now, typing is what it takes. By the way, if you don't already know how to type or need to brush up, there are computer programs available that will teach you, that is, if you don't mind learning something from a machine that can't think for itself.

Mac versus IBM

Computers now come in a number of different styles and they are evolving faster than the speed of light. About thirty years ago the first computers, with names like UNIVAC and RAYDAC, were as large as army tanks. They consisted of thousands of television-like vacuum tubes, took hours or even days to wade through difficult mathematical functions, and cost millions of dollars. Today, for less than $1,000, you can buy a new computer that sits comfortably on your lap and calculates the most complex of mathematical problems in a matter of seconds. Hardly a month goes by without the development of yet a new computer component that is faster, smarter, and ultimately cheaper than its predecessor. In choosing what type of computer to get, you might as well relax. No matter how much you spend today or how carefully you study up before making your purchase, the model you've selected will be obsolete in a matter of months. For that reason, when buying a new computer, simply make sure the one you pick can easily be upgraded as new technology comes out, and you won't have too much to worry about.

We will briefly discuss the most common types of computers to assist you in selecting your own. At the outset, however, we wish to emphasize that just about any kind can be used successfully to make money on the I-way. The latest bells and whistles may expand your marketing options and add to your enjoyment, but they are rarely a business necessity. Computers come in different sizes, from mainframe computers that fill a room (which are becoming obsolete) to laptop portables that can fit under a plane seat. This discussion will limit itself to microcomputers better known as personal computer systems, or "PCs." These are the ones most individuals use and are what you will find being sold at your local store.

There are two basic types of PCs. One is the Apple system, known mostly as Macintosh, or Mac for short. The other is the IBM-based system, including IBM clones such as Dell, Compaq, and Packard Bell. When we refer to IBM here, we mean a general type of computer, not necessarily a product directly manufactured by the IBM company. Styles of IBM computers differ according to the kind of processor they contain. The processor is actually the brain of the computer, although physically it is about the size of a soda cracker. Interestingly, processors for most IBM machines are not even made by IBM but by another company known as Intel. The most common processing system is the Intel Model 486. A model number 486 on an IBM computer indicates that it contains this type of Intel processor. The newest Intel processors are called the Pentium. Accordingly, there are Pentium-model IBM PCs. The various IBM models differ in the speed and efficiency with which they handle data. Speed of data transmission is measured in megahertz. The speeds available for 486 models range from about 20 to 100 megahertz, while Pentium model speeds begin at about 60 megahertz. The type of processor, however, also affects the speed of the computer. Therefore, a Pentium running at 60 megahertz will be much faster than a 486 operating at the same speed. The Pentium chip processes data in a more efficient manner.

Both the Mac and IBM systems, in their most complex configurations, are extremely powerful and versatile. You can easily access the Internet or any other part of the I-way from either type of machine. If you already have one or the other, there is no reason to change. If you are buying a computer for the first time, you should consider that Macs are inherently more user-friendly and handle computer graphics brilliantly, while IBMs are thought to be better business computers, manipulating non-graphical data more efficiently than Macs. At present, there is also more business software available for IBMs, but this may be changing. New computer processors are under development that will allow you to run either Mac or IBM programs from the same machines. Microsoft Windows, the best-known computer software package in existence, is used in IBM-type computers to assist you in moving easily between the various other programs you have purchased and installed on your PC. One thing that Windows can do is make an IBM look and act much like a Mac. The Mac purists, however, insist that their operating system is superior. In fact, the two systems look more and more alike all the time. We won't enter into the ongoing debate about which system is better. In reality, we believe that in the end, it is purely a matter of personal preference.

Memory

When purchasing a new computer, one important question you will be asked is how much "memory" you will need. A computer has two kinds of memory. One is internal and deals with the capacity of the computer to process data. The other refers to the amount of data itself that the computer is able to store. The internal memory is also called Random Access Memory, or RAM for short. You will remember that each general function you want your computer to perform, word processing, for example, requires a different program. The more sophisticated the programs you use and the more programs you install into your computer, the more RAM you will need. Most modern PCs are equipped with a minimum of four megabytes of RAM, but can be increased to many times that amount simply by adding additional memory chips that plug into a special slot. RAM is expensive, so when comparing prices of computers, make sure you are comparing systems with comparable configurations, including RAM. How much RAM you will require depends again on the type of software you will be using and whether or not your computer is part of a network. For most personal and simple business uses, four megabytes will probably be adequate, but eight is better. Here again, though, there is not much to worry about if you make a mistake. Increasing a computer's RAM is one of the simplest types of upgrades. If your software seems to run very slowly, increasing the amount of RAM may cure the problem.

Operating Systems

Another essential component of all computers is the operating system. An operating system is a special computer program that tells the machine how to handle basic functions. Software that you buy, such as word or data processing programs must be purchased in versions compatible with the operating system you select. The most common operating systems are DOS, OS/2, Apple, and UNIX. Macs almost always run on their own proprietary system made by Apple Computer. IBMs usually run on an operating system called DOS (Disk Operating System). The overwhelming majority of DOS systems come from Microsoft. Indeed, this product started Microsoft owner Bill Gates on his way to becoming the fourth richest man in America. Other operating systems can, however, be used with IBMs. IBM itself, in an effort to steal some of Microsoft's thunder, has now developed an operating system called OS/2 which requires a rather powerful computer to work properly. You can also put a UNIX operating system on an IBM-type computer or a Mac if you want to. If you use DOS, which is still the most common operating system, you should also use the Windows program mentioned earlier. Most of the large Internet computers that keep the Net going run on the UNIX operating system. It is unlikely that when you get started you will use UNIX on your own computer.

Generally, if you are a beginner, we recommend you select the most common operating system, DOS. DOS is the one that has the most software available for it. Because it is used so predominantly, it is also easier to find people who can help you with it when you get stuck. Almost all the software being written for use on an IBM computer requires having Windows in place. As a practical matter, then, a DOS system by itself is inadequate to run most modern software. You will have to install Windows as well. As you get more experienced with a computer and have a better feel for your particular needs, you may decide that a different operating system will better serve your needs. For starters, DOS is the simplest way to go.

Only those who have advanced Internet business interests need to look at the UNIX operating system. You should consider a UNIX operating system if the type of Internet access you are planning is the very high-level leased line, which we discuss, along with other types of access, in the next chapter. As we mentioned earlier, the Internet networks are based on UNIX. Most individual and small-business computer users will have little or no familiarity with UNIX and could probably care less about that system because common software does not usually come in a UNIX version. Nonetheless, UNIX, having been developed in the 1960s, is actually one of the oldest, not to mention the most powerful computer operating system around. UNIX is far superior to the other common operating systems for computer networking. This is because UNIX was specifically designed to allow many computers to access the same programs and files at the same time.

Most UNIX systems usually operate on larger, more powerful, and therefore more expensive computers than Macs or IBM PCs. There are now, however, versions of UNIX that can even be installed on the less powerful PCs. Two of the most popular versions are SCO UNIX and Novell's Unixware. We run Unixware on our Pentium computers with no difficulty. Installing UNIX is considerably more complicated than the other operating systems and is therefore best left to a hired computer geek.

Often, depending on the Internet access provider you have selected, UNIX computers can be accessed and run by other computers not operating with UNIX. The easy-to-use Internet software coming out now, for use on Macs and IBM PCs, allows you to work on a UNIX network without knowing anything about UNIX. You simply execute DOS or Mac commands while the software then invisibly converts your commands to UNIX.

Even though you will probably not buy a UNIX-based computer as you begin your money-making trip down the I-way, you should still at least know that they exist, since UNIX is the language of the Internet. There are other networking systems out there, including AppleShare for Macs, Novell's NetWare, and Windows NT from Microsoft. The latter two, as you may have guessed, run on DOS-based computers. If, however, you ever do want a computer network and intend for it to be hooked into the Internet, UNIX is still the way to go.

If the Internet access you choose is a fairly low-level variety, then, for Net marketing purposes, which operating system is on your own computer won't make any difference. That is because most people accessing the Internet will be doing so through the computer of an intermediary network or access provider. The commands you enter from your keyboard are actually manipulating programs that sit on the intermediary computer, which is almost always UNIX-based. Your operating system does not come into play. When you retrieve data from the Internet, it is sent to the provider's computer, although you may elect to copy it on to yours later. With this type of Internet access, it does not make a great deal of difference what sort of computer you are using, since all the real action takes place somewhere else.

Data Storage Capacity and Disk Drives

Some of the earlier personal computers stored data only on floppy disks. Earlier we discussed RAM memory. RAM is the memory used internally by the computer to process data. Floppies are a way of storing the actual information the computer processes. This includes your e-mail, customer information, inventory, accounting—any data you wish your computer to store. Floppy disks also are used, at least initially, to store the software you have chosen for various functions. Almost all software you purchase will come on floppy disks.

Floppy disks are small circles of magnetic tape, much like the tape used in a tape recorder. They are housed in plastic containers that are flexible, hence the name "floppy." These disks are inserted into a portion of the computer known as the disk drive. The floppy comes in two basic sizes, 5¼ and 3½ inches in diameter. Its use as a repository for data is often convenient in many situations, because floppies are inexpensive and removable. All computers come with at least one floppy drive. Floppy disks, however, have extremely limited storage capabilities, and operate rather slowly on the computer when compared with the more advanced hard disk drives we'll be discussing in a minute. There are now new high-density floppy disks that hold about five times as much data as the older ones did. They are still very slow, however, by comparison with hard disks.

Virtually all computers today have hard disk drives in addition to floppy drives. A hard disk drive looks somewhat like a miniature record player. A circular magnetic disk, housed in a metal cabinet, is accessed by a needle-like apparatus. Hard disks are usually installed inside the computer and are not meant to be removed (though there are now removable versions available as well). Hard disk drives operate very fast and can hold huge amounts of data. A typical, large hard disk drive, containing 540 "megabytes" of storage, will hold as much data as nearly 400 of the new, high-density floppies, and 1500 of the older kind. Because of the large program size of most modern software, you'll need a hard drive to take advantage of it. The larger the storage space on the drive, the more it costs. You'll be surprised at how quickly even the largest of disk drives can fill up, so you should buy the biggest one you can afford. If you are using a very early model PC that does not have a hard disk drive, you can still access the Internet, but you will be unable to use Windows or most of the fancier software now available, since the size of these programs just can't be accommodated with floppy disks.

Truth in labeling is becoming important to the computer industry, just as it has with packaged food. There is now software out that compresses computer data, enabling a hard disk drive to store as much as double its normal capacity. For example, we recently saw an ad for a hard disk claiming it could hold 850 megabytes. The fine print, however, said that the actual disk size was 425 megabytes, but could hold twice as much with data compression. The trouble is that you probably won't want to compress the data on your disk, even though it's easy to do, because hard disks do not work as well when they are compressed, and there is greater danger of losing your data due to a malfunction or system crash. Moreover, not all data can be compressed. Certain types of computer files, particularly those containing nothing but text, such as e-mail or most word processing files, will safely compress into about half the space. Other types, including most program files, may not compress at all. It is quite likely that the majority of disk space is taken up by non-compressible files. What's important to understand here is that when you consider your purchase, the only figure that counts is the true disk size.

You've probably heard of Compact Discs, or CDs, which have all but completely replaced phonographic records and cassette tapes for music lovers. These are round, plastic disks with digitized data permanently recorded on them. CD drives are, obviously, computer drives that can play back CDs. Unlike other types of data memory we've been discussing, the data on a CD is permanently encoded and cannot be erased, written over, or changed. All you can do is read the data on the disk. Hence the name ROM, meaning Read Only Memory.

As computer software programs become more sophisticated and complex, they are taking up more and more disk space. Some of the newest software programs fill up literally dozens of floppy disks. Besides just recorded music, CDs can be used to store any type of digitized data, including computer programs, and a single CD disk can hold as much data as 500 floppy disks. Therefore, some software programs are now being made available on CDs, and, of course, that means you need a CD-ROM drive attached to your computer to use them. CD's are many times faster than the fastest hard disk drives. They are becoming especially popular for multimedia functions, such as video, animation and sound. You can probably get a good deal on a new computer equipped with a multi-media package, which might include a CD-ROM drive, speakers, and special computer parts to improve the quality of sound that is generated. If you have a use for those kinds of features, by all means indulge yourself. A CD-ROM drive, however, is not at all necessary to the goal of making money on the I-way.

The Software Factor in Choosing Hardware

The key to which computer you should buy lies to a large extent more in the software you want to use than anything else. You will remember that it is the software you select which will control what tasks your computer can perform. The operating system, the memory size, the speed and type of processor, all these features are there only to see that the programs run at peak performance. We happen to use IBM-style Pentium computers made by Zeos, a mail-order manufacturer, because they are powerful and so handle UNIX, as well as our many business and Internet programs, efficiently. If you know you will be using a particular type of software, a good idea would be to pick your computer system on the basis of which machine will run your favorite program best. If you haven't yet decided on your software, then, when shopping for your computer, the simplest strategy is just to look for the best bargain.

Monitors

Now let us move away from the computer itself to the monitor. A monitor looks much like a television screen. Your computer would be virtually useless without one, since everything you send or receive on your computer will be in the form of an image and the monitor enables you to see that image. Monitors, like televisions, come in many sizes, in color or monochrome, which is a single color, usually green or orange. They are also identified by their degree of resolution which, in English, means the sharpness or clarity of the image. Most of today's color monitors have a resolution much greater than that of your television set. Your new computer will probably come with a color monitor, called either VGA (Video Graphics Array) or SVGA (Super Video Graphics Array). Super is better. When it comes to I-way marketing, the monitor is another piece of equipment where what you select doesn't matter much. With the exception of looking at the World Wide Web, which is based on graphics, the type of monitor is not particularly important for most Internet functions.

Keyboards, Cursors, and Mice

Remember, we said that typing is the most important skill needed to work with a computer. All computers are equipped with a keyboard, which looks like the main part of a typewriter. If you are buying one separately, you may test it by pressing the keys to see if one feels better than another. Beyond that, once again, it doesn't particularly matter which one you select.

When you press a key on the keyboard, the letter or symbol on the key should show up on the monitor. The cursor, appearing as a blinking light, will also be flashing on the monitor screen to show you where you are. You can move the cursor around by pressing assorted keys on the keyboard, or you may acquire another piece of equipment for this purpose called a mouse. The "mouse," or pointer, first became popular when they began being used with the early Apple computers. A mouse is a plastic device with two or three buttons. Except for the absence of fur, this device really does look in size and shape like the rodent after which it is named. By sliding the mouse on a table, you can move the cursor on the monitor screen. This makes it easy to jump around the screen without having to hit a lot of keys. Mice are particularly useful with graphical programs, including all Mac and Windows applications. With graphical programs, instead of a cursor, you usually see an arrow. We've already explained how point-and-click graphics operate. To execute any computer task, you simply move the mouse until the little arrow points to a picture representing the function you want to perform. Then you press one of the mouse buttons.

The computer does the rest. You do not need a mouse if you are using only a UNIX shell without graphical software. Otherwise, because it makes the handwork so much easier, you should definitely get one. Again, a mouse is almost always included with new computer systems.

Modems

The modem is perhaps the single most important piece of hardware you will need for your venture down the I-way. A modem is an electronic device that takes data from your computer, converts it into electronic impulses, and sends it through telephone lines to the I-way. At the end of the line, another modem receives the impulses you sent and converts them back into the same format the data was in when it left your computer. That is how computers communicate. Speed is the key element to consider when choosing a modem. You will be happiest with a high-speed modem of at least 14,400 "baud" or "bps" (bits per second). Not that it really matters, but baud and bps are a measure of speed, the computer version of miles per hour. The faster your modem, the easier it will be for you to communicate with the Internet. If your computer is not already equipped with a modem, you can buy a high-speed one at a discount store for between 100 and 150 dollars, with prices dropping all the time.

Over and above speed, there are two types of modems you can choose from: internal and external. You will probably not be surprised to learn that internal modems reside inside your computer while external ones sit outside. External modems have a series of colored lights that blink on and off as data is being transferred. This gives a spaceship like appearance to your computer and will make you feel vastly superior to those having only internal modems. Actually, the lights serve a variety of diagnostic functions. Most importantly, if the lights are blinking, you know you have a connection to another computer. This is useful information, especially if you seem to be having problems in this regard. With an internal modem, you cannot tell for sure whether you have made a connection or not. An additional benefit to external modems is that they are easier to install. You only have to plug it into the back of the computer. Installing internal modems can be tricky. On the other hand, internal modems usually cost a bit less.

Most new computers come already equipped with internal modems, but don't assume you will want to use it. Very often such a modem handles data transfer at only 2400 baud, a painfully slow speed for cruising the Internet. Some computer manufacturers try to mislead you by claiming high-speed *fax* access with the included modem. What the manufacturer is hiding from you is that computer data transfer is a completely separate function from that of sending faxes and all faxes transmit at high speeds. Always check the *data transfer speed*. That is what really counts. It is probably listed in fine print somewhere on the computer or modem carton. If the data transfer speed is not at least 9600 baud, don't even consider buying it. The brand of modem you use is not very important as long as it is "Hayes" compatible. Hayes is a brand of modem that is considered the industry standard.

Printers

A computer monitor lets you look at everything one screen at a time, but it does not let you carry the information away from the computer or give you a hard copy. For that you will need a printer. We should mention here that computer printers are not absolutely necessary for doing business on the Information Superhighway, provided you will only be communicating with your customers electronically. If you want to take full advantage of your computer, however, for such tasks as word processing and record keeping, a printer is required.

There are three basic types of computer printers. The first type is called a dot matrix, because it forms letters and other characters with little dots that strike a ribbon, much like a typewriter. Dot matrix printers are the least expensive, but they have many drawbacks. First, they are very noisy. If you use one, keep your telephone in a different room. You won't be able to hear a conversation while the printer is running. Second, the quality of print they produce is very poor. Actually, they make things look like they were printed on a computer. Lastly, they are slower than the other types of printers. Dot matrix printers are designated by how many ink pins they have. The more pins, the higher quality of print. Twenty-four-pin printers are the highest quality dot matrix and we wouldn't consider anything less.

The second and newest type of printer is called an ink jet printer. Like a dot matrix, the ink jet forms characters by using tiny dots of ink, but the way ink jets transfer the ink to paper is very different. Instead of having a pin strike a ribbon, ink jets have tiny nozzles and the ink is actually sprayed onto the paper. The result is an extremely sharp-looking image that produces a print quality close to that of the top choice, the laser printer, discussed below. Ink jet printers can be purchased for about $250, and the most popular models are made by Hewlett Packard or Canon. They are much quieter than dot matrix printers, but are still a bit on the slow side, especially if you are printing out graphics. A new feature available with ink jet printers is color. You can now buy a full-color model for about $500! The quality of output is surprisingly high, though it can take several minutes or more to print out a single color page.

The third type of computer printer is called a laser printer. Laser printers offer the best of everything, except color, which hasn't really been perfected yet. Laser printers work very much like photocopy machines. An image is thrown on a developer drum, and heat causes toner to bond to the paper. The higher end laser printers can print out more than 8 pages per minute, with a quality that, until a few years ago, could only be obtained with very expensive offset printers. Slower models can be purchased for under $500, with top of the line machines, like the Hewlett Packard Laser Jet 4, selling for around $1400. If you can afford it, a laser printer is by far the best choice.

Another type of printer that should be mentioned is a Post Script printer. These are special types of laser printers that operate with a computer language known as Post Script. They have more graphical capabilities than regular laser printers, and cost quite a bit more. Post Script format is frequently used to store files on the Internet, so having a Post Script printer may be handy. It is not absolutely essential to have one, however, because there are numerous software programs available that will automatically convert Post Script files into formats that other types of printers can recognize.

Key Software Selections

Communications software is next on your list. Software, as we've said, is the name for a program that tells your computer or modem, both in the hardware category, what to do. Neither your computer nor your modem can work without software. The most basic software is the operating system, which is what allows the computer to function at all. Beyond that, each specific application you want your computer to undertake requires separate software. Word processing, database management, accounting, or Internet access are some examples. There is really no limit to how many different programs you can buy for your computer.

The ability to transmit and receive data between different computers or networks is a separate computer task that requires its own software. Since that is the function we need most to travel down the I-way, communications programs are key. Most modems and many computers come with free communications software. Some of the more common programs you may get for free include Comit, Smartcom, and Quicklink. Much of the free software is designated as "Lite," meaning it lacks a few features of the full-priced version. All will work, however, and are good places to start. There are also excellent communications programs you can download free from the Internet itself or many commercial on-line services. Telix is our personal favorite of these because it is extremely easy to use and has most of the features of the upper-end commercial programs.

Any of the communications programs we've mentioned so far will work satisfactorily. However, if you expect to be sending or receiving lengthy files, such as computer software or graphical material, you will want to make sure your software supports "Zmodem" protocol. The word *protocol* is more computerese, meaning a type of computer program used to send and receive data. Zmodem protocol is currently the fastest way to transfer data. Telix has Zmodem, which is another reason why we like it. Most of the lite versions of communications programs leave Zmodem out. Other transfer protocols you may hear of include Xmodem, Ymodem, and Kermit. All are useful but are very slow when compared to Z. For example, a one megabyte file may be transferred by Zmodem in less than sixty seconds, whereas with Xmodem it might take more than ten minutes.

There are software programs that are designed specifically for using the Internet. These programs usually take advantage of the graphical capabilities of Windows or Macintosh, and are easy for novices to use. Some on-line services, including America Online and Prodigy have their own graphical software that is wonderful for working strictly within each of those particular systems. They are, however, specific to one network. You cannot use them to access other networks like the Internet. Several Internet access providers have started putting out graphical software for use with their services only. These programs eliminate the need to execute UNIX commands, but they usually sacrifice speed and the capacity to handle large volumes of mail efficiently. On the plus side, these proprietary programs are usually free. There are some commercial programs coming out now that offer graphical interfaces to the Internet. The next version of Microsoft Windows, which is expected to be called "Windows 1995," but is being given the code name "Chicago," is also expected to contain this feature. Once the all-powerful Microsoft gets a grip on the situation, it is likely that other Internet programs will fall by the wayside and the Microsoft product will create a uniform standard.

Where to Shop

Where should you go to buy your new money maker? Assuming you want the latest system and are not considering a used computer, there are three types of computer dealers from which to buy: discount department stores, mail-order houses, and specialty computer stores. If you know exactly the items you want to buy, then price is your only consideration. In such cases, you will probably choose to deal with a mail-order house. That is because you can easily shop by telephone until you find the best deal. You can locate the larger computer mail-order houses by looking for their advertisements in any computer magazine. There is absolutely no reason to fear dealing with a mail-order house. Their main drawback is that there will be no experienced sales people to assist you. Returns can also sometimes be problematic with mail-order purchases, not because these companies are dishonest, but due to the time and hassle of repackaging the equipment, shipping it back, and then waiting to receive credit.

Discount department and electronic stores that have computer sections are another option. Examples of these are Sears and Best Buy. You will find that they usually offer a rather limited selection of brands and features, but generally have good prices on name products. In addition, the sales people will probably be able to give you at least limited help. If there is a problem later on with the system you bought, you will have no trouble exchanging it or getting a refund. If you are only comfortable buying mainstream brands, don't need anything fancy, and want to see what you're getting before you lay down your money, the discount department store is your best bet.

Last, but certainly not least, are computer specialty stores. These include national chains, such as CompUSA and Computer City. There are also numerous locally owned and operated specialty computer dealers. These stores, like mail-order houses, usually have a wide array of products to choose from, and in some cases may even be competitive price-wise. The larger chain dealers will offer name-brand products. Sometimes, however, a specialty dealer may be selling brands you haven't heard of. They may have been made by a larger company. On the other hand, they may also be locally assembled. It is not difficult to assemble computers from purchased components, and there are some computer "manufacturers" that are actually working out of basements, garages, or dorm rooms. This is not to say that the computers from such sources aren't any good. The problem is, you never know. The sales people at specialty stores are likely to be more knowledgeable than at the other types of dealers. If you want an unusual configuration of computer components, such as an especially large disk drive to increase your computer's storage capacity, the larger computer specialty store should best be able to meet your needs.

Used computers are another option, attractive if you are on a budget. Many people buy computers and then never bother learning to use them. Tired of having them gather dust, they offer them for sale, sometimes at bargain prices. The main problem with used computers is that they are likely to be at least a few years old, and so not as powerful as those you can buy today. Also, because prices for new computers are steadily declining, even though the person selling a used computer may be discounting it considerably from what he or she originally paid, it may still turn out to be nearly as expensive as a brand-new, more powerful model. Finally, you won't have the comfort of a warranty that you get when you are a computer's first owner. Buying a used computer is a great option if your immediate financial resources are very limited. Besides, you can always move up to a newer one, once you've made your fortune on the I-way. Still, as with anything you may purchase from a private individual, let the buyer beware.

Ford or Cadillac

How much computer should you buy? As we have previously said, virtually any computer can be used successfully for accessing the Internet and making money on the Information Superhighway. Nonetheless we always recommend buying the most powerful computer you can afford. Computer software is becoming increasingly complex and requires more and more sophisticated equipment to run it properly. Then, too, your expectations will probably change fast as you become more familiar with using a computer and more aware of how much it can do for you. Just because you don't need all that power today doesn't mean you won't want it in the near future. Although most computer systems can be upgraded, upgrading is always more costly than buying the more powerful system in the beginning. Upgrading is an inexact science at best. Sometimes the upgrades just don't work because of a system incompatibility, and you end up buying a whole new computer anyway.

Our first computer was an early version IBM PC with one floppy disk drive, 64K of memory, and an ugly monitor that produced a virulent shade of fluorescent green. We paid about $3,000 for that system. Today, the same amount of money will buy the highest-powered PC with the vaunted new Pentium processor that can zip through data with impressive speed. Compared to those early IBMs, which cost a small fortune, the new and cheaper computers have over 100 times the memory capacity, hard disk drives that will store 1,000 times as much data as the old IBM floppy drives, and incredibly high-resolution full-color monitors that will put your color television to shame. You can purchase new or used computers in virtually every price range, with market prices for brand new, respectable, 486-based systems readily available at under $1000. Still, don't forget that with some minor upgrading, you could probably access the Internet with an old IBM. The system memory could be increased to its 640K limit and a modem added. The total cost would be under $150. You would be quite limited in the type of software you could use and Windows wouldn't even be an option, but it would still work. How much computer you need depends on the type of Internet access you want, the software you will run, the size of your pocket book, and your personal pleasure.

You have now digested a sufficient amount of knowledge about computers to convince a computer store salesman that you actually know what you're talking about. You've also learned all you need to make your way to riches on the Information Superhighway. Our final word on all of this is to once again remind you to relax. No matter what you do, you're not going to make a fatal error. Any computer can get you on the I-way. A recent perusal of the Phoenix Sunday newspaper showed used computers being sold for less than $200, equipped with all the hardware and software you'll need. Of course, if you want to be at the forefront of the newest technology, feel free to indulge yourself. A computer system costing thousands of dollars will work well too.

13

HOW TO GET YOURSELF ON THE NET

Now you're ready for that final big step. Your computer and modem are bought and in place. It's time to actually get on the I-way. But how? For years, finding your way on was a mysterious process, generally available only to people affiliated with governments, universities, and a few select corporations. The rest of us were limited to commercial networks like CompuServe and Prodigy. There are certainly money-making opportunities within these closed networks, but they aren't anywhere near as large as the Internet. The largest commercial Net, CompuServe, has about two million users versus more than thirty million on the Internet, and access to the commercial networks does not come cheap.

The first things to consider as you look for Internet access are your particular needs. Your purpose is to market a product or service on the Internet. How many people do you think will be contacting you by computer? Hopefully, a lot. What type of marketing program do you have in mind? Will you need more than just e-mail and Usenet access or do you plan to use Gopher and the Web? There are more than 10,000 Newsgroups available on the Net, but some access providers elect to carry only a fraction of them. This can greatly affect the buying audience you can reach. If your provider decides to exclude groups that offer sales potential for your product, you are stuck. How about costs? What are you willing to spend? How sophisticated are you with computers and networks? What type of computer do you have? What services are available in your area? With these questions in mind, we will next consider the types of Internet access you may choose.

Free Access

If you are affiliated with a university, you might begin looking for Internet access by going to the school's computer science center. There, you should ask if you are entitled to a free Internet account. Many universities provide them to all students and faculty members. Be aware, however, that there may be severe restrictions on what you are allowed to do with such accounts. Typically, universities will permit uses consistent only with academic purposes. Money making is strictly taboo. There have been several documented cases on the Net where entrepreneurial students attempted to sell products or services over their university accounts, and quickly had those accounts pulled. Consider yourself warned.

A number of "Freenets" are now cropping up all over the United States. They are usually operated by city or state governments. Freenets, as the name implies, provide free Internet access to anyone with a computer and a modem who is a resident of the area served by the network. The Cleveland Freenet is the most famous. The state of Maryland recently announced formation of a Freenet that will be available to any of its residents. Most Freenets offer e-mail and bulletin board services and many give Usenet access as well. Call the office of your state or city commerce department to find out if now or in the not-too-distant future, free Internet access will be available to you.

It's hard to resist anything that is free. However, if you intend to log onto the Internet frequently or for long periods of time, as you will when you utilize the Internet for marketing purposes, Freenets are not a good business solution. Freenets are not set up for volume use. They can handle only a limited number of users at a time. That is why you should not be surprised if you find yourself getting busy signals when you try to dial-up. On a recent Sunday afternoon, it took us nearly thirty minutes to get an available line to the Cleveland Freenet. Once you do make a connection, many Freenets limit the amount of time you can stay on line. Again, looking at Cleveland as an example, you are permitted only one hour per day of on-line time, not nearly enough to do serious business. Freenets also offer only very limited space in which to store files and messages you receive. This is yet another serious drawback when you anticipate large numbers of responses from potential purchasers of the product or service you are selling. Finally, as with college and university accounts, you will find yourself limited in the marketing that can be done, due to restrictions on types of usage. Freenets may be a good Internet learning tool, and a means of inexpensive recreation. Overall, it is not what you will probably want for business purposes. If free service is unavailable to you or if it is too restrictive, you will want to go to paid access.

Paid Access

One of the fastest-growing business opportunities in this country is supplying paid access to the Internet. Simple Internet accounts can be opened for less than $20 per month, often permitting unlimited use at no extra charge. Dialup accounts, those that you can access with a modem over a standard phone line, typically cost $1 to $2 per hour for time you spend online. Some companies charge a flat fee of $20 to $30 per month including unlimited on-line access. Other more powerful types of access can run into thousands of dollars per month. How much you spend depends entirely on your needs.

There are five main types of Internet access accounts: UUCP, Shell, SLIP, PPP, and leased lines. With the exception of leased lines, all of them utilize transmission through a standard telephone line and a modem. We will explain the pros and cons of each one, including typical costs. In selecting your access provider company, be aware that all types of services are not available from every provider. Another related consideration in choosing an access company is the software you must use. It is software that tells the computer how to access and utilize the Internet, and it is the access provider that gives you this software. Some Internet programs are easier to use than others, depending on the type of account. Then, there is the matter of the telephone or long-distance charges you may have to pay. Using a modem carries with it the same charges as you would pay for any other telephone call. Some access providers also levy a surcharge. A number of the larger access providers, like Delphi, offer local dialup numbers in most major cities. Smaller outfits have dialup service only for limited areas or the one place where they are physically located. If you choose a company without a local dialup for your area you will be paying long-distance charges every time you log on. That in itself will cost much more than the fee you pay for Internet access itself. If you are on-line twenty-four hours a day as we are, those long-distance charges can quickly become prohibitive. It is, therefore, essential to choose a company that offers a local dialup for your area, if one is available.

UUCP

UUCP stands for UNIX to UNIX Copy. UNIX, you will remember, is the computer operating system or language that ties together most computer networks. UUCP accounts lack speed, flexibility, and availability of the more sophisticated Internet features such as Gopher and the Web. UUCP accounts also frequently charge on a per message basis, which can make them very expensive if you are doing extensive business on the Net.

UUCP is what is known as a file transfer system. Technically, it does not give you true Internet access. Instead, you dial into a remote computer, in this case the one owned by your access provider. This remote computer transfers the data from Newsgroups, as well as e-mail, and sends it back and forth from the Internet at regular intervals. When you log on, the data from your provider's computer is copied to your own, where you can then read it. If you want to send data out, the procedure is simply reversed. UUCP, then, really only gives you e-mail functions to the Internet. Even your Newsgroups come in the form of e-mail.

Direct access to the most popular search tools like Gopher or the World Wide Web are not available with UUCP systems. Neither will it allow you to engage in talk or chat. Most such accounts do have a method that allows you to research Internet databases by retrieving files on other systems through FTP. Once again, this is accomplished by sending an e-mail request to your UUCP access provider's computer. This computer then forwards the message to a second computer that does have a direct Net connection. It is the computer second down the line that actually carries out the search or retrieval you requested. Then the result comes back via e-mail to your provider's computer. There it will sit until you log on and retrieve it to your own computer. If the thought of all this makes you dizzy, it won't surprise you to learn that the process can take a number of hours or sometimes even days. When you have a more direct access to the Net, you can do the search yourself, perhaps in a matter of minutes.

The most important thing you need to be concerned with here is that the circuitous procedures of the UUCP system limits the type of marketing you can do. FTP by e-mail may allow you to research databases. It does not, however, allow you to create your own data sites that others can access. Therefore, you cannot develop Web or Gopher sites for your customers to reach. Remember, too, that everything on a UUCP account must go through sporadic e-mail transmissions which get sent out to the Net itself only as often as your access provider chooses. In many cases, that is only once a day. One thing computer customers don't like to do is wait, but they will have to wait with UUCP. Finally, let's not forget those charges. If you are retrieving a lot of data, perhaps as many as thousands of e-mail messages from your customers each day, the per message or per minute charges of UUCP accounts can run up a significant bill.

Why, then, would anyone ever want a UUCP account? There are two reasons that we can think of. First, these accounts are very simple to operate. The easy-to-use graphical software we discussed earlier that runs under the standards Windows or Mac operating systems is usually available free from UUCP providers. If you are an extremely inexperienced computer user, or are interested only in e-mail and very limited employment of the Usenet, these accounts may make sense. The other reason to choose a UUCP account is that it may be the only one available with a local access number. Remember, the business of providing Internet access is a new industry. The day when all types of services are available to everyone, everywhere, is in the future. Under most circumstances, the few advantages of a UUCP account rarely outweigh the many limitations. For cyber-selling, a UUCP account is not a good choice. If, however, you have other, less demanding plans in mind for your use of the Internet, or you simply have no other local dialup option, a UUCP account may best serve your needs.

Shell Accounts

Shell accounts are probably the most common type of Internet access. With them you can use the marketing techniques supported by e-mail and the Usenet. Like UUCP, you cannot create World Wide Web or Gopher sites with a Shell account, although you can access and look at the sites of others. All other Internet features, including talk and chat are available. They are also among the more difficult to use. With a Shell account, you are connecting to what is known as an Internet host computer. Since the host is used for heavy commercial purposes, it is very powerful. By using just your PC and a modem over a standard telephone line, you can connect with the host computer and utilize space on it, making that power your own and thereby getting access to most Internet features. By access, don't forget we mean you can look. As we said, you still cannot develop your own data site with a Shell account.

To tie into the host computer, which is the one you will in reality be using, you will need a standard communications program. Pro-com and Telix are the names of two such programs in wide use. When you operate a communications program, the only thing you control is whether your own computer sends or receives data. Other than that, your keyboard acts as if it was connected directly to the computer of your access provider. Your provider has actually set up a directory for you there. In fact, when you decide to store a file, you are storing it not on your own computer but on that of your provider. If you want to send e-mail, you must first place the message on his computer, and then send it. You cannot send anything to the Internet directly.

Shell accounts do not really give you a direct connection to the Internet. When accessing the Internet with a Shell account, your own computer is, in effect, a dummy terminal, but a Shell account is a giant step closer to the Internet than UUCP. The difference is easy to understand. With UUCP, data is simply being transferred back and forth between you and the Internet, with the access provider's computer acting as a stop along the way. With a Shell account, you actually obtain space on your access provider's computer for the time you are on-line. You can do almost anything from your computer that your access provider, with his heavy-duty equipment, can do. UUCP is slow and limited. Shells, utilizing the powerful host computer, can be quite fast and versatile. E-mail sent from a Shell goes directly to the Internet via your provider's computer in a matter of seconds. E-mail on a UUCP account sits on the provider's computer until someone or something decides to send it out, maybe once or twice a day. Shell accounts, besides affording you easy access to virtually all Internet goodies, are usually very inexpensive.

The word "Shell" is a UNIX term for a special kind of program. If you ever see strange names such as Bourne and Korn pop up on your screen, they simply refer to two of the more popular types of UNIX Shells. The software you use to access features of the Internet is the software on your provider's computer. Forget about Mac or Windows. Forget the programs you've installed for yourself. You are now using UNIX. The UNIX language, if you were to see it written out, would look to you like a series of weird codes and general gibberish. A UNIX Shell allows you to tell the computer what to do, using plain English. As we said earlier, UNIX is a powerful computer language but it is also quite advanced. Even though through the Shell, you can execute UNIX commands in words that will be recognizable to you, you still must learn those commands. Most of us are too busy struggling with DOS and Windows to digest UNIX in any depth. Never fear, however, you can master enough UNIX commands to meet your cyberselling needs without too much trouble. Alternatively, you can always fall back on the option of hiring someone to help you out until you learn what you need to know.

One of the most useful features of the Shell account is the ability to use UNIX scripts. Scripts are extremely simple automated programs meant to carry out special functions. We were able to place our Green Card message in 6,000 Newsgroups by typing only one word, "masspost," because we had someone write a script for us that would post that message to all groups automatically. The script then took over and sent our message to each group, one at a time, in a matter of about 90 minutes. To do this manually would have taken many hours, if not days. Script programs are written in English, not computer language. If you want to use scripts but don't have programming ability yourself, once again, think geek. If you're only interest, however, is in creating a script to post to the Usenet, just call us. No use reinventing the wheel.

As time goes on, more and more ways are being offered to free you from the need to learn even a few commands in the relatively complex UNIX language. Several access providers are now offering their own graphical software that will allow you to use commands from Microsoft Windows, translating such commands automatically into the UNIX language. All these programs feature easy "point-and-click" graphics. The next version of Windows is expected to have an Internet access program. At present, though, most graphical programs can be obtained only if you have your access account with the provider who developed the software. When you choose a company offering such a graphical program, you do not need to know any UNIX yourself. You don't even have to know that UNIX exists.

In many respects graphical software programs are a joy to use, especially for the person who is not technically oriented, but this ease of usage comes at a very significant price. As we explained in our chapter on the World Wide Web, graphics require the computer to operate huge files of electronic instructions. This really slows operations down. It has been our experience that these software interfaces cause your computer to work so slowly that handling volumes of mail or other data becomes virtually impossible. In addition, remember that with a Shell account, you are going through a host computer. This puts one more computer between you and the Internet, one more machine that could break down or garble the huge file of data graphical interfaces require. You are also limited to the particular features the software will allow, and that often means fewer functions are possible with your account.

In addition to the limitations of graphical software, there are other possible problems with Shell accounts. Your provider may limit the storage space you can use on his computer. A five or ten megabyte maximum is typical. If you exceed that amount, you may incur additional charges. Our main Green Card Lottery posting resulted in more than 1 gigabyte of mail in the first few days. This is equal to a thousand megabytes. Many providers charge a storage fee of a dollar per megabyte. Keep this in mind when comparing prices.

Graphical Shell accounts are great for personal use, to play with the Net, and learn how it works. You may want to consider one for your first steps into Cyberspace. You can certainly do Usenet postings from them. Windows even has a special feature called Recorder that allows you to write a script that will work on a Shell account without knowing how to program. It works by entering into memory a series of the keystrokes you first performed manually to achieve a certain function, and then playing them back over and over. In the long run, though, as you become more comfortable with the Internet we do not believe you will be satisfied with a Shell. You will then probably want to lose the pretty software in exchange for more power and flexibility.

SLIP and PPP

SLIP and PPP connections are answers to the limitations of the graphical software UNIX Shell account. SLIP, which stands for Serial Line Internet Protocol, and PPP, standing for Point to Point Protocol, are two relatively inexpensive ways to become your own Internet host. Here, for the first time, we are talking about acquiring a direct link to the Net. SLIP and PPP accounts, are, therefore, the first types of accounts that allow you to market by putting up your own Gopher or World Wide Web site in addition to selling with e-mail and Usenet. SLIP and PPP accounts allow full access to all Internet features.

For your purposes, assume that SLIP and PPP are similar. PPP is a more updated system and should work more efficiently that SLIP. Because it is new, however, there may be fewer software options available to take advantage of PPP's benefits. If you have a choice, you should probably select PPP. It's almost always best to go with the latest technology in a field where obsolescence happens so quickly.

SLIP and PPP, like Shell accounts, are available through dialup services. You may also choose dedicated access, a special phone line for use only with your computer. In either case, this time your access provider acts as no more than a connection point between you and the Internet. Your own computer connects out to the Internet by itself, again by use of special software. Once this is accomplished, your only limitations on what you can do on the Net comes from the software you select. Some good SLIP and PPP programs are available free on the Internet. Others can often be obtained at a nominal charge from your access provider. There are now a number of SLIP and PPP programs you can buy, which will run under both Windows and Mac. We've already told you how much easier it is to use software under these common operating systems than it is to function under UNIX. Commercial Internet access programs are sold at prices ranging from $100 to more than $400. The higher-priced programs usually allow you to operate your own network of computers, something you will want to consider as your financial success on the I-way grows.

Frequently SLIP and PPP accounts include a Shell account at no extra cost. The Shell account may be necessary in order to have a place to put your arriving e-mail when you are not on-line. Remember, with SLIP and PPP, you are now connected directly to the Internet. With Shell accounts, you have the advantage of an always on-line host computer, where your mail can come in and wait for you. With SLIP or PPP cutting out the middle man, the mail has nowhere to go while you are off-line. The addition of a Shell to your SLIP and PPP solves this problem. It also simplifies some of the processes you would need to undertake for the sending and receiving of mail and Usenet data. When you are on the Net alone, without the aid of a Shell, you normally have to create your own news and mail sending and receiving system, something well beyond the scope of a beginner. The addition of a Shell takes this big technical burden off your shoulders. Be sure to check if the SLIP or PPP access provider you are considering offers this important added service.

If you expect to be on-line for more than a few hours per day, rather than relying on a dialup account, it may be cheaper to get a dedicated telephone line for your SLIP or PPP access. The access provider can help arrange this at a flat fee per month. Costs for a dedicated line frequently involve initial setup fees of up to $1,000 and continuing charges of around $300 per month. You will then be on-line 100% of the time, and you will never have to dial into your provider to reach the Internet.

The main marketing advantage of a dedicated line is that you can allow potential customers to access your sales information through World Wide Web and Gopher 24 hours a day. It is certainly possible to set up Gopher and Web data sites without a dedicated line, but doing so puts real limits on your customer's ability to reach your information. They will be able to get it only when you are on-line. Keeping normal business hours is not enough when you are dealing with varying time zones around the world and customers that often don't turn to computers for recreation and shopping until evening. Let's also not forget the large audience of obsessive Netters who stay on-line during all their waking hours and traditionally never sleep.

Other than full-time on-line marketing benefits, dedicated access has the same features, good and bad, of any dialup SLIP and PPP account. The biggest limitation are the speeds of standard telephone lines and your modem. SLIP and PPP accounts probably can handle up to one thousand messages per day with respect to e-mail. In terms of Web or Gopher access the SLIP or PPP can comfortably accommodate one or two people at a time. If you think of this as a two-line telephone, that should tell you if it will accommodate the business volume you have in mind, or if you need to move up one notch to a leased line.

Normally with dedicated SLIP or PPP access you will want to register your own domain name. Domains indicate the name of the Internet host computer. Since you have a direct line to the Internet, in this case the host computer is your own. Our domain name is cyber.sell.com. As we explained in our chapter on e-mail, all Internet domain names end with designation of the type of business or organization owning the host computer. Com is used for commercial addresses. In the computer world, there is prestige attached to having your own domain. Registration of domain names is done through the Network Information Center (NIC), a private voluntary corporation affiliated with the University of Virginia. You can obtain an application for a domain registration by writing to:

Network Solutions
InterNIC Registration Services
505 Huntmar Park Drive
Herndon, VA 22070
Telephone: 703-742-0400

Most access providers will arrange this for you as part of their service.

Symptomatic of the Internet's still untamed character, name theft is now becoming a problem with domain registration. When a company applies to be given a certain domain name, InterNIC grants it to them without question, as long as that name has not already been assigned to someone else. It has now become common practice among those with questionable ethics to register the names of established companies that have not yet begun to do business on the Internet. The hope is that when these companies do discover the commercial potential of the I-way and want to register domains, they will buy back their own names from the techno-pirates, finding it cheaper to do that than sue. Coca-Cola, NASDAQ, and Viacom are among the companies whose names have already been pirated. When Cybersell™ went to register its domain name, we found that we, too, had been victims of this practice. The names of our own pirates will come as no surprise. Bill Fisher and Mike March of Internet Direct, the Phoenix access company that earlier had reneged on its promise to give us notice to stop before cutting off our access to the Internet.

ISDN: A New Breed

The reason why SLIP and PPP deliver data transmission that is relatively slow is that standard telephone lines weren't really invented for this purpose. Telephone lines usually handle what is called analog data, which works well for voice transmission. Computer data is digitized to occupy a much smaller space than analog data. Therefore, a lot more of it can go over a line at one time. The only problem is that a special line able to carry digital rather than analog data is required. Digital phone lines are only just starting to be installed around the country. The availability of these transmission lines is giving a high-speed twist to SLIP and PPP, called Integrated Services Digital Network, or ISDN. ISDN telephone lines carry data at a speed of 64 kilobits per second. Compare this with the 14 kilobits per second speed of so-called high-speed modems. An ISDN link to the Internet will operate 4 times faster than a traditional SLIP or PPP over regular phone lines.

One of the first companies to offer ISDN service is Performance Systems International, or PSI, located in Herndon, Virginia. They call their ISDN program On Ramp. It is available with either dialup or dedicated lines. PSI's fees for ISDN services are $2 per hour on a dialup basis and a flat fee of $400 per month with a dedicated line. Undoubtedly, other access providers will soon be offering comparable service. It does cost a bit more than dedicated SLIP and PPP access, but should be well worth the difference if you anticipate significant volumes of traffic from your cyberselling efforts. An ISDN account should be able to handle a number of different users at the same time with no sacrifice in speed.

SLIP and PPP accounts are excellent ways to connect your computer directly to the Internet. They give you all Internet marketing options and work well when only a few people are accessing your computer or sending you data at one time. However, if you anticipate having a lot of customers contacting you and many employees, all of whom need to be on the Net at the same time, SLIP and PPP will not be adequate, even with a dedicated line and ISDN. If you generate 30,000 e-mail responses in a few days, as we did, your messages are likely to become choked in the narrow bandwidth of your connection and you may lose much of your mail. For this reason, if you don't mind limiting your marketing feature to e-mail and the Usenet, you may be better off using a dialup Shell account. It will handle masses of e-mail better than PPP or SLIP, since you are getting the benefit of your host computer's strong Internet connection. Still, under any of these circumstances, your account remains subject to any restrictions placed on it by the access provider, and your allocated storage space may be limited. If you are handling the volume of messages that we believe is possible, you probably won't want to trust another company's computer anyway. You'll much prefer to control everything yourself. For that you need a leased line.

Leased Lines

A leased telephone line is the ultimate solution to marketing freedom on the Internet. It is a permanent connection between your computer and your Internet access point, usually an access provider. A leased line keeps your Net connection up around the clock. The size and power of your own computer is the only limitation on what you can do. Since you are on-line all the time and control your available storage by the capacity of your own computer disks, you may have hundreds of customers contact your computer directly to retrieve information through Gopher and World Wide Web Servers. All Internet features are available. With respect to speed, a leased line provides a full range of options. Speed of data transmissions is measured in units known as bits. You may select the speed or size of your leased line, ranging from 56,000 bits per second (known as a 56K line), to 1,540,000 bits per second or even faster.

This speediest of options is known as a T-1 connection. The faster the line, the higher the cost, but the greater the volume of traffic it can manage. A T-1 connection will probably set you back at least $10,000 in start-up expenses, including needed equipment. Another $2,000 to $4,000 per month will be spent in operating costs. However, you will be able to put hundreds of people on the Net at the same time. With a T-1, you can even rent out space on your own computer network to outsiders, thereby becoming an Internet access provider yourself!

In deciding whether to proceed with a leased line, you should keep in mind that, in addition to the higher cost, leased access also requires the greatest level of technical expertise. Leased lines are for those on the Internet fast track. It is unlikely that you will be able to set up your own system without a lot of help. A few hours of geek time aren't going to do the job. Using leased lines almost always requires you to work with networked computers, called Local Area Networks or LANs. These function best under the UNIX operating system. Although it is technically possible to do it with DOS, Windows, or Mac computers as well, the result will be disappointing. It is also more difficult to find leased-line Internet access than it is simpler types of accounts. If you are interested, we would suggest that you contact one of the following national Internet providers for assistance:

Performance System International
703-620-6651

SprintLink
703-904-2156

UUNET
703-204-8000

Choosing the right type of access and the right access provider is a difficult decision. Costs may narrow your choices significantly. If you are new to the Net, you will probably want to dip your toe into the water first before jumping in all the way. Shell accounts with graphical software programs are a good choice for this. If you are a bit more adventuresome, you may want to start with either a straight UNIX Shell or dialup SLIP/PPP. After you have been on the Net for a while and can see what direction your business is taking, you can better decide if a stronger and more expensive Internet connection is warranted.

A word of caution in evaluating costs: per hour fees on any type of account can mount up faster than you think. Long-distance charges, however, will probably add up even faster than the charges from your access provider. A number of access providers offer toll-free 800 dialups, but be careful. They always charge a per minute fee for the 800 service. This can sometimes be even higher than the actual long-distance charges. In considering the comparative costs, take a good look at your long-distance carrier's discount plans. Sprint, for example, offers a very large discount to the number you call most. Such discounts might bring long-distance charges down sufficiently to make an access provider, with many good features to offer but no local dialup, competitively priced with a local company.

Money-Making Prospects from the Commercial On-Line Services

We've already mentioned several times that the commercial on-line services are separate networks from the Internet. Due to the pressures of the marketplace, some of these on-line services are beginning to offer varying degrees of Internet access. Delphi and America Online, as of this writing, already offer Usenet access but are limited to excruciatingly slow modem speeds. Having a fast modem at your end doesn't help because you are still limited by the speed of the modem at the receiving end of your connection. Hopefully such services will be increasing their access speeds soon. Speed notwithstanding, America Online does not yet provide full Internet access. Delphi provides its own Shell accounts, but the cost is considerably more than you would have to pay for full access from other companies. CompuServe, another giant-sized on-line service, has plans to offer full Internet access in the very near future.

Although they may not be well connected to the Internet, the commercial networks are still part of the I-way and do offer additional money making opportunities. CompuServe alone has two million subscribers. The primary problem with promoting products or services on the private networks is the fact that their main reason for being is to make money for their owner. To accomplish this, they must charge you—a lot! If you already have an account with one of these companies and are not quite ready to get on the Internet itself, a good use of your commercial access might be a test run of your sales messages. All of these commercial networks have bulletin boards or forums, which work much like the Usenet. On certain boards, it is permissible to post commercial messages. Try it on those where such postings are allowed and see what happens. The numbers you will be reaching will be considerably less than with the Usenet itself. However, we are certain that you will have enough success to make you eager at the prospect of jumping in head first on the Internet. For those of you who have yet to make your first connection with a network of any kind, we believe that you should look at the commercial services as money making outlets only after you have established your main I-way storefront. Once you are firmly entrenched in the larger part of the market, you may then want to consider reeling in the important but much smaller group of potential customers who can be found on the commercial services.

The "Friendly" Provider

Remember that our objective here is getting rich on the Information Superhighway. We want to advertise. We are not accessing the Internet to read jokes, play games, or download sexy pictures. We may choose to do those things in our spare time, but that is not our primary purpose. You already know that due to the historical development of the Internet, many oldtimers are not happy about its recent commercialization. We've described some of the roadblocks we ran into during our first I-way ventures with the Green Card Lottery. We believe that we have helped pave the way for you. Still, not all access providers, knowing that your goal is heavy Internet marketing, will welcome your business. Pipeline and Netcom, companies that have their own proprietary graphical software for Shell accounts, were two of our own earlier access providers. Both were extremely uncooperative with our advertising venture. Netcom, a Bay area company, was even abusive, influenced no doubt in part from the veteran Netters in Silicon Valley with whom they are in close physical proximity.

As the National Science Foundation takes permanent leave of its authority over the Internet in April 1995, we will see greater tolerance for advertising. More and more people are starting to do what we did. Those providers who will not adopt an open policy toward advertising will soon have to change their tune, or risk perishing altogether. There are hundreds of Internet access providers. Until the dust settles in the commercialism controversy, check with any access provider whose service you are considering to find out company policy on marketing. If you don't like what you hear, waste no time. Move on.

14

DO IT YOURSELF OR FIND A GEEK

Maybe you're really turned on by what you've just read in the last two chapters. If, instead, the technical aspects of cyberselling serve only to bring on a violent headache, there is a solution—the geek. Geeks don't mind the use of the term. To them, it is not an insult but a badge of honor. Computer geeks aren't like you and me. Cyberspace may be a fictional place, but the true geek is trying to move there nonetheless. This probably accounts for the other-worldly aura that surrounds them and explains why they have difficulty communicating through speech. You probably knew a geek in high school or college. You remember, the one with the thick glasses and silly laugh. He who laughs last, laughs best. Now, thanks to the computer revolution, many geeks make ten times as much money as you do. Were you nice to the geek when you both showed up at your last class reunion? If not, you'd better change your attitude fast. At some point, unless you're already an Internet computer expert who can understand UNIX, you're probably going to need him.

How much technical expertise is required to make your fortune on the Information Superhighway? It really depends on where you are starting from and the degree of your dedication to knowing the technical end of the business yourself. If you've never even used a computer before, there is certainly some learning required, although, in the general scheme of things, not that much. If you can turn on your computer, operate Microsoft Windows or the Macintosh desktop, and memorize a few short commands, you can easily start a profitable marketing campaign with Usenet and e-mail. The Internet, however, is a vast resource and some of its features require more expertise than others. If you wish to venture out into sophisticated areas, such as building Gopher and World Wide Web sites, you may need some professional help.

Finding that help is not one of the easiest tasks you will ever face in

Cyberspace. Perhaps it is because the medium and technology are so new. Perhaps the old-time Netters want to keep you confused. You can't beat the independent feeling that comes from being able to do everything for yourself, but if you are eager to get started and don't want to take the time needed to scale the learning curve, finding some technical support may be the answer.

When we first landed on the Internet, we did it the hard way. We had been using CompuServe for a number of years, but the Internet was unexplored territory. No one told us how it worked. We didn't understand from a technical standpoint what access providers did. We weren't in the position to choose between types of accounts because we knew nothing about any of them. More to the point, we had found the name of only one company to call and so we called it. We managed to arrive on the Internet without much difficulty. We also figured out how to send individual e-mail as well as post to Usenet groups easily enough. Soon, however, we were faced with a situation we could not readily handle. Our earlier Green Card Lottery postings resulted in nearly 1000 responses and we had no idea how to deal with answering that kind of volume efficiently. We knew what needed to be done. We hadn't the vaguest idea how to do it. Shortly after our first Usenet postings, we got an e-mail message back saying "just what we needed, geeky lawyers on the Internet." Unfortunately, we weren't sufficiently geeky to solve our own technical problem. We need a technical expert to help us automate both the posting and mail answering tasks.

We started looking for our expert by studying the Yellow Pages. There was no shortage of listings under the heading "Computer Consultant." This was going to be easy, we concluded smugly. We were not concerned that none of the ads we saw mentioned the Internet. A computer's a computer, we thought. We started calling around. About half the consultants didn't know what the Internet was. Most of the rest recognized the term but had never actually accessed the Internet themselves. The remaining few claimed to know all about the Internet and to have had extensive experience. We began interviewing. Eight different allegedly experienced individuals came to our office. Seven could not identify the Usenet.

The Expert

Then there was number eight. He was a little more mature than the average applicant. He was not at all typical of the usually arrogant computer jocks that had been parading through our office so far. He was professorial-looking. He knew the Internet terminology better than we did (which wasn't saying much at the time) and he told us what an expert he was. He said he could have everything worked out for us within a week. He wanted a minimum of $2,000 for two weeks' work, half-time only. The Green Card Lottery would be over soon and we didn't want to lose a golden opportunity to get rich. We agreed.

Day One. Our secretary, who had worked with computers herself only a few months, had to help him install Microsoft Windows on the new PC we had just purchased. It didn't work, and Mr. E couldn't figure out why. We looked at the computer ourselves after he had fussed with it to no avail for several hours, and realized that DOS wasn't installed. Windows will not run on an IBM PC without DOS. Of course, you already know that. Our expensive computer consultant didn't.

Day Two. We opened a new Internet SLIP account. We didn't know what that meant, but the access provider had recommended it. This new program would put pretty pictures on the computer screen that we could point at, freeing us from having to worry about troublesome UNIX commands. Setting up a SLIP account requires a bit of technical knowledge. Actually, it's quite easy for anyone who has done it even once before, but somewhat confounding to those who haven't. The software used is available free from the Internet itself, meaning there are no instruction books or manuals. Mr. E was lost. He kept getting error codes every time he tried to log on to the Internet. He suggested that we didn't really need this fancy type of account and maybe we should try something "easier." He forgot that we chose SLIP because easier is exactly what it was supposed to be. Cheerfully, he told us not to worry. He was having the same problem setting up his own account at home. He said he was working directly with the access provider who would make it all better. We became nervous. When were we going to see a demonstration of his self-claimed brilliance? The clock was ticking on the Lottery program.

Day Three. Mr. E stayed home. He was waiting to hear from the access provider who would give him some pointers. We progressed from nervous to severely agitated. Later in the day, we called Mr. E and learned to our amazement that he had shifted mental gears. He was no longer concentrating on posting news and answering e-mail. Instead, on our behalf he was searching for a new pre-installed computer system, something we had never asked him to do.

Day Four. No Mr. E again. He was still waiting to be bailed out by the access provider, who still had not telephoned. He had tried to call us but couldn't remember the phone number, so he sent us a note via e-mail. Unfortunately, we were not yet able to access e-mail on the account he had used, so we never got the message. We pictured him lost and roaming aimlessly in the Arizona desert.

Day Five. Mr. E continued to await salvation from the access provider, but he came to our office anyway, bringing us up to date. It would take several more weeks to sort out these problems, he said. He could sense our distress. He then announced he had been studying the situation and we needed to work with a more knowledgeable access provider. He immediately suggested he could have us up and running in a matter of days with Prodigy. Prodigy, we happened to know, did not provide Internet access. When we pointed this out, Mr. E looked puzzled and hurt. He said that perhaps he had been given bad advice and would look into it further.

Day Six. Mr. E wanted his first week's paycheck, a day early. He then informed us that he would be attending a party the access provider was throwing the next day, where he would not only finally learn how to install SLIP, but where he would meet with the owner who had agreed to prepare special software that would allow us to easily mass post to Usenet and automate our mail.

Day Seven. At the party, a good time was had by all. Mr. E enjoyed himself, eating and drinking with the Netters. Some of the partygoers overindulged on the free libations and engaged in minor acts of vandalism. Pieces of computer equipment turned up missing and damage was sustained to a valuable potted plant. Complaints from the owners of the access company about the bad behavior of the partygoers appeared on their Gopher server the next day. In all the excitement, however, our new special computer program was somehow forgotten. "Don't worry," Mr. E told us reassuringly. If nothing else, he now knew how to install SLIP. We paid Mr. E for his week's efforts and fired him.

The Pseudo-Geek

Soon enough we hired expert number two. We found him through the word-of-mouth-network at a local university. He was in his late 20s, old enough presumably to have acquired some sense. He possessed the requisite long hair and T-shirt, standard markings of the true geek. In spite of this, the fact that he had a family to support indicated, we hoped, a modicum of stability. He also talked a great game. He had wonderful ideas—robo spammers, chat robots, World Wide Web, home pages with hyper-graphics, auto mailers—the works. He had, he told us, taught the local access provider how to set up its system. Pseudo Geek walked around with a laptop computer in hand, two cellular phones, and a beeper. He told us he was on retainer for big corporations and was flown all over the country to straighten out their computer networks. He had a little free time just then, however, and he would love to help us. He truly admired what we were trying to do. He could get the job done. Mr. Pseudo Geek got paid top dollar, he told us, but was so enthralled by what we were trying to achieve that he would do what we needed for the low fee of three thousand dollars. Having been burned once, we told Mr. P that we'd accept his terms but would pay only $250 a week until the work was completed. No problem, he said.

Mr. P would call on the phone and talk for hours. He loved to talk and he really loved Macintosh computers, so much so in fact, that he had never, we learned later, gone near an IBM. We had IBMs. He suggested we immediately replace all six of our IBM PCs with new Macs. We said no. Mr. P panicked for a brief moment, but then regained his composure as well as his pervasive, geek-like swagger. He said he'd develop the programs we needed. By that, we discovered, he meant he had friends who could create the programs. He informed us that certain people were prepared to do the work for him as favors because they all owed him. We didn't really care who wrote the programs. We waited. Nothing happened.

The problem was beginning to become clear. Mr. P could talk the talk, but he wasn't delivering. Certain kind souls had, apparently, pulled his fat from the fire in the past. No one was going to do it this time. After wasting several more weeks and another thousand dollars, Mr. P followed in the ignominious footsteps of Mr. E. Interestingly, several months later, after news of our mass posting had made the papers, the Pseudo-Geek publicly claimed credit for developing our mass-post program. Just to be safe, he also denied having any idea of what we were planning to use it for. Nothing had changed. Talk was still this guy's chief talent.

The Genuine Article

Our third attempt finally turned up the real thing. He was only 20 years old. He had started college but dropped out temporarily for financial reasons. Besides, all the hours he spent accessing the Internet left little time for school. Mr. Genuine Article had been cohabiting with a computer since he was nine years old. He absolutely loved computers, loved the Internet, loved UNIX, and thought the $12-an-hour salary we offered him was a fortune. Mr. G designed all the programs we needed in a matter of days.

He was having so much fun, it didn't really matter much to him whether he was paid or not.

Mr. G was not, however, problem-free. As with most geeks, his ability to communicate on a real-life human level was limited. He evidenced no appreciation of our business concerns. He was operating on a different level. As long as our needs and his happened to coincide, all was well. If he had something better to do, we had to wait. We've told you about the Net fanatics we encountered. Mr. G was one of them. In addition to getting our programs written, he undertook to indoctrinate us with the gospel of the Net. "We must respect the Internet," he would preach to us. We didn't much care for being lectured to by our twenty-year-old employee, especially when he was telling us it was morally wrong to mass-post to the Net, even as he was having the time of his life creating the program that would help us do it. The program worked, as you already know, but when the media took hold of the story, our Genuine Article began to fear that his friends on the Net would find out the role he had played and ostracize him. No other form of banishment could be worse. Mr. G flew back out into Cyberspace where he came from. He requested anonymity and we were happy to oblige.

Hard Lessons

Even though it took a while, we did finally manage to find effective help. It may have been no picnic, but the results were worth the effort. If you don't want to learn about computers and the Internet yourself, there are geeks out there you can hire to do the work for you. Moreover, you can benefit from our experience. We found out a lot that should help you to avoid our mistakes. Anyone can call himself a computer consultant. We discovered that most who do know little more than how to use a few mainstream computer programs, like the ones with which you probably are already familiar. In the case of some, like Mr. E, even that is asking too much.

Be aware that you are looking for help in an area of computerdom that is so new, there are relatively few people who know their way around it. Don't make the mistake of believing, as we did, that someone with extensive general computer experience is at all familiar with the Internet. The Internet, its programs and functions, are highly specialized. You, yourself, now know a little about the Usenet, the World Wide Web, and other assorted special Internet features. If you run into a computer consultant who is unable to talk knowledgeably about these subjects, don't assume that because of experience in other areas, he will be able to figure out the

Internet any better than you can. We learned the hard way that just isn't so. When you interview a prospective geek for hire, ask direct questions about the Internet specifics we've described to you. If you see no sign of recognition in your prospective consultant's eyes, go on to the next candidate.

An Internet expert knows UNIX. There is a special problem in finding the right kind of help in this area because UNIX comes in so many different versions, some operating only on larger computers than you can't buy at the local computer store. Although all UNIX versions are similar, there are sufficient differences that someone with experience in one cannot be presumed to know how to work with another.

There are all kinds of people out there billing themselves as computer consultants, and the prices they charge careen wildly over a huge spectrum. If someone asks you for a fee of $100 per hour and tries to tell you that is the going rate, don't listen. From everything we have observed, there is no going rate. More important, a high price tag on a consultant's time is no assurance that you are getting what you pay for. Just because someone has a lot of degrees or years of computer experience doesn't mean he or she should automatically be paid a high salary. The ability to produce results in a specific area, the Internet, is what counts. Fancy credentials are in themselves meaningless. In negotiating with computer consultants, arrange for payment based on results, not time. Anyone who is a true expert will have confidence in his or her ability to get the job done and will not mind being paid on this basis. Those who object to being paid only for results are telling you they aren't sure they can deliver. The technical knowledge you will need for executing the marketing techniques we've described in this book is not extensive. The most unusual thing we required was the writing of the simple script that did our mass-posting. Unless you are trying to achieve something truly exotic, a real Internet geek should be able to help you reach your goals quickly and easily. Anything else is an unnecessary waste of your money.

Overall, your best bet in locating an effective computer geek is to contact a college or university. Try the student employment office or go directly to the computer department. Remember, these days almost every institution of higher learning provides Internet accounts to its students free of charge. While knowledge of the Internet may not yet be widespread among the public in general, it is common to college students. When there is a computer department at a university, there is usually a veritable hotbed of geekdom. You are much more likely to find people who know the territory here than anywhere else, and the prices they charge, pizzas included, are usually quite reasonable.

Stereotype humor aside, many computer wizards have unusual personalities. If you want to hire someone who is really good with computers and the Internet, you may find the individual possessing such skills difficult to deal with. A cousin of ours who is head geek for a large New York financial firm says all of them suffer from attention deficit disorder. Real computer buffs tend to care only about the fascination they find in exploring areas of the computer field they deem interesting. Your deadlines and business requirements mean little to them. Often, even money doesn't provide a truly effective incentive for giving you what you want. If you find a truly talented person, it is worth it to show some tolerance for the quirky geek personality. At the same time, you must be firm or you will find yourself covered with geek footprints. It often takes a strong and forthright approach to get through to someone living in Cyberspace. When your geek flies too far into orbit, say what you must to bring him back down to earth.

Your own skills, time availability, and personal preferences will dictate how much you rely on the technical skills of others. There is help out there if you want it. You just have to look until you locate the right person. Perhaps you will decide to delegate all the computer chores to someone else and concentrate only on marketing and other aspects of your business. It is possible to do this and make a fortune on the Information Superhighway without ever knowing how to operate a computer. Maybe, though, you will become fascinated with computers and want to master it all yourself. Books, computer tutorials, classes, and your access provider can all assist you in learning what is essential. To engage in cyberselling you don't need to be a computer engineer. In addition to helping you get started, one thing a geek can do is teach you what he knows, so that eventually, you won't need him anymore. The day you say good-bye to a geek will probably bring you warm memories for the rest of your life.

15

CRIMES IN CYBERSPACE
Why the Net Needs You

You've now learned what you need to know about how to make a fortune on the Information Superhighway. You understand why it works so well and how to execute the marketing techniques available. You have a fine, salable product or service ready to go. You are aware of what you can expect in the way of both risks and rewards and you've made the decision to go forward, even though there are forces in Cyberspace who would like to stop you. All of the information we've given you so far is related to solid, practical considerations that can lead to a satisfying financial result. Now we'd like to offer you a not-so-practical reason for seeking your fortune on the I-way: Cyberspace needs you. When you've finished reading this chapter, it won't be hard to see why.

Our own trip down the I-way has been an eye-opening experience. Not only have we had the opportunity to find an excellent money-making method, we've also gotten to see first hand the influences that computer technology is having on society. The speedy availability of enormous amounts of information can fuel any number of worthwhile endeavors from comforting the sick to curing the disease that created the need for comfort. The potential for good is truly wondrous. But, like the Old West with which analogies are often drawn, Cyberspace is going to take some taming before it is a completely fit place for people like you and me to spend time. There is a small but extremely vocal group that will do almost anything to keep out the new settlers.

The Community That Isn't

It is important for you to understand well that the Cyberspace community is not a community at all. It is simply a huge and heterogeneous group of people accessing the Internet for an endless variety of reasons. A lot of folks watch television for entertainment. That doesn't make them a community. A lot of people go to the library for either entertainment or educational purposes. That doesn't mean all library patrons form a community just by checking out a book. Almost everyone uses a telephone. Picking up a receiver does not equate with the instant purchase of a residence in Phonesville. The Internet is no more than a library, entertainment center, and telephone all wrapped up into one. You don't join a community by using it.

The idea that there is a separate Internet community with special laws and standards of behavior differing from those that you will find in actual society is a notion harking back to a set of circumstances that no longer exists. In the days when the Internet was only a way for defense department employees to communicate among themselves, there was arguably a small and like-minded enough group to which the term community could be applied. Even when usership expanded to include academic and industrial researchers, there were still severe limits to the vocations and group affiliations of people who could access the Internet. It was understandable, then, why certain conventions arose that were well suited to the interests and temperament of most Internet users at that time. The National Science Foundation's no-advertising policy existed primarily because the U.S. Government cannot, by law, finance private commercial ventures. Still, the computer geeks loved the idea that they had something of value which the slick, commercial outside world couldn't touch.

Then, the Clinton administration got into the act, developing a split personality about the Internet. On one hand, they were thrilled to have it around. They could see in it the potential for a badly needed boost to the sagging economy and an even more badly needed tool for improving the American educational system. It became Al Gore's adored baby and he talked about it like a proud papa everywhere he went. As much as the Clinton people loved the Internet, they hated paying for it. They were willing to do anything to encourage its growth except spend money. The baby needed to be offered up for adoption to the corporate parents who could afford its support. Once commerce was allowed on the Net, supplying Internet access became a legal business in which to engage, and the general public began to come in droves. It was then that the vanishing community of original Internetters started down the path to extinction. When we refer to the Net community in this chapter please understand that we use this term for convenience, and are talking only about the small, mainly academic and technological community established before the Internet opened to the general public. The limited group that sees itself as the Net community has little to do with the tens of millions of users who participate in the Internet today.

Above the Law

The reaction of the already entrenched Netters to the influx of new users is a mixed bag of negatives. In these days of uncontrolled Internet expansion, the Net community often finds itself provoked. Some are satisfied to express their displeasure in a legal and civil manner. Others take the next step and become electronic sociopaths. The death threats and mailbombs that were aimed at us are only a sampling of what the Net community can do. We soon learned that forged messages are a common Usenet practice. In our own case, people would electronically sign our names to messages that we never sent. One of those messages advocated the assassination of President Clinton. We, however, are hardly the only ones to experience this sort of activity. The regular Netters, many of whom are college students, find the practice extremely amusing and do it all the time. They do it so much, in fact, that they have succeeded in creating an atmosphere of paranoia amid themselves. They live in an world of doubt, constantly questioning the origin of any message they receive.

Those who don't want to be bothered with the creativity that forgery demands simply send messages through the Anonymous Server located in Finland. We mentioned this Scandinavian-based computer earlier as a vehicle by which pornography can be distributed without fear of police intervention. Another major use of the Anonymous Server is for the purpose of defamation. The Anonymous Server can "launder" messages in the same spirit that money is laundered through small Caribbean Island nations. Once sent through the Finnish computer, no one can tell where the message came from. In short, you can say anything you want about anyone, true or false, and never have to worry that a lawsuit will deter you from acting unethically.

Being able to do things with complete anonymity in an environment already free of any real rules invariably creates the potential for abuse. In a well-publicized software piracy case not too long ago, the FBI was unable to arrest most of the perpetrators because they were sending the software all over the world via the Anonymous Server in Finland. If the FBI couldn't trace it, it's doubtful anyone else could either. Still, the Cyberspace crime family is not safe, as you will see.

Among the most flagrant criminals in Cyberspace are the hackers. The hacker stereotype is well known: young, male, brilliant, introverted, badly dressed and poorly socialized. Like most stereotypes, the perception of the hacker as a human cartoon isn't altogether accurate. Still, one thing does seem to be typical of many hackers, they don't care about breaking the law. The two most famous examples of this are Craig Neidorf and Michael La Macchia. Neidorf went down in the annals of hacker fame for stealing a program that detailed the operations of Bell South's emergency 911 telephone system. For this Neidorf was arrested and convicted, although he received only a year's probation as punishment. Michael La Macchia, an MIT student, ran an electronic bulletin board out of an MIT workstation. At one point, he invited his subscribers to post to the bulletin board software manufactured and sold by private companies so that anyone wanting it could simply take it free of charge. The companies who produced the software viewed this as piracy and La Macchia was criminally indicted. Somehow, it seemed the dark forces of "evil" at work in the American criminal justice systems did not understand, as did the Net community, that distributing stolen property was a noble endeavor.

In his book *Cyberia*, which chronicles the behavior of the Cyberspace culture, author Douglas Rushkoff paints a chilling picture of the computer devotees who deem themselves part of the entrenched Net community. In describing the crimes of the hackers, Rushkoff quotes former Arizona assistant attorney general Gail Thackery. "I see a ruthless streak in some kids. Unlike a street robbery, if you do a computer theft, your victim is unseen. It's a fiction. It's an easy transition from Atari role-modeling games to computer games to going out on the network and doing it in real life." Maybe the hackers can't tell the difference. The rest of us, including law enforcement authorities, obviously can.

Sex, Drugs, Rock 'n' Roll

Probably the most publicly condemned behavior practiced on the Internet has to do with sex. We've already described the vast array of pornography readily available on the I-way that has parents up in arms and police in hot pursuit. Here is yet another example. In July of 1994, Robert and Carleen Thomas, a California couple, were convicted of sending pictures showing acts of bestiality and sexual fetishes over a computer bulletin board they ran out of their home. They charged $99 a year for their services. Business was apparently good. Very good. The pictures reached everywhere. In Tennessee, where the California state of mind that tends to accept almost all manner of alternative lifestyles isn't operative, the pictures didn't play well. Internet users there complained. The court that tried the case was located in Memphis. The Thomases were convicted of 11 counts of transmitting obscenity over phone lines. Each count carried with it a jail term of up to five years and a fine of $250,000. The Net community was outraged.

California also leads the way in another favorite pastime of the Net community: drugs. In spite of the "Just Say No" initiative of the '80s, the as yet unfinished war against drugs still rages on, with so-called designer drugs coveted as boutique items and psychedelics enjoying a major comeback. While Net denizens are hardly the only group engaged in heavy drug use, they are in the forefront of the movement. Based primarily in San Francisco, maintaining close proximity to Silicon Valley, the true believers engage simultaneously in computer development and substance abuse. Indeed, they see a relationship between the two. Just as LSD is purported to expand the mind with new perceptions of the world around you, connectivity to the vast reaches of the Internet supposedly does the same thing. Just as you may shape your computer environment through virtual reality, so too can your real surroundings be altered to suit by taking the correct combination of drugs. It is not for nothing that drug takers of today call the acquisition of new insights they receive by distorting their minds with chemicals "downloading."

To those of us who were there for the first psychedelic drug wave in the '60s, the repeat performance with a computer twist that we are now witnessing is as funny as it is frightening. Timothy Leary, the tune in, turn on, drop out professor of LSD who was a '60s icon, is being trotted out for another round of hero worship by the young computer crowd. This dubious intergenerational role model is now past seventy. Douglas Rushkoff explains that it is trendy among the Net set to buy psychedelic drugs in the parking lot of a Grateful Dead concert and then spend the evening tripping to the rock and roll of these men who are old enough to be their fathers. He describes such a scene, following the activities of a typical drug dealer. "Leo is an LSD dealer from the Bay Area who believes that his distribution of psychedelics is a social service. Leo [at a Grateful Dead concert] is well into his own acid trip of the evening (he says he's been tripping every day for several months) and sits in a makeshift tent explaining his philosophy to a young couple who makes falafel and beaded bracelets. He does express the psychedelic concept of interconnectivity and networking from a modern cyberian standpoint." Observing this incredibly exact replica of the '60s hippie scene being recreated thirty years later by the children of the generation where it was first formed, you really don't know whether to laugh or cry.

Taking Charge

Some members of the inbred Net society may like to take drugs and break laws. All of them love wielding power. It is standard propaganda of the Net community that no one controls the Internet. A picture is drawn for outsiders of a Utopian village where the residents function peacefully together without the restraints of formal control. In practice, however, human nature takes over, and there are none more determined to run the Internet than members of the presently entrenched group. If you think about who makes up the old Net community, it is not difficult to understand why this is so. The Internet started as a government pursuit and soon evolved into a purely research environment. Every person on the Internet came from a strongly academic background. Free accounts at universities promoted heavy usership among students as well as faculty. Even when industry got involved, it was only the research and development people who were permitted, by law, to be Internet participants. The Internet population, then, was made up almost entirely of people who in our society often receive among the least in the way of worldly recognition and financial rewards. The images of the nutty professor, the weird scientist, the nerdy computer hacker, best fit the public perception of who the Net community was.

Enter Vice-President Gore and suddenly a favorable and extremely bright spotlight was turned on the Internet under the sobriquet Information Superhighway. And who were the experts in this new medium that was fast becoming an obsession with the international press? The nerds! Suddenly, they were yanked from their normally obscure life into prominence. The newspapers sought their quotes. Publishers sought their manuscripts. People wanted to know what hackers thought. Howard Rheingold, a San Francisco-based journalist who is one of advertising's fiercest critics, wrote about members of a Bay Area network called the WELL (Whole Earth 'Lectronic Link) of which he is part and parcel. The WELL, another group near to Silicon Valley, appears to be still one more throwback to the sixties—a commune with a computer spin. Rheingold, Rushkoff, and all the other Internet genre writers related the adventures of the Netters, new objects of curiosity who gave themselves nicknames like Acid Phreak, Phiber Optik, and Poptart. (Nicknaming is a standard Net practice, a custom similar to the one observed by CB radio operators, although we doubt any CBer ever saw the wisdom in calling himself "Poptart.") A librarian at Boston College wrote a book about how to do business on the Internet. This university denizen who had been in an academic environment for the past twenty years, was often quoted by the press as an authority on her subject, even though she'd worked in business hardly a day in her life. The Net community had come into its own.

Also catapulted into prominence were two organizations representing the Net community: The Internet Society and the Electronic Frontier Foundation. The Internet Society is currently composed of 3700 members, corporate and individual, most of whom are either college students or computer technology companies, their leaders and employees. The Internet Society originally contented itself mainly with a very important job. It assumed the highly complicated technological task of keeping an enormous international web of computers, all using different languages and different operating systems, networking successfully. It set uniform technical standards to insure that this would be achieved. It further undertook to see that new applications for the Internet would be developed. Now, faced with Internet usage from people who are not Net community insiders, this private organization of individuals who banded together voluntarily and have received public sanction from no authorized source, are preparing to issue a set of behavioral standards for you, the Internet user, to follow.

Now, you might think that with all the electronic vandalism, criminal activity, profanity and pornography being sent over the Net, that the Internet Society would be coming up with standards aimed at controlling this objectionable behavior. If that is what you believe, you are wrong. The Internet Society decided standards of behavior were necessary as an immediate and direct reaction to our own mass posting. These codes of behavior appear to be designed mainly to insure that they maintain business control of the Internet for themselves.

If you want some idea of what the Internet Society's standards of behavior are, consider the case of Brock Meeks. Mr. Meeks is a freelance journalist who writes for a number of computer publications. Early in 1994 he took pen in hand against Benjamin Suarez, a direct marketer who owned a company in Ohio. Mr. Suarez offered a plan for money-making on the Usenet. Mr. Meeks, concurring with the widely held belief of the small Net community that any company advertising on the Usenet must certainly be crooked, decided to call Mr. Suarez a few choice names in print. Mr. Suarez, not thinking of himself as a crook, but simply as a businessman placing an advertisement, sued Meeks for liable. Immediately the Net community began coming up with reasons why defamation laws should not apply to speech on the Net. Freedom of speech would suffer, they contended, if people using the Internet had to demonstrate the same sense of responsibility for their words as everyone else does who chooses to badmouth another. The Internet Society promptly began a Brock Meeks defense fund to insure that this would not happen. Conveniently, they forgot that the First Amendment applied to Mr. Suarez when he advertised just as much as Mr. Meeks when he wrote about it.

The Electronic Frontier Foundation is another private group. Their alleged purpose is advocating freedom of speech on the Internet. The organization is the brainchild of Mitch Kapor and John Perry Barlow. Kapor is a recognized Net guru, former hacker, and founder of the Lotus Development Corporation, one of the most successful software companies in the world. Barlow is a Wyoming cattle rancher and another recognized Net guru. He is best known, however, for his place in rock and roll history as a lyricist for—the Grateful Dead! Both men, long past the need to be concerned with the state of their finances, were disturbed by the fact that the FBI had begun to consider hacker infiltration of government materials a problem. They feared this would bode ill for freedom of speech in Cyberspace. The EFF was born to protect the hackers.

In May of 1994, believing that the EFF really did support freedom of speech in the same broad and democratic manner as did the ACLU, we initiated a discussion with Mike Godwin, an EFF lawyer. We wanted his views on the censorship issues raised by the behavior of electronic vandals and access providers who had pulled our account for performing the perfectly legal act of Internet advertising. We were amazed when Godwin stated to us that he was so busy sympathizing with those who opposed us, that he had no sympathy left for the other side. So much for freedom of speech. Considering the Meeks case, it was becoming ever more apparent that, according to the Net community, just about everyone was entitled to First Amendment protection except advertisers. In July, 1994, Godwin who, by this time, had expanded his duties to include becoming a contributing journalist for *Playboy* magazine, offered a portion of his limited sympathy quotient to the enterprising Robert and Carleen Thomas. Upon learning of their conviction on multiple counts of disseminating pornography, Godwin told the Associated Press that the judge's decision represented "one community attempting to dictate standards for the whole country." Mr. Godwin seemed not to realize that, unlike the Internet Society and other loud voices in the Net community, the Memphis judge who sentenced the Thomases wasn't trying to dictate standards. He was upholding the law.

Occupying positions as front men of the Net community are the Internet access providers. Most of them as individuals find their roots in the old Internet guard. Vinton Cerf, the president of the Internet Society, owns the access company CerfNet. James Gleick, author of the computer classic *Chaos*, owns Pipeline, where we had one of our early accounts. Yet, for all their purity of origin, the fact is that the access providers are, in large part, responsible for and profiting handsomely from the influx of newbies. This, however, also puts them in the unenviable position of having a foot in two opposing camps.

The role of the access providers is especially uncomfortable when the Net community asks them to assume the task of controlling the pesky newcomers. Whether Internet access providers should or should not be able to control the speech of those who use their services is an issue that will certainly lead to lawsuits. When you consider that the Internet is a free resource, it hardly seems appropriate that private companies who have no proprietary connection with the Internet should decide what those who access it may and may not say. Nonetheless, they try. In our own case, two companies, Internet Direct and NetCom closed our accounts. Others didn't go that far but simply insisted we curtail our activities. The refusal of access providers to limit their role on the Internet to that of a common carrier which, like the telephone company, does nothing more than convey communication without censoring content, is a truly terrifying aspect of how the Internet is now operating.

What is more frightening still, however, is that there are many access companies that would prefer to take the non-judgmental role of the common carrier, but the members of the Net community won't let them! In every case, when we encountered a problem with an access provider, it was because that company had been pressured to stop us. What they stated to us in private and their public stance were very different matters. When the church of the Internet warns that an access provider may be excommunicated, it is no idle threat. Some of the smaller providers we had used were told if they did not stop us, their Usenet signals would be cut off by the universities that controlled them. Our current access provider, PSI, the largest company of its kind, immediately became the subject of much open criticism from the Net community the minute we opened an account with them. A number of administrators from other network systems made it clear that if PSI cooperated with us, they would block any messages that came from PSI customers. When PSI threatened to sue any systems administrator who tried it, a new plot hatched. This one came from Austin Kelly at the University of Chicago:

Since PSI feels that they can threaten administrators at will, isn't it time to threaten them appropriately? I understand that PSI is wiring Cambridge and, I would bet, has bids in to wire lots of other towns. If your town happens to be one of them, shouldn't you send a note to your elected representative, town council, local newspaper, etc., questioning whether or not this is the kind of outfit you want being approved to provide you access?

Once again, the Net community displayed its disrespect for the freedom of others, especially when faced with the unpleasant prospect that a company might choose to deal in an even-handed manner with those whom it considered its enemies.

As we investigate the wielding of power on the Internet, it is easy to see the limited size and unlimited inbreeding of those who claim leadership. EFF founders Mitch Kapor and John Barlow are active participants in the WELL electronic commune, where Internet writer Howard Rheingold is a leader. Ex-WELL director Cliff Figallo became the first director of EFF when it opened its Washington office. EFF attorney Mike Godwin writes columns for the Internet Society News. The Internet Society makes sure that access providers, all of whom are Society members, uphold the party-line philosophy, and so it goes. As the waves of outsiders continue to roll in, the little, besieged Net community hangs together, trying to consolidate its hold on the Internet in the glare of the public spotlight.

Original Sin

Each individual has his or her own personal idea of what constitutes the most deeply offensive type of behavior imaginable. In Cyberspace there is much to choose from. For us, we found the canceler robot as reprehensible as it gets. The application period for the Green Card Lottery was nearing its close and we went about the business of doing one last Usenet posting to alert possible clients that time was running out. We completed the posting but, unlike before, we got few responses. We wondered why. In short order, we learned that a twenty-five-year-old Norwegian computer specialist had written a program designed to cancel automatically the Usenet messages of whomever he chose. Whom he had chosen was us. We were getting no replies because all the postings we had put up were gone before anyone could read them. Usenet is designed in such a way that the only one who is able to cancel a message is the person who posted it. In order to eliminate our messages, the "cancelbot" as it came to be known, had to first electronically forge our name and then perform the standard cancellation procedure.

When we learned what had occurred, we immediately put the postings back up. Since the so-called robot didn't really work automatically, the Norwegian had to expend time and effort in seeking our messages out. Each time he canceled them, we would post again. The messages would stay up for a brief time and some inquiries would come in before they were once again canceled. This game of tag kept on until the deadline for the Green Card Lottery registration was finally over.

There is no telling how many clients we lost because of the canceler robot. To view it from the customer's perspective, it is hard to estimate the number of people who might have wanted information on the Green Card Lottery but were unable to get it. Everyone was stopped due to interference from an individual who had no consideration for the rights of parties on either side of a transaction that was none of his business in the first place.

The most striking feature of the cancelbot episode, however, was what it showed about the attitude of the Net community. As soon as word of the Norwegian cancelbot reached the press, Peter Lewis of *The New York Times* wrote an in-depth article about examples of censorship on the Net, with the canceler robot incident as its centerpiece. A picture of the Norwegian, the long-haired, T-shirted, bespectacled self-appointed protector of the Net appeared for all to see. Lewis pointed out the seriousness of the questions raised by one person's ability to silence another on the Internet at will.

The Net community responded to the cancelbot episode with a staggeringly shameless display of hypocrisy. When Prodigy had tried to respect its large audience of children by limiting the use of profanity, the Netters were outraged. When a University of Florida student had had his Internet access yanked by the school for repeatedly posting copies of a political argument, there were screams of protest. When Brock Meeks and the Thomases were silenced by the courts, the Net community flew to their defense under the banner of the First Amendment. There was no criticism, however, for the cancelbot. The Internet Society, would-be purveyors of standards for Internet behavior, said nothing. Equally silent was that alleged bastion of free-speech advocacy, the Electronic Frontier Foundation. Individuals in the Net community were not silent. The old gang immediately climbed on their soap boxes in the various administrative Newsgroups where they usually aired their thoughts, and began praising the Norwegian as the man of the hour. Not one of them saw anything wrong with what had been done. None of them seemed to understand or care that free speech, in order to remain free, must be for everyone equally, not just those who said what they wanted to hear. The Norwegian himself expressed surprise to the press that his actions had found no critics among the Netters. We were not surprised. We'd seen this two-faced attitude before.

It seems, however, that there may have been more to the cancelbot story than we'd suspected. Along with congratulations all around, there were constant suggestions in the various Newsgroup threads discussing this matter to the effect that the Norwegian hadn't thought up or executed the cancelbot plan on his own. As talk continued, it was stated that he'd had a lot of help from his counterparts in the United States. It was further suggested that the Norwegian had been especially selected as front man for this operation because he was located an ocean away from us, where we could never reach him with a law suit. Whether or not there was a well-thought-out plot behind the canceler robot is something we'll probably never know. There is one thing, however, that does emerge crystal clear. The entrenched Net community knew, when it supported the canceler robot, it was advocating actions prohibited by the laws in most real communities. It knew it was going against the most basic principle on which the American culture rests. That didn't matter at all.

Joining enthusiastically in the criticism of our money-making efforts were others who themselves actively engaged in earning large sums off the Net. While a number of access providers, acknowledging their own commercial interest, had expressed to us their reluctance to limit our activities, others were not as egalitarian. Some, like NetCom, a company whose attitude was no doubt shaped by its proximity to the Bay Area Silicon Valley crowd, expressed particular distress that we had been able to make money from the Internet without having to pay someone for advertising. They had no problem, however, when they took money from us and everyone else to gain entrance to the Internet, which was supposed to be a free resource.

Attacks from other Internet businesses followed. A company called Meckler was developing a Web site aimed mainly at blue chip companies. The charge to be part of it is a minimum of $25,000 per year. Yet, a representative of Meckler appeared on an NBC news feature discussing the Internet and criticizing what we had done. Perhaps the gentleman was sincere about the views he expressed or perhaps it occurred to him that if others did what we had done, there might be fewer customers for Meckler.

We'll let you decide for yourself. Meckler also puts out its own Internet publication called *Internet World*, where we were often criticized. One of the most scathing articles there was published by the ubiquitous EFF lawyer Mike Godwin, who, in choosing his editorial stance, never mentioned that Meckler and Cybersell are direct competitors. Indeed, most of the publications serving the Net community jumped on the bandwagon. Every one of these publications is a money-making venture that profits from the Internet. Every one profits from advertising. If we'd advertised on the Internet in exactly the same manner as we had before, but paid an Internet insider for the privilege, we presume they would have found such a situation eminently satisfactory. In fact, one writer, Bob Metcalfe of *Infoworld* even applied for the job. Metcalfe offered his suggestions on how to "handle" the situation we created. His solution? "It's also time the Internet got itself some publishers—like me . . .—who can afford to pay their editors by carefully selling the hard-earned attentions of their readers to advertisers." All those interested in paying Bob before you decide to advertise on the Internet, contact us and we'll be happy to refer you to him.

Over the months that followed our mass-posting, we read or heard about an endless number of Internet money making schemes. Many of them tried without much success to differentiate their plans from ours. The premise that except for what Canter and Siegel did, anything goes, is not one that will stand up to much scrutiny. Don't tell that, however, to one Joel K. Furr. Mr. Furr, a student at Duke University, came up with a truly creative idea for making money on the Internet. He produced and sold T-shirts about the Green Card lawyers who spammed the Net for profit. Can you guess how Mr. Furr chose to market his product? Sure you can. He posted advertisements to Newsgroups on Usenet. Look around the I-way and you will see a grand array of money-making projects underway. Everyone engaged in his or her own electronic gold rush understands very well that advertising on the Internet is bad—unless, of course, they're the ones doing it.

Nowhere are the pervasive double standards of the Net community more evident than in the application of Netiquette. Those who feel the newbies require initiation into the sacred order of the Net usually begin the process by trying to imprint the plebes with Netiquette basics. Once again, because currently recognized Net authorities come from the old guard, they are the ones to whom the press turns when they need input for the endless number of articles now being written about the Internet. This set of circumstances provides an excellent opportunity for the Net community to spread propaganda on Netiquette. Most of the Netiquette rules that receive press coverage have to do with behavior while posting to Usenet. Here is the standard dogma:

1. Spend several weeks reading the Newsgroups in which you are interested before contributing any of your own messages. That way you will have an idea of what is going on and will, therefore, be better able to make yourself fit in.
2. Don't ask stupid questions. "Stupid" refers to those questions that have been asked before. Each group maintains an FAQ file (frequently asked questions). It is strongly recommended that you read these before saying anything that your new found Net friends might deem offensive.
3. When replying to a Newsgroup article, summarize the article to which you are replying so others will be able to follow the conversation.
4. Don't put a word in all capital letters. It's considered shouting.
5. Don't break the law by posting copyrighted works.
6. Keep your messages short.
7. Don't post off topic of the group.
8. Don't clutter up Newsgroups with empty statement such as "me too" or "I agree."
9. Don't use poor grammar and spelling.
10. Don't flame someone who uses poor grammar and spelling.
11. Don't post private messages meant for one person to a Newsgroup.
12. Keep your signature short.
13. Don't be rude and abusive to others. Be polite and show some consideration.
14. Keep in mind that what you are saying is public and will be read all over the world.

Whew! If you had to worry about that much every time you opened your mouth in the real world, you would probably never say anything at all. It is equally true that if everyone to whom you spoke criticized your behavior for failing to follow all these rules, there would be more fist fights than conversations. The arrogant tone here is not hard to perceive.

The rigorousness of the Netiquette rules offers at least one possible explanation of why the Net community, so anxious to see you indoctrinated, doesn't follow those rules themselves. If you tune into a Usenet group, recalling the elements of Netiquette we've just listed, you will see that asking you to abide by them is a question of "do as I say, not as I do." Netters stray from the topic being discussed all the time. They are routinely rude and abusive. They reveal the contents of private e-mail whenever it suits them. Making fun of someone else's bad grammar or spelling is common. In fact, it has been a widely made observation that because those engaged in computer conversations are not standing face to face with the people to whom they are "talking," they tend to lose their inhibitions and behave more rudely than they ever would otherwise. Sometimes they try to excuse themselves. Among the most widely used phrases you will find as you peruse Usenet groups is, "I know I shouldn't be saying this, but . . ."

The very existence of the practice of flaming demonstrates the dual standard by which the Net community routinely operates. Flames, as you already know, are critical and insulting messages. Now, we've all told off a few people in our day, when they've really deserved it, and so, we're certain, have you. But flaming in Newsgroups is not limited to the rare outburst. In Cyberspace, flaming is the national pastime. Let us consider the following typical flame exchange. This one is taken from the *alt.flame.hall-of-flame* Newsgroup. In it, one Netter reposts a conversation between two other Netters whom we'll call Mr. X and Mr. Y. Mr. Y has his Internet access account with America Online (AOL). Apparently, Mr. Y had criticized AOL's posting system. Mr. X thought Mr. Y's comment stupid. He, therefore, concluded that Mr. X must be a newbie and sent him an unsolicited beginners' guide on how to act on the Internet. Here Mr. Y lets Mr. X know he was not happy to receive the guide and Mr. X demonstrates his disdain for Netiquette as well as Mr. Y.

```
Newsgroups: alt.flame.hall-of-fame
Subject: A nice one

. . . .

Mr. Y   Obviously, I'm not the first person you've sent this
        [new users guide] to, and it seems I'm not the first
        person who has been offended by your accusation of
        ignorance.

Mr. X   It wasn't an accusation of ignorance until you began
        your whiney little tirade. It isn't even an accusation
        of ignorance now. It's a simple fact, one that you have
        proved beyond the shadow of a doubt: AOL users in
```

general, and YOU, in particular, are worthless, whiney, clueless fuckstains who should be driven off of a tall bridge on the ''information superhighway'' and left to crash to the jagged rocks below.

Mr. Y   Maybe you should take the angry responses to your mailing as a clue.

Mr. X   I have. I now am clued to the fact that you're the stupidest whiner I've ever corresponded with.

Mr. Y   If you want to be helpful, perhaps you should ask first if the person would like your assistance.

Mr. X   Sure thing. I'll send mail to guy who probably doesn't know which button to push if he wants to answer it. Brilliant fucking idea, son.

Mr. Y   Certainly better than randomly sending off mail that says, ''First of all, welcome. [. . .H]ere's a little introduction I wrote a while back for new users,'' to someone who has a definite history with the Internet and is by no means a new user.

Mr. X   Ohhhh, would YOU QUIT FUCKING WHINING ABOUT HOW GODDAMN EXPERIENCED YOU ARE?

If you were not a novice, you'd know better than to get this hissy-pissy attitude with someone who, I remind you AGAIN, was trying to help you.

Mr. Y   I skimmed through your little guide and found the tone to be overwhelmingly condescending and the advice to be barely useful to someone who had been online more than a week.

Mr. X   Yes, fuckstain, it might appear so. But if today was your first time online and you don't know what the fuck you are doing, it won't help you very much if email you source code for a newsreader and tell you to compile it. It WILL help if you know how things work, where to go for help, etc.

Mr. Y   Nobody wants that kind of help . . .

```
Mr. X    Do me a favor. Since you represent only
         1/5,500,000,000th of the population of the earth,
         don't tell me what ''nobody'' wants.

         Here is your final clue, pal.

Mr. Y    I'm not your ''pal.''
```

We don't think we need to comment further on the above exchange. It speaks eloquently for itself. There is, however, one additional point to make about flaming. It is more of a departure from Netiquette than first meets the eye. In many cases a flame will have nothing to do with the topic of the Newsgroup in which it appears. When a flame war erupts, the rule that Newsgroup discussions must be kept on topic is quickly forgotten.

You may have noticed in the argument between Mr. X and Mr. Y the use of words in all caps. The fact that, according to Netiquette, they were supposedly shouting at each other, is no worse than their other infractions. It does, however, raise some interesting questions not only about whether Netiquette is observed, but whether a special code is really necessary for behavior on the Net.

The argument has been made that all Newsgroup messages, because they are mainly text, require conventions such as the "capitalization is shouting" rule so that nuances of the speaker's meaning can be transmitted without the listener having the benefit of hearing voice intonation or observing body language. There are other symbols meant to serve the same purpose. For example, if you type a colon, followed by a dash followed by a closing parenthesis, you get :-), which is called a smiley. Turn this page ninety degrees to your right and you will see why. A smiley at the end of a sentence indicates that you were only kidding about what you just said. If you replace the parenthesis with a capital D and you get :-D, a smiley that is laughing. Replace the colon with a semi-colon and you get ;-), a smiley that is winking. Had enough? We don't blame you.

We do not feel any sort of special convention is required for successful transmission of ideas on the computer. After all, expressing thoughts through writing is nothing new. Think of newspapers, letters, or the book you are now reading. If we put a word in all caps, will you feel we are shouting at you, or will you understand that we are trying for EMPHASIS? If we mean something in a joking manner, can you tell that from context, or do you require the use of a smiley face lying on its side to make you understand? We have great faith in your ability to perceive the meaning of written words without extra help from the folks who bring you Netiquette.

Likewise, do you really need a special code telling you to mind your manners when you turn on your computer? If you resent the condescending attitude inherent in Netiquette, you are not alone. You probably learned more than enough about how to be polite and considerate to others from your parents, even though clearly the parents of some Netters didn't have much success in that regard.

During our own experience with the Net community, we have been constantly surprised at the pervasive lack of ethics we have witnessed. We have been even more surprised, however, that this group, most of whom deem themselves intellectually superior, fail to see that anything is wrong here. In the weeks that followed our universal posting to the Usenet, complaints were sent to both the Tennessee and Arizona Bars, attacking our law licenses. Our home address was published on the Net with a suggestion that our house be burned down. Numerous messages forging our names were circulated, one, as we've already mentioned, containing a death threat to the President of the United States. Lies of all kinds filled the "administrative" Newsgroups where most of the discussions on our activities were taking place. If the Net community didn't like the facts as they were, they simply changed them until the scenario that emerged suited them better. They repeated constantly that we had received no positive replies to our Green Card Lottery posting, although they were certainly in no position to know. In the next breath they would change their position and threaten to report us to the IRS if we did not pay the taxes on all the money we had made from advertising on the Internet. Those who favored electronic dirty tricks speculated with relish on the horrible fate they planned to inflict on us. We also started to receive hate mail expressing bigotry for both us and the clients we represented. Hundreds of magazines and mail-order products we never sent for arrived at both our home and office, in an effort to clog our mail box and cause us inconvenience. Through it all, no one in the Net community ever acknowledged that such acts were both immoral and illegal.

None of it really came to anything. Our house is still standing. The Tennessee and Arizona Bar Associations quickly concluded we had done nothing wrong and so informed the parties who had written the complaints. Predictably, this immediately triggered discussion in Newsgroups of plots on how the Net community could harass members of the uncooperative Bar Associations. As for the hate mail, the fact that there are bigots loose in the world is always disturbing but, sadly, nothing new. We haven't even canceled all the magazine subscriptions. Some of them are interesting and quite useful. Overall, we went on unscathed. The only thing that remained with us and does so until this day is the unshakable conviction that the Net community is the last bunch on earth who have the right to tell anyone else how to behave.

As we went through the process of getting to know those with whom we were dealing, an obvious question kept going through our minds. What *was* their problem with advertising? Aside from those who had an obvious financial interest in stopping us, why did they care so much? People could scream at each other, lie, swear, and break every rule of Netiquette. That was just fine. Perhaps courts of law didn't condone stealing, slander, and pornography, but the Net community would defend it to the death. Freedom of speech was, theoretically, an Internet sacrament, but not when it came to advertising. In their zeal to stop us, the Net community never gave one ounce of consideration to the rights of the thousands of people who very much wanted to receive our messages about the Green Card Lottery. When magazines subscriptions and other items were falsely ordered in our name, no one gave thought to the money being lost by the innocent publishers and manufactures who sent the unwanted goods. The Net community had a point to make. It was us they wanted to attack, but if someone else got hurt in the process, so what?

On occasion, we would ask some of the calmer-voiced protesters who called in how they justified the fact that nearly every form of human behavior, kind or unkind, honest or dishonest, legal or illegal, was condoned by the Net community except advertising. The answer we got most often was that, well, maybe mailbombings and bigotry and other forms of sociopathic behavior were not exactly right, but advertising on the Usenet was so terrible that those who did it deserved anything they got. One young gentleman, whose name we never knew, summed it all up. Yes, he said, electronic vandalism, arson, pornography, and the rest were all sins. But advertising? That was original sin.

Flying Like Superman

Think about the description you've just read of what we call the Net community. Where do you fit in? Chances are good that, like us, you don't. The one feature that distinguishes the Net community from the rest of those who access the Internet is that for them, the Internet is the dominant force in their lives. Many who belong to groups like the Internet Society and the Electronic Frontier Foundation, have made a career of the Internet. Others, although they do not earn a living from the Internet, have adopted it as their home away from home. They access it every available waking hour that they aren't forced to be elsewhere. Much has been written about the strong emotional attachment certain individuals develop to their computers and the possible harm inherent in substituting a mechanical relationship for the personal kind most of us have in the real world. When you consider the exaggerated role the Internet plays in some lives, the reasons why there are those who have violent reactions to an unfamiliar presence on-line, become, if not more tolerable, at least easier to understand. We have no interest in passing judgment on those who make the Internet a near obsession. How people choose to live their lives is their business, as long as they don't harm others. The Net community crosses that line on a regular basis.

We hope you've found your darkside tour of the Net community informative. It is always valuable to see all aspects of the environment in which you are dealing. What we did not intend was to scare you. There is no reason why the crimes in Cyberspace should intimidate you, even though that's what they were meant to do. Those who deem themselves part of the Net community are in the overwhelming minority. Of the tens of millions of Internet participants, probably less than a few thousand exhibit the criminal or anti-social behavior we've described here. Only a very small group are prepared to trade their homes and families on earth for a room with a view of the I-way. It would certainly be better for all concerned if the strident, criminal factions in Cyberspace were gone. Like our real-world society, there are some elements we could well do without. Still, the number of those who commit crimes in Cyberspace is small. They are just very noticeable because, in addition to being the most undesirable, they are also the loudest.

Owing to the fact that they were the first to develop and populate the Internet, a certain group of professional computer researchers and academicians have assumed the role of authorities on the subject. It is to them that the press turns when they need commentary for their endless outpouring of I-way stories. Accordingly, the opinions of one tiny group are heard over and over again. The millions of Internet users who don't share the same view are not asked what they think, and most of them don't place enough importance on the battle for control of Cyberspace to participate. The Internet is, after all, just a convenient way of sending and receiving information. To most, it hardly seems an all consuming passion worth fighting over. What a relief to know that is how the majority sees this wonderful new tool. What a welcome breath of sanity. It is time everyone knew the feelings of the majority.

We know very well that the millions of people on the Internet don't hate advertising. If they find merit in the product or service you present, they will buy it. They will not become psychotic over the posting of an advertisement to a Newsgroup. They will not take it all seriously enough to think there is a moral issue involved. As we watched the Newsgroups where discussions of us were going on, we saw the same names appear over and over again. In all but about five of the approximately 10,000 existing groups, talk stopped a few days after we posted. Looking at the final numbers, we received somewhere over 20,000 polite e-mail requests for information. We received about an equal number of flames. Of these, often several hundred or even several thousand would come from a single person. Strictly counting heads, the vote came out in our favor. What, then, can we assume about the 9,600,000 who didn't bother to weigh in on one side or the other? We can assume they went out and mowed the lawn, caught a movie, or read a book. Then they got into bed and went to sleep, totally unaware that the Internet community believed it was facing Armageddon in the form of a 191-word Usenet posting.

Of the supposed moral issue, there is little left to be said. Making money on the Internet in whatever way seems best to you is not a moral question as long as you conduct yourself with basic honesty and obey the law. The inappropriateness of those who are at best rude and at worst criminally inclined dictating standards of behavior to others is all too obvious. The attitude of those who make large sums of money from the Internet but don't want you to do the same should not be tolerated. Anyone who dislikes you simply because you are new on the block or will not play by their rules is not worthy of your consideration. You don't owe them obedience because they were there first. You don't have to buy into their rituals. You were taught good manners years ago. You don't need to be reprogrammed. The Internet is public property. It belongs to everyone equally. Go about your business and leave the childish squabbles to those who have the time and inclination. There is no avoiding the contempt that the Net community has for commercial enterprise on the Internet. Go ahead and make your fortune anyway, secure in the knowledge that most people who access the Net are not part of the steadfastly anti-commercial Net community.

Not long ago Penn Jillette, one half of Penn and Teller, the popular magician duo who often appear on television, wrote a column about the evolution of the Internet. Jillette, a nine-year Internet veteran, gave two examples of the influx of undesirable new elements onto the Net. We were one of them. The other was Teri Hatcher, a stunning actress who plays Lois Lane in the television series "Lois and Clark: The New Adventures of

Superman." Jillette, it seems, did a guest shot on an episode of "Lois and Clark" and during the course of the taping, Miss Hatcher, learning of Jillette's Internet expertise, invited him to her apartment so she could learn more about it. Was Jillette happy to help out? Was he gracious? No way. He was suspicious of Hatcher's motives. He waxed sarcastic, observing that Hatcher could certainly, to use his words, "do better than a big ugly son of a bitch with a square head" like him. He complained that she wanted him only for his Net access. Then, he exultantly addressed his Internet compatriots about how great all of this was for them. "She invited me because I know people like you! Get it? It's more proof that we have won. The beautiful people want to be us. Even our Deadhead vice president is talking about how hip it is to be on the Internet." Jillette worked Teri Hatcher over verbally for a few more paragraphs before moving on to us. When he was finished, he concluded that once the advertising lawyers and the Teri Hatchers of the world wanted onto the Net, the party was over.

Well, there it is in a nutshell. The "nerds" want the "beautiful people" to want to be like them. When the smoke clears, it's an old story. Those who view themselves as underdogs want to be on top. Everybody wants control. The Net community thinks, or at least hopes, that because you want to be part of the Internet, you must be like them. The fact is you don't. Personally, if we had to pick a role model we'd be more partial to Superman. Besides being strong and able to fly, he's also a law-abiding citizen and a really nice guy—more than you can say for many members of the so-called Net community. Anyway, Superman was created by a fellow named Jerry Siegel who, we're sure, must be a long lost relative somewhere down the line. Whoever it is you may admire, whatever your personal code of behavior, you don't need to transform yourself in order to utilize the Internet. On the contrary, the Internet is lucky to be getting you. There are some on the Net badly in need of a good influence. You have every right to seek your fortune on the Information Superhighway. If anyone tells you otherwise, let them know it's a bad idea to tug on Superman's cape—or the hem of Lois Lane's skirt.

16

WHAT IT MEANS TO BE A PIONEER

When you become a cyberseller, you're jumping head first into uncharted territory. The Internet and other parts of the I-way are a new frontier, and it has been said that those of us who are among the first to undertake its exploration are pioneers. If the word *pioneer* conjures up romantic images of the Wild West, wagon trains forming circles to protect the settlers from attack, singing around a camp fire, and looking up at the stars while feasting on the day's kill, well, that's not at all what Cyberspace is like. This is about as far from a natural setting as you can get. The only similarities to the Old West you'll find here are a small degree of lawlessness, and the desire of most I-way travelers to see a better tomorrow for themselves and their families. In that, the goals of cybersellers and others on the computer frontier are one.

The computer revolution, especially the spread of networking, is impacting society like no other recent event in history has. As a business person, your future success will depend on how well you understand what is happening and learn to fit in. We're going to end the description of our plan for making a fortune on the Information Superhighway with a tour, not of the future, but of the present. While we describe the computer-driven changing scene, think of what opportunities you might find for yourself there.

You can begin by realizing what many technical developers of the Information Superhighway can't grasp: The basis for pioneering is usually economic. This is as true for the frontier of Cyberspace as any other. Even in its relative infancy, the computer revolution is affecting the worldwide monetary picture. Countries fail or flourish based on the extent of their ability to develop and apply computer technology. The stark contrast between rich and poor, both individuals and nations, is reflected precisely in the differences found between the technological haves and have nots. Even in the United States, we have seen our economic fortunes rise, fall, and then rise again with new achievements in the computer field. Alan Greenspan, chairman of the Federal Reserve, has pointed out that our nation's salable output is consisting more and more of information products like computer software, instead of durable goods like automobiles. The world's best and most advanced computer components and software are now invented and manufactured in the United States. America is also far ahead of its industrial peers in overall computerization and networking. As a result, this country, after several decades of falling behind less developed nations in manufacturing jobs, has again taken a leadership role.

The computer revolution is not only good for our country as a whole, but for you as an individual as well. Computers have put us back on top, and as a result, you, the marketer, now have many healthy areas of the economy in which to operate. Moreover, if you are a business person just starting out, you won't need huge amounts of money to stand a chance of success. The emphasis on information means your ideas will be valued as much as your ability to raise venture capital. The Information Superhighway, where you have ample opportunity to market any product or service you can think of without a huge cash outlay, is the perfect example of this principle in action.

Your Work Life

To plan how you can take your place as a successful pioneer on the computer frontier, you must look hard at the impact computers are already having on daily life. Most of us sense what is happening, but never really give much thought to its dynamics. Let's step back for a moment and observe the events taking place in our world that, among other things, probably led to your reading this book. Computers are taking over, much as science fiction accounts of them that proliferated in the 1950s predicted they would. In the workplace, the resulting decrease in the need for human labor has completely and permanently altered the job market. Alan Greenspan observes that the need today for the physical labor of the unskilled worker has all but disappeared. Everything is done by machine and even the machines are operated, not by people, but by computers. The well-paid assembly-line worker is becoming a thing of the past. And why not, when the jobs of 100 semi-skilled workers can be replaced by a handful of highly trained technicians and a computer or two? Even a simple job like that of cashier in a fast-food restaurant requires some computer ability. More and more, finding work is tied to computer skills. Prospects for the computer illiterate are becoming increasingly bleak. It is equally true that the future is bright for any who will take the trouble to absorb the necessary knowledge.

Nowhere is the influence of the computer more apparent than in the office. Word processors have cut the need for secretarial help easily in half. Automatic banking machines, not live tellers, now hand us our money and receive our deposits. Telephone voice-mail systems have replaced switchboard operators. So pervasive have these systems become that many of us face on a daily basis the frustration of never dealing with a live person. Everyone has experienced telephone gridlock, where answering machines leave messages for other answering machines and two people who need to have a discussion can never reach each other. However exasperating we may find this, it is clear that anything that can be mechanized will be mechanized.

Even those who do so-called "white collar" work are not immune to the effects of computerization. Accounting software has greatly reduced the need for bookkeepers and accountants. A business that fifteen years ago required a full-time bookkeeper can now manage with one person entering data into a computer for an hour a day. Desktop publishing programs and high-quality laser printers are significantly cutting into the sales of the printing industry. With graphics software, an artist can put together a complex design for a magazine or book cover in a few minutes without ever picking up a pencil or paintbrush. No matter, it still takes the artist to develop the concept. The articles for the magazine cannot write themselves. As we said in the beginning, computers can't think. Intellectual ability and human creativity are not devalued but heightened by what the machine can achieve.

Computers are not only eliminating certain types of office workers, they are eliminating the offices themselves. Virtual offices, where workers spend most of their day at home or in their cars, telecommuting with portable PCs, cellular phones, pagers, and fax machines, are becoming commonplace. Such virtual offices depend on networking capabilities just like the ones supporting the structure of the Internet. A corporate buzzword of the '90s is "downsizing," the term given to cost reduction strategies. Virtual offices accomplish this goal. Not only has computerization enabled many companies to lower their work forces without decreasing work production, but, with virtual offices, physical plants can be made smaller, saving on rent and other office overhead. As more employees work away from the physical office, the location of that office becomes less important, and companies may save even more money by putting plants in lower-rent districts. Meanwhile, you get to stay at home and avoid rush-hour traffic.

Everyone today is dealing with the realization that to keep up and stay competitive, computers absolutely must be integrated into his or her daily existence. If you are contorting your face into a grimace at this prospect, stop. It is not a difficult or unpleasant adjustment to make. Remember the vast difference between inventing a computer and learning to use one. The learning process can be interesting and exciting. The evidence of this is how readily people are making computers a part of their home life. Surprisingly, the fastest growing segment of the personal computer market is not for business, but home use. Instead of buying a set of encyclopedias for the children, parents now purchase a personal computer, and, by the way, an entire set of encyclopedias can be had on a CD-ROM disc for less than $50. IBM recently made the startling announcement that selling to the home market will now become its top priority. Most schools have already accepted the reality that learning how to use a computer is as much a necessity as knowing how to read and write. Instruction in computer operation has evolved from an educational innovation into a basic, and the kids love it.

As you contemplate these changes, do not imagine finding your economic place has become more difficult. To the contrary. If you will think about the scene we've just described, you won't covet the jobs computers do. Most of them are tedious. That's why computers were invented, so that you could escape boring tasks and perform work taking full advantage of your talent and intelligence. In addition, the more situations change, the more chances for those who make the most of the changes to prosper. While computers eliminate many jobs, they also create others. Whole new industries are springing up. Someone, after all, must make the computers, program them, service them, and, of course, operate them. Someone must train the operators. Someone must even take on peripherally created jobs such as office relocation for downsized companies. The increasing reliance on computer networks gives rise to the need for businesses like our own that adapt services traditionally obtained elsewhere to the new networking facilities. The computer marketing plan we've described for you here is only one way of profitably fitting into the technological evolution taking place.

Your Personal Life

In personal terms, a common condition of Cyberspace frontier existence is a marked reduction in face-to-face human contact on every level. The advent of the virtual office means the absence of water-cooler camaraderie. The growth of the virtual mall means a decline in the social sport of mall crawling. Video conferencing, still in its infancy, will all but eliminate the need for most business travel. Time with the family may increase, but interaction with everyone else will become more and more dependent on the computer itself. Computers as communication devices, when depended upon too much, seem to detach us from our fellow man, creating a feeling of emptiness and a craving for interpersonal connectivity. This has been observed in some of the larger corporations, such as IBM and Arthur Anderson, during their efforts to convert many of their employees to telecommuters. Suddenly, the executive who finally gets the corner office after years of climbing the corporate ladder finds it taken away. Instead, as a reward, he or she is sent home with a PC and a modem. The satisfaction of walking through oak-paneled hallways with the admiring eye of those with lesser positions turned in his or her direction is taken away. Ultimately, if users are eased into this new situation carefully, they usually grow to prefer the freedom offered by the virtual office. Still, there is a wrenching change in the adult system of relationships and rewards to which we are accustomed. It may be that in the near future, one way of making a fortune on the Information Superhighway will be to offer new face-to-face gathering places to those who have been on-line one day too many.

For those to whom computers are becoming a drug, they can never get enough. Cyberfanatics living in their virtual communities on-line, breaking away from their computer screens only long enough to sleep, are the new addicts and there are plenty of fortune seekers who unwittingly act as their supplier. That computers enable a person to interact with others but not to really see or talk to them is a mixed blessing. The painfully shy or those suffering various physical and psychological disorders may thrive in a computer environment, where they can maintain a high degree of privacy. They also may lose incentive to deal with problems in a direct manner. The practice of flaming is thought by many psychologists to be a manifestation of the particular type of personality that built the Internet and now uses it as a shield from the real society where they feel unwelcome. For those who really want to envelop themselves in their computer terminals, several companies are now contriving so-called virtual-reality helmets. This headgear puts a small screen directly before your eyes, providing a 3-D view of Cyberspace, while blocking out the physical world completely. For those who watched the futuristic murder mystery, *Wild Palms*, on television not long ago, you may have seen such a device demonstrated. Like much high-tech fiction, it is all closer to reality than you might believe.

The fact that computers can isolate people from face-to-face encounters is widely recognized as one of the main reasons Cyberspace crime is so rampant. Those who are comfortable using computers draw a sense of power or control from the experience. Some handle the power correctly, deriving from it a useful, confidence building experience. To others, like the Cyberspace criminals we've described, power is a feeling with which they are unaccustomed and they misuse it. This is a dangerous situation that must be controlled. By bringing real-world law to the computer frontier, there are attorneys whose fortunes are starting to be made addressing these serious problems. Those who mourn the passing of the early days in Cyberspace, nostalgically thinking of it as a golden era, will be relatively few. The anarchy that is the old buzzword for freedom on the Internet is giving way to an order and values that are comfortable for its new, wider audience. As the transition progresses, everyone will have increasingly better opportunities to make a fortune on the Information Superhighway.

Beating Computer Phobia

Perhaps the biggest challenge of the computer frontier is to eliminate computer phobia. Don't imagine this is just a casual or humorous term. It is a real problem and there is now a whole raft of psychologists studying it. People seem to be either enamored of or completely repelled by computers. Many enjoy using them because they provide direct and immediate feedback. If you make a mistake carrying out a computer function, you'll find out about it right away. Likewise, if you do something correctly, you'll get the instant reward of seeing it work. Those who don't enjoy feedback find computers their natural enemy. If they make a mistake, they'd rather not know. Computers don't allow for that kind of escape unless you turn them off.

Everyone who may be computer phobic can take heart in the fact that a good deal of the fear originally came about from a difficult situation that no longer exists. Computers are not inherently user friendly. It takes a lot of specialized know-how to make them that way. In past years, as computer processes became more complex, the knowledge required to operate them increased as well. Original programs like those that run the Internet were written by computer technicians for their own use. They didn't care if others could understand how to use them. In fact, they may even have preferred to keep it all a convoluted mystery in order to ensure their own technological supremacy. Those not falling into the geek category, then, were somewhat at the mercy of programmers, who might or might not choose to undertake simplifying the incomprehensible.

In today's computer world, populated not only by the technological elite, but by just about everyone else, a goal of programming is user friendliness. Since most civilians are now insisting on access to all the advantages computers and computer networks offer, there is plenty of motivation for the technology crew to pursue this objective. The greatest fortunes in the computer business have been made by those who have devised effective solutions to the user friendliness problem. Thanks to this profit-driven initiative, extensive technical skill is not even close to being necessary in order for you to find your place in computerdom. The complexities of UNIX we have so feverishly tried to shield you from in this book were faced by all computer users until Apple came out with point-and-click graphics. Even typing, which had been so essential to efficient computer use, is now less important with the advent of Mac and Windows. As a result, children who can barely read or write, let alone type, can now be taught to use computers. Learning about computers at such an early age insures that it becomes second nature. The generation growing up now and those that will follow won't ever have to deal with computer phobia.

Staking Your Claim

As the excitement over computers and computer networks grows, what everyone with a pioneer outlook is going to see is not a lessening of job possibilities but a broadening of opportunity for wealth. Prospects for those tuned into the computer revolution, even in a largely non-technical way, will skyrocket. The gap will continue to widen between the technology haves and have nots, but that is no different from what happens in any age to those who choose to let new developments pass them by. Today's technology "haves" are well educated, with promising futures ahead of them. As a consumer group, they are among the most desirable for marketers to reach. Soon, it is inevitable that cyberselling will be the main way marketing is done. A report from Forrester Research Inc. of Cambridge,

Massachusetts, has predicted that on-line shopping will grow more than 20-fold between 1994 and 1998. What other words of encouragement need be said to you, the computer marketing pioneer, than that.

The early pioneers faced a dangerous existence. They didn't experience the romanticized frontier we all enjoy watching in movie westerns. Instead, they underwent tremendous hardship for one main reason: the federal government literally gave away land by the acre, to anyone willing to stake a claim and work the property. Homesteading typically resulted in ownership of 40 acres or more. That land was about as raw as it gets. No electricity. No roads. No well-mapped-out plan for the future. The earliest settlers formed the foundation of great wealth for their descendants, but struggled mightily in their own lifetimes. In Cyberspace, the homesteading race is on. Hoards of anxious trailblazers are prospecting for the best locations in Cyberspace. At the moment, everything seems up for grabs. We've staked our own claim. We've explained to you how to do the same. While you may need some of the pioneer spirit to get involved in cyberselling, the good news is that you won't have to live in a tent and brave the elements to make your fortune. The worst you will have to deal with is some misguided electronic vandals and the foolishness of a few flames. You won't be laying your life down for the enjoyment of your grandchildren. You'll see results quickly. That's one thing about the I-way, it's built to make things move fast.

Anything can be sold on the Information Superhighway. As for how to go about it, you are limited only by your own imagination, and, in this early stage, where the newness of the medium makes even the most standard marketing practices controversial, acceptance of your role as a pioneer. We advise you to act fast. There is still plenty of room, but the ground-floor opportunities won't last much longer. Fortunes are in the making right now. The largest retailers are starting to move in. A new position being established in the upper management levels of the retailing giants is that of Director of Interactive Technology. It takes no contemplation at all to understand what that means.

Right now, all companies, even the big ones, are starting out on the Information Superhighway from largely the same place. In a sense, all fledgling business ventures involve pioneering. Every new product or service is initially an experiment. The smartest business gurus cannot flawlessly predict the future. Companies spend millions test marketing products before offering them to the public. In spite of those efforts, many new products fail. The largest companies can ride out the failures, but most of us can't. This is the single biggest reason start-up businesses falter. It's not because some big company necessarily knows something they don't. Rather, the cost of trial and error eats up resources faster than revenues come in. One of the most attractive features about I-way marketing is that it is so inexpensive, you can afford to make mistakes. A small business might drown in the cost of a few big city newspaper advertisements. On the Internet, the expense of experimentation, test marketing, and general advertising, becomes negligible. The single greatest resources required are no longer money, but creativity and the willingness to try something novel. You can give your pioneering instincts full range of expression without risking the family farm in the process.

In our own experience, we just took a product with which we were familiar and brought it to an audience we thought would want it, and we were right. If we had been wrong, we could have survived nonetheless. We didn't have to worry about spending a year's worth of house payments on advertisements. Not only did our voyage on the I-way cost very little, but we found what we were looking for. Cyberselling works! We made a fortune, and we got an amazing bonus, too. We discovered a completely new and largely uncharted world where you can sell virtually anything at minimal cost. The so-called Green Card incident defined the future of I-way commercialism for nearly everyone, friend or foe.

Those who invented the I-way technology are understandably reluctant to see their creation pass into the hands of others. Sadly, they won't take the wide public use of their invention for the compliment that it is. They can't understand that unless their creation is utilized to change lives for the better, it will never be more than a technological curiosity. Those who utilize the I-way for all sorts of purposes, including marketing, will complete the job the computer technologists began. Cyberselling is the future of marketing. We've tried to share what we've learned with you so you can be among the first to try it out. We encourage you to stake your claim to your piece of Cyberspace. Cyberselling is new. It is unknown. Think back to those early homesteaders and the vast family fortunes that were created. Some people say there are no more good opportunities left in the world, but how can you know about the Information Superhighway and still believe that is so? Sit down at your computer and begin the journey to a dazzling future for yourself and your family. Not only will you make a fortune, but you'll have a good time on the trip.

SAMPLE USEGROUPS

ab.general
ab.jobs
acs.magnus
adobe.market
ads.comp.periphs
ads.comp.systems
ads.comp
ads.config
afmc.cmd.pol
air.bboard
air.unix
alt.abortion.inequity
alt.abortion
alt.abuse.offender
alt.activism.death-
  penalty
alt.adjective.noun.
  verb
alt.adoption
alt.agriculture.fruit
alt.agriculture
alt.aldus.pagemaker
alt.algebra.help
alt.alien.visitors
alt.amateur-comp
alt.amazon-women
alt.amiga.demos
alt.anagrams
alt.anarchism
alt.angst

alt.animals.foxes
alt.animals.humans
alt.animation
alt.anybody
alt.appalachian.
  literature
alt.architecture
alt.art
alt.arts.nomad
alt.asci-art.animation
alt.asian-movies
alt.astrology
alt.atari
alt.atheism.satire
alt.authorware
alt.autos.antique
alt.autos
alt.bad.clams
alt.banjo
alt.barney
alt.basement
alt.bass
alt.bbs.doors
alt.bbs.internet
alt.bbs.lists
alt.bbs.pcbuucp
alt.bbs.searchlight
alt.bbs.unixbbs
alt.bbs.waffle
alt.bbs.wildcat

alt.bbs.wme
alt.beer.like-molson-
  eh
alt.beer
alt.best.of.internet
alt.bigfoot
alt.binaries.doom
alt.binaries.pictures.
  anime
alt.binaries.pictures.
  cartoons
alt.binaries.pictures.
  erotica.cartoons
alt.binaries.pictures.
  erotica.oriental
alt.pictures.fine-art
alt.pictures.furry
alt.binaries.pictures.
  supermodels
alt.binaries.pictures.
  tasteless
alt.binaries.sounds.
  misc
alt.binaries.sound.
  movies
alt.bio.hackers
alt.bio.minority
alt.birthright
alt.bitterness
alt.books.deryni

alt.books.review

alt.books.toffler

alt.boomerang

alt.brain

alt.buddha.short

alt.business.misc

alt.business.multi-level

alt.business.seminars

alt.business

alt.butt

alt.buttered.scones

alt.cable-tv

alt.Cajun.info

alt.california

alt.cancel.bots

alt.cars.Ford-Probe

alt.cellular

alt.censorship

alt.cereal

alt.chess.ics

alt.chinese.computing

alt.chinese.text

alt.chinese

alt.christnet.christnews

alt.christnet.ethics

alt.christnet.evangelical

alt.christnet.hypocrisy

alt.christnet.public

alt.christnet.sex

alt.clearing.aquaria

alt.clothes.sneakers

alt.clubs

alt.college.food

alt.college.fraternities

alt.comedy.british

alt.comics.batman

alt.commercial-hit-radio

alt.comp.compression

alt.comp.databases

alt.comp.hardware.home

alt.comp.consultants

alt.computer.workshop

alt.config

alt.conspiracy

alt.cooking-chat

alt.cows.moo.moo

alt.creative-cook

alt.cuddle

alt.cult-movies

alt.culture.hawaii

alt.culture.internet

alt.culture.kuwait

alt.culture.us

alt.current-events.bosnia

alt.current-events.usa

alt.cyberspace

alt.data

alt.dcom

alt.delete

alt.desert-storm

alt.destroy.the.earth

alt.deutsche

alt.dev

alt.duke.basketball.sucks

alt.education.bangkok.theory

alt.education.disabled

alt.education.research

alt.emulators.ibmpc

alt.engr.explosives

alt.evil

alt.fairs.renaisssance

alt.fan.addams

alt.fan.brie

alt.fan.clarence.thomas

alt.fan.disney

alt.fan.elvis.presley

alt.fan.goons

alt.fan.letterman

alt.fan.lightbulbs

alt.fan.monty-python

alt.fan.nathan

alt.fan.robert

alt.fan.rush-limbaugh

alt.fan.spinal-tap

alt.fan.TTBS

alt.fan.vejcik

alt.fashio

alt.fax

alt.filepro

alt.flame.eternal

alt.flame.landlord

alt.flame.parents

alt.flame.spelling

alt.folklore.gemstones

alt.folklor.info

alt.food.cocacola

alt.food.veg.live

alt.foolish.user

alt.forgery

alt.forsale

alt.freedom.of.information

alt.french

alt.fun.with

alt.games.air-warrior

alt.games.dragons-inn

alt.games.whitewold

alt.geek

alt.good.morning
alt.good.news
alt.gossip
alt.graphics.ctl
alt.guitar
alt.hackers.malicious
alt.happy.birthday
alt.health.cfids-action
alt.hi.are.you.cute
alt.history
alt.horror.cthulhu
alt.housing.nontrad
alt.humor.puns
alt.hurricane
alt.gypertext
alt.image
alt.india
alt.industrial
alt.info-science
alt.internet.services
alt.internet.talk.haven
alt.irc.questions
alt.japanese.text
alt.journalism.
   criticism
alt.killfiles
alt.lang.cfutures
alt.lang.sas
alt.lawyers.sue.
   sue.sue
alt.letter
alt.linux
alt.machines.misc
alt.magnus.and
alt.make.money.fast
alt.manufacturing
alt.mcdonalds.
   ketchup
alt.med.allergy

alt.meditation
alt.mothergoose
alt.motorcycles.harley
alt.music.enya
alt.music.monkees
alt.music.pink-floyd
alt.music.queen
alt.music.ween
alt.my.crummy.boss
alt.national
alt.necktie
alt.net
alt.newgroup.for.
   fun.fun
alt.online-service
alt.out-of-body
alt.paranet.psi
alt.pcnews
alt.personals.ads
alt.pets.rabbits
alt.pictures.fuzzy
alt.politics.
   datahighway
alt.politics.italy
alt.politics.org.covert
alt.politics.usa.
   constitution
alt.president
alt.privacy
alt.psychology.
   personality
alt.punk
alt.radio.scanner
alt.rave
alt.religion.all-worlds
alt.religion.islam
alt.revolution
alt.rock-n-roll.hard
alt.rodney-king

alt.romance
alt.save.the.earth
alt.sci.physics.spam
alt.scooter
alt.security
alt.sex.bestiality
alt.sex.bondage
alt.sex.exhibitionism
alt.sex.fetish.amputee
alt.sex.intergen
alt.sex.movies
alt.sex.pictures.female
alt.sex.wanted
alt.sex.wizards
alt.sexy.bald
alt.sharon.tate
alt.shut
alt.silly-group.radish-
   therapy
alt.society.civil-liberty
alt.society.generation-
   x
alt.spam
alt.sport.bowling
alt.sport.paintball
alt.sport.baseball.
   cinci-reds
alt.sport.baseball.sd-
   padres
alt.sports.basketball.
   ivy.penn
alt.sports.basketball.
   ny-knicks
alt.sports.darts
alt.sports.football.pro.
   sf-49ers
alt.sports.pro.la-
   raiders
alt.sports.hockey.ihl

alt.sports.hockey.mtl-
   canadiens
alt.startrek.creative
alt.stupidity
alt.suicide
alt.superman
alt.support.arthritis
alt.support.depression
alt.support.jock-strap
alt.surfing
alt.tasteless.jokes
alt.technology.
   obsolete
alt.test.test
alt.thinking.hurts
alt.toys.lego
alt.rv.beavis-
   n-butthead
alt.tv.dinosaurs.
   barney.die
alt.tv.infomercials
alt.tv.mash
alt.tv.roseanne
alt.tv.simpsons
alt.tv.tiney-
   toon.fandom
alt.unix.wizard
alt.usenet
alt.uu.lang.esperanto
alt.uu.math
alt.visa
alt.war.civil.usa
alt.windows.text
alt.world
alt.znet
amiga.hardware
apple.hot-ads
athena.forsale
atl.jobs
att.unix

aus.archives
aus.bicycles
aus.computers.linux
aus.education.rpl
aus.footy
aus.games
aus.music
aus.net.directory
aus.personals
aus.pyramid
aus.rail
aus.sources
aus.sun-works
austin.forsale
austin.news
ba.announce
ba.food
ba.israelis
ba.jobs.offered
ba.motss
ba.seminars
ba.wanted
ba.windows
bc.bcnet
bcm
bionet.agroforestry
bionet.drosophilia
bionet.journals.
   contents
bionet.molbio.
   genbank
bionet.molbio.yeast
bionet.parsitology
bionet.women-in-bio
bionet.xtallography
bit-listsefv
bit.listserv.3com-1
bit.listserv.basque-1
bit.listserv.cdromlan
bit.listserv.cinema-1

bit.listserv.csg-1
bit.listserv.easi
bit.listserv.edtech
bit.listserv.gaynet
bit.listserv.geograph
bit.listserv.hytel-1
bit.listserv.infonets
bit.listserv.isn
bit.listserv.lis-1
bit.listserv.mdphd-1
bit.listserv.muslims
bit.listserv.pakistan
bit.listserv.por
bit.listserv.quaker-p
bit.listserv.snurse-1
bit.listserv.test
bit.listserv.wp51-1
bit.listserv.wx-talk
bit.mailserv.word-mac
bit.tech
biz.books.technical
biz.comp.services
biz.digital.articles
biz.newgroup
biz.pagesate
biz.sco
biz.tadpole
bix.zeos.general
bln.general
bin.net.statistik
brn.test
br.astro
br.opera
br.redes
brasil.ciencia
bu.wanted
ca.driving
ca.news.group
ca.wanted
caltech.cco

can.ai
can.forsale
can.test
can.uucp
capdist.announce
carleton.chinese-news
cern.lep
cern.sunflash
cernvaxusers
ch.general
ch.si
chch.chat
chi.mail
chi.news
chi.weather
chicago.news.stats
chil.revistat.ssi
chil.tes
chile.comp.pc
chile.economia
chile.varios
chinese.newsgroups
chinese.talk.politics
cl.adressen
cl.afrika
c.asien.suedasien
cl.atom.muell
cl.allgemein
cl.datenschutz
cl.europa.eg
cl.frauen.diskussion
cl.frieden
cl.geschichte.
  allgemein
c.gruppen.spd
cl.kultur.allgemein
cl.medien.allgemein
cl.menschenrechte.
  europa
cl.religionen.christen

cl.umwelt.allegemein
c.userforum.hilfe
cl.wirtschaft.geld
clar.news
cle.misc
club.general
cmh.jobs
cmu.cs.market
co.ads
co.politics.amend2
compt.ai.edu
comp.ai.philosophy
comp.arch.storage
comp.archives.
  msdos.d
comp.bbs.tbbs
comp.binaries.atari.st
comp.binaries.ibm.pd
comp.bugs.2bsd
comp.bugs
comp.dcom.isdn
comp.dcom.telecom
comp.editors
comp.emulators.cbm
comp.graphics.
  raytracing
comp.home.
  automation
comp.ibm.pc.
  soundcard
comp.infosystems.
  wais
comp.lang.ada
comp.lang.basic
comp.lang.fortran
comp.lang.ml
comp.lang.prograph
comp.lang.visual
comp.mail.elm
comp.mail.snail

comp.msdoa
comp.newprod
comp.next
comp.org.eff.talk
comp.org.usenix
comp.os.coherent
comp.os.linux.
  development
comp.os.misc
comp.os.ms-
  windows.apps.misc
comp.os.ms-windows.
  networking.tcp-ip
comp.os.ms.
  windows.
  programmer.
  memory
comp.os.
  ms-windows
comp.os.os2.bugs
comp.os.os2.
  programming
comp.parallet.pvm
comp.programming
comp.protocols.nfs
comp.protocols.time
comp.publish.cdrom.
  hardware
comp.publish.
  prepress
comp.simulation
comp.soft-sys.matlab
comp.sources.amiga
comp.sources.
  games.bugs
comp.sources.testers
comp.std.lisp
comp.std
comp.sys.68k
comp.sys.acorn

comp.sys.amiga.
  datacomm
comp.sys.amiga.pirate
comp.sys.atari.st.tech
comp.sys.cdc
comp.sys.convex
comp.sys.ibm.games
comp.sys.ibm.pc.misc
comp.sys.ibm.pc
comp.sys.mac.app
comp.sys.mac.
  graphics
comp.sys.mac.scitech
comp.sys.mac.wanted
comp.sys.macintosh
comp.sys.ncr
comp.sys.next.
  sysadmin
comp.sys.palmtops
comp.sys.ridge
comp.sys.sinclair
comp.sys.sun
comp.sys.unisys
comp.test
comp.theory.cell-
  automata
comp.unix.appleIIgs
comp.unix.internals
comp.unix.pc-c
comp.unix.xenix
comp.wanted
comp.windows.ms
comp.windows.x.pex
consumers.auto
control.rmgroup
cor.forsale
courts.usa.federal
crl.mud
cs.bboard
cd.sports

csn.ml.pubnet
csu.stats
csulb.gate
cu.cs.clim
cu.cs.ugrads
dc.driving
de.admin.lists
de.alt.astrologie
de.alt.binaries.
  picture.male
de.alt.cdrom
de.alt.drogen
de.alt.fan.warlord
de.alt.games
de.alt.sources.huge
de.comm.gatebau
de.comp.databases
de.comp.lang.misc
de.comp.os.os9
de.comp.sys.pcs
de.etc.lists
de.mag.chalisti
de.markt.jobs
de.newusers.
  questions
de.org.ccc
de.rec.fahrrad
de.rec.music
de.sci.electronics
de.sci.medizin
de.soc.misc
de.soc.umwelt
de.talk.jokes.funny
demon.ip.support.
  amiga
depewnet.misc.legal
dfw.news
dobag
edm.news
essug.telco

eunet.misc
eunet.works
fdn.comp.sys.next
fido.ger.antifa
fido.ger.btx
fido.ger.control
fido.ger.isdn
fido.ger.movie
fido.ger.storage
fido.ger.wissen
finet.asiointi
finet.helsinki
finet.koulutus
finet.salaliitot
finet.viestinta
fj.archives.answers
fj.binaries
fj.comp.dev.cdrom
fj.comp.oops
fj.editor.emacs
fj.forsale
fj.lan
fj.lang.perl
fj.living
fj.news.announce
fj.news.group.rec
fj.rec.autos.sports
fj.rec.fine-arts
fj.rec.ham
fj.rec.mystery
fj.rec.sports.american
fj.rec.sports.soccer
fj.sci.chem
fj.sco.culture
fj.soc.smoking
fj.sources
fj.sys.sgi
fj.unix
fj.wanted
fl.jobs

fl.test
fluke
fr.announce.divers
fr.bio.biolmol
fr.comp.os.vms
fr.comp.sys.next
fr.doc.magazines
fr.news.8bits
fr.news.distribution
fr.rec.oracle
freenet.govt
ga.amnet.suche
geometry.college
git.cc.help
git.lcc.class
git.ohr.jobs.digest
git.politics
git.talk.abortion
anu.bash
gnu.g++.lib
gnu.ghostscript
gnu.smalltalk.bug
gnu.utils
hiv.aidsweekly
hiv.resources.
  addresses
houston.personals
hsv.flame
hy.fori
ieee.fidonet
ieee.tab
in.ham-radio
info.firearms
info.jethro-tull
info.slub
info.wisenet
ingr.forsale
ita.test
junk
k12.channel12

k12.ed.comp.literacy
k12.library
k12.sys.projects
katana.flimmerkiste
knox.weather
kw.housing
ky.motorcycles
la.forsale
la.slug
list
maus.bremen
maus.kites
maus.mathe
maus.oecher
maus.politik
maus.recht
maus.sys.ql.ger
mercury.general
milw.unix
misc.comp.forsale
misc.forsale
misc.forsale.
  computers.others
misc.invest.funds
misc.jobs.resumes
misc.legal.moderated
misc.taxes
mit.lcs.announce
mn.map
mod.compilers
mod.computers.vax
mod.mac.sources
mod.philosophy
mod.politics.arms-d
mod.rec.guns
mod.recipies
mod.std.mumps
motrpg.pit
nara.general
ne.food

ne.motss
ne.org.neci.software
net.ai
net.auto
net.comics
net.games.hack
net.garden
net.lang.forth
net.lang
net.micro.68k
net.microapple
net.news.sa
net.puzzle
net.rec.wood
net.sport.hoops
net.veg
neworleans.general
news.announce.
  newgroups
news.config
news.newsites
news.software.nn
nj.market.autos
nj.politics
nijit.for-sale
nlet
no.alt.arkiv
no.alt.gledesutbrudd
no.general
no.nuug
no.uninett.diverse
no.x
nordunet.edu
ny.forsale
ny.test
nyc.food
nyu.decstations
nyu.popbb
nz.soc.green
oar.users

oc.forsale
oh.chem
ok.announce
ont.singles
orst.cs.public
osu.faculty
osc.forslae
osu.opinion
ott.online
pa.general
pagesat.stats
pdaxs.ads.computers
pdx.books
pdx.singles
pdx.utek
phl.config
phl.music
phl.weather
pnw.news
princeton.grad
psi.psinet
psu.jobs
purdue.cc.staff
queens.events
rec.antiques
rec.arts.erotica
rec.arts.poems
rec.arts.sf.marketplace
rec.arts.sf.written
rec.arts.startrek.misc
rec.arts.theatre.plays
rec.arts.tv.uk
rec.audio.high-end
rec.audio.tech
rec.autos.subaru
rec.aviation.ifr
rec.aviation.stories
rec.bicycles.rides
rec.colling.stamps
rec.equestrian

rec.food.drink
rec.games.design
rec.frp.cyber
rec.games.hack
rec.games.mud.admin
rec.games.mud.tiny
rec.games.
  programmer
rec.games.roguelike.
  nethac
rec.games.video.
  classic
rec.games.xtank.play
rec.golf
rec.huns
rec.humor.flame
rec.hunting
rec.models.rc
rec.music.alternative
rec.music.beatles
rec.music.country
rec.music.funky
rec.music.jazz
rec.music.makers.
  marketplace
rec.music.reggae
rec.music.video
rec.nude
rec.outdoors
rec.pets.dogs
rec.photo
rec.radio.amateur.
  swap
rec.radio.shortwave
rec.scuba
rec.skydiving
rec.sport.baseball
rec.sport.football.
  canadian
rec.sport.midget

rec.sport.
  snowboarding
rec.sport.volleyball
rec.toys.lego
rec.travel.europe
rec.video.production
relcom.banktech
relcom.commerce.
  consume
relcom.commerce.
  estate
relcom.commerce.
  products
relcom.commerce.tour
relcom.comp.demo
relcom.comp.
  os.windows
relcom.demos
relcom.fido.su.general
relcom.games
relcom.netnews
relcom.talk
rhein-netz.umwelt
rpi.announce
rpi.sys.amiga
rpi.union
sac.swap
sanet.adverts
sanet.flame
sanet.talk.politics
sas.misc
sci.agriculture
sci.astro.planetarium
sci.data.formats
sci.energy
sci.engr.
  manufacturing
sci.geo.eos
sci.lang.japan
sci.mech.fluids

sci.military

sci.physics.
   accelerators

sci.physics

sci.skeptic

sci.space.shuttle

sci.techniques.
   microscopy

sco.opendesktop

scot.test

sdnet.eats

sdnet.forsale

sdnet.wanted

seattle.test

sfnet.atk.kerhot

sfnet.atk.tex

sfnet.csc

sfnet.funet

APPENDIX **B**

SUGGESTED INTERNET COMMERCIAL SPEECH GUIDELINES

Explanatory Preface

The Internet is the most powerful communication tool in the world, today and for the forseeable future. Recently, the circulation of an advertisement by two lawyers for their legal services raised tremendous controversy as to the manner and location that ads should be placed on the Internet.

Two years ago the National Science Foundation lifted the ban on Internet advertising that they had previously imposed. Yet, the idea of commercialism and advertising in this increasingly pervasive medium is still controversial. The primary anti-ad forces can be found among the academics and technical workers who were the early residents of the Internet. Where advertising is an integral part of all other mediums, this highly vocal faction is attempting, not without some success, publicly to characterize advertisers as inferior to others who supply information via computer.

While the ad critics do not speak with a single voice, but rather express a diversity of opinions, several elements emerge with some consistency. First, there is an overall presumption that advertising is unwanted and useless. Even though those who have made the pioneering forays into Internet advertising have met with financial success (proving that advertising messages are indeed accepted) the vocal minority continues to insist otherwise. Based on this faulty premise, advertisers are told that custom demands they approach potential customers only in an indirect manner. Specifically, advertisers are told it is appropriate to place ads only on channels set aside to carry nothing but advertising. Mixing advertising with other types of content, as is done in newspapers and on television, is considered unacceptable. Alternatively, an advertiser may place a message at a fixed locale in cyberspace but must use other mediums such as billboards or television ads to announce the computer location and ask the customer to go and look for it.

It is unanimously agreed that no one controls the Internet and there is no legal requirement to follow these dictates. Nevertheless the vocal Internet minority insists that custom requires adherence to its outdated philosophy.

The guidelines presented here refuse to recognize the unreasonable stance of those who are anti-advertising. Commercial activity on the Internet is a valuable and worthwhile use of this resource and advertising is a key element of such commercial use. It should be recognized that virtually no business can be successful without advertising. The old-think view of some Net extremists that advertising is as an unwanted and unpleasant annoyance to be marginally tolerated is not good for the development of the Internet, nor healthy for the world economy.

Recently special groups and networks devoted exclusively to product and service promotion have begun to be established. While these are an exciting part of the development of the Information Superhighway, it is not acceptable or practical for advertising to at all times be kept in a restricted area, separate from other Internet activities. Advertising is not relegated to such an inferior position in any other medium, thus it should not be so with respect to the Internet.

Neither should those who advertise on the Internet be forced to do so passively. In no other medium is it required that a potential customer deliberately seek out an advertisement rather than having it placed before him or her. The idea that the only acceptable way to advertise on the Internet is a system where a non-computer medium is utilized to request that a potential purchaser look for commercial information at a particular site in cyberspace is a totally unacceptable limitation. Such convoluted methods are not effective or convenient for either the advertiser or the consumer.

The easy, free flow of information is the goal of the Internet. Advertising is valuable and useful information. It is the concept of free flow that should govern any Internet advertising policy.

Guidelines

- ## Usenet
  It is recognized that the Usenet is the only public gathering place currently existing on Internet. It is a legal and appropriate forum in which to place commercial messages.

- ## Distribution
  Distribution of advertising messages to newsgroups on the Usenet will be based upon the demographic and/or interest of users of the newsgroups, insuring that the newsgroups selected are those most often used by people likely to be interested in a particular commercial message.

- ## Identity
  All commercial messages should be readily identifiable so users can read them in a fully informed manner. For example, a conventional, easily recognizable "AD" identifier in the title of all commercial message offerings may serve this purpose.

- ## Filtering
  Advertisers shall respect the right of all individual Internet users to, through the use of current or evolving technology, filter out commercial messages if they so choose. However, any upstream provider short of the end users should refrain from making that decision for the individual, who may welcome a particular commercial message. Anything else would amount to censorship.

- ## Sincerity
  Commercial messages should be offered only when there is a sincere belief that the information will prove useful to Internet users. The inclusion of useful information with the advertising copy content is encouraged. However, it is also recognized that solicitation of purchases and directions on how to make such purchases are a valid ethical pursuit of the advertiser, as well as a useful convenience for the customer.

In addition to the above Internet-specific guideline, the following suggestions are based upon time-tested, proven codes already in existence. (Sources from which guidelines have been derived are included with each entry.)

• Truth

Advertising shall tell the truth and shall reveal significant facts, the concealment of which would mislead the public. ("The Advertising Principles of American Business," the American Advertising Federation.)

• Responsibility

Advertising agencies and advertisers shall be willing to provide substantiation of those claims made. ("*The Wall Street Journal* Guide to Advertising Policy and Production.")

• Taste and Decency

Advertising shall be free of statements, illustrations, or implications that are offensive to good taste or public decency. ("*The Wall Street Journal* Guide to Advertising Policy and Production.")

• Substantiation

Advertising claims shall be substantiated by evidence in possession of the advertiser and advertising agency, prior to making such claims. ("The Advertising Principles of American Business," the American Advertising Federation.)

• Omission

An advertisement as a whole may be misleading although every sentence separately considered is literally true. Misrepresentation may result not only from direct statements but by omitting or obscuring a material fact. (Better Business Bureau Code of Advertising.)

• Testimonials

Advertising containing testimonials shall be limited to those of competent witnesses who are reflecting a real and honest opinion or experience. ("The Advertising Principles of American Business," the American Advertising Federation.)

• Composition

The composition and layout of advertisements should be such as to minimize the possibility of misunderstanding. (Better Business Bureau Code of Advertising.)

- ## Price Claims
  Advertising will not knowingly create advertising that contains price claims that are misleading. ("Standards of Practice of the American Association of Advertising Agencies," the American Association of Advertising Agencies.)

- ## Unprovable Claims
  Advertising shall avoid the use of exaggerated or unprovable claims. ("*The Wall Street Journal* Guide to Advertising Policy and Production.")

- ## Claims by Professional/Scientific Authorities
  Advertisers will not knowingly create advertising that contains claims insufficiently supported or that distort the true meaning or practicable application of statement made by professional or scientific authority. ("Standards of Practice of the American Association of Advertising Agencies," the American Association of Advertising Agencies.)

- ## Guarantees and Warranties
  Advertisers of guarantees and warranties shall be explicit, with sufficient information to apprise consumers of their principal terms and limitations or, when space or time restrictions preclude such disclosures, the advertisement should clearly reveal where the full text of the guarantee or warranty can be examined before purchase. ("The Advertising Principles of American Business," the American Advertising Federation.)

- ## Bait Advertising
  Advertising shall not offer products or service for sale unless such offer constitutes a bona fide effort to sell the advertised products or services and is not a device to switch consumers to other goods or services, usually of higher price. ("The Advertising Principles of American Business," the American Advertising Federation.)

"Advertising Can Save the Internet from becoming a Utopia Gone Sour," by Bob Metcalfe, *Infoworld*, San Mateo, California, May 30, 1994.

"Author Broke Netiquette Law," by Karen McCowan, *The Register-Guard*, Eugene, Oregon, August 20, 1994.

"Brew Pub Beer on the Internet," by John Whalen, *Internet Business Journal*, Ottawa, Ontario, Canada, June 1994.

"Censors Become a Force on Cyberspace Frontier," by Peter H. Lewis, *The New York Times*, New York, New York, June 29, 1994.

"Couple Convicted of Computer Porn," *Meridian Star*, Meridian, Mississippi, July 19, 1994.

Cronin, Mary J., *Doing Business on the Internet*, New York, New York: Van Nostrand Reinhold, 1994.

"The Do's and Don'ts of On-Line Advertising," *PC Today*, Lincoln, Nebraska, September 1994.

"Electronic Poser for Copyright Laws," *Financial Times*, London, England, August 22, 1994.

"E-Mail Gains Cachet among a Certain Crowd," by Steve Lohr, The New York Times Service, *Middletown Press*, Middletown, Connecticut, June 6, 1994.

"Entrepreneurs Flock to On-line Shopping," by Dan Gilmor, *Knight Ridder Tribune*, *Arizona Republic*, Phoenix, Arizona, June 26, 1994.

"Free Access to Maryland's Internet Line Ready for Unveiling," *Danville Register*, Danville, Virginia, June 26, 1994.

"Getting Down to Business on the Internet," by Peter H. Lewis, *The New York Times*, New York, New York, June 19, 1994.

Gibson, William, *Neuromancer*. New York: Ace Science Fiction, 1984.

Gleick, James, *Chaos*. New York: Penguin, 1987.

"Government Steps Back from Internet," by Jonathan Groves, *Arkansas Democrat-Gazette*, Little Rock, Arkansas, August 14, 1994.

Hahn, Harley and Stout, Rick, *The Internet Complete Reference*. Berkeley, California: Osborne McGraw-Hill, 1994.

">kj> Signs Off, With Intensity," Rob Pegoraro, *Washington Post*, Washington, DC, August 18, 1994.

Krol, Ed, *The Whole Internet Users Guide & Catalog*. Sebastopol, California: O'Reilly & Associates, 1992.

"Loyalists Want Plug Pulled on Internet Advertising," *Newsday, Arizona Republic*, Phoenix, Arizona, April 15, 1995.

"Mind Your P's and FAQ's," by David Landis, Gannet News Service, *Bellingham Herald*, Bellingham, Washington, April 26, 1994.

"MTV Battles Former VJ Who Used Station Name in Internet Site," by Joshua Quittner, *Newsday, Star Tribune*, Minneapolis, Minnesota, May 19, 1994.

Remarks by Vice President Al Gore at National Press Club given December 21, 1993.

"Restaurants Offer E-Menus, More On-Line," by Hollie Hartman, *Des Moines Register*, Des Moines, Iowa, June 20, 1994.

Rheingold, Howard, *The Virtual Community*. Reading, Massachusetts: Addison-Wesley Publishing Company, 1993.

Rushkoff, Douglas, *Cyberia*. New York, NY: HarperCollins, 1994.

"Shop till You Drop from Your Chair, *Information Week*, Manhasset, New York, June 13, 1994.

Siegel, Martha S., and Canter, Laurence A., *U.S. Immigration Made Easy*. Scottsdale, Arizona: Sheridan Worldwide, Inc., 1993.

"Sneak Peek at Windows 4," *PC Magazine*, New York, New York, July 1994.

"Stark Company Sues Internet Newsletter Writer," by Jared Sandberg, *The Wall Street Journal, Akron Beacon Journal*, Akron, Ohio, April 23, 1994.

"Technology Briefs," from staff and wire reports, *Plain Dealer*, Cleveland, Ohio, June 26, 1994.

"Tolls for Thee?" by Penn Jillette, *PC Computing*, Foster City, Pennsylvania, August 1994.

"Tuesday Ticker," *Chicago Tribune*, Chicago, Illiniois, August 23, 1994.

"Where There's a Will There's an A," Professor Claude Olney, Chesterbrook Educational Publishers, Inc., 1991.

"Whose Standards? Whose Community?" by David Loundy, *Chicago Daily Bulletin*, Chicago, Illinois, August 1, 1994.